Developing the Emotionally Literate School

Developing the Emotionally Literate School

KATHERINE WEARE

PCP
Paul Chapman
Publishing

Paul Chapman Publishing
A SAGE Publications Company
6 Bonhill Street
London EC2A 4PU

SAGE Publications Inc
2455 Teller Road
Thousand Oaks, California 91320

SAGE Publications India Pvt Ltd
B-42, Panchsheel Enclave
Post Box 4109
New Delhi 100 017

Library of Congress Control Number: 2003109191

A catalogue record for this book is available from the British Library

ISBN 0 7619 4085 6
ISBN 0 7619 4086 3 (pbk)

Typeset by Dorwyn Ltd, Rowlands Castle, Hants
Printed in Great Britain by Cromwell Press, Trowbridge

Contents

Figures and Tables

Acknowledgements

There are many people to thank for helping make this book a reality.

To Marianne Lagrange of Sage for both keeping the faith that I would finish it and giving me the space to do so during an unexpectedly challenging time in my life.

To the Research and Graduate School of Education, my department at the University of Southampton, for providing me with some time and space to write the book, and in particular to Torhild Hearn for proofreading, to Mary Thomas for help with finding materials and searching websites, and to Jenny McWhirter for holding the fort at work while I wrote.

To Sarah Stewart-Brown of the University of Oxford for sharing the results of her work on assessment of emotional and social competence which has helped shape and inform Chapter 6.

To James Park of Antidote for providing some examples of practice and assessment that are used in the book, and being a valuable sounding board for ideas.

To Nick Boddington of Essex Local Education Authority for helping me connect my interest in emotional literacy with his interest in work on accelerated learning, and for running the conference on 'The Emotionally Intelligent School' which has provided some examples of teachers' thinking for this book.

To Mark D. Weist of the University of Maryland School of Medicine, for help with compiling the list of contacts at the end of the book through providing help with contacts in the USA. To Bernie Marshall of Deakin

University for help in identifying with Australian contacts.

To the Department for Education and Skills in London, and especially to Helen Kay, for giving me the opportunity and funding to work on the project 'What works in promoting children's emotional and social competence?' that informed some of the thinking for this book.

To Gay Gray for working with me on the project, seeking out material for me to work with and commenting on drafts of chapters.

To those who advised the project and who gave ongoing support and wise counsel. They are Pauline Forrest, Gill Frances, Liz Morris, Dinah Morley, James Park (again!), Amanda Sasia, Peter Sharp, Marilyn Toft, Maria Walmer, Allan Watson, Mog Ball, Adrian Faupel, Harriet Goodman, Candida Hunt, Edmund Sonuga-Barke, Bob Stratford, Susan Tarlton and Jo Wright.

To those who were interviewed from the five Local Education Authorities whose work informed the project and provided a case study for Chapter 7 of this book. As we assured them of confidentiality I cannot, sadly, thank them by name.

To my husband, Barry, for reading drafts of the book, and for looking after our three children on many a long wet weekend while I tapped away. To my children, Conner, Shannon and Shelby for being so patient with 'mummy's book'.

Introduction

Our society has traditionally been frightened of emotion, but now we are realizing its importance. Work on what, in the UK at least, is often called 'emotional literacy' is developing at an extraordinary pace in education, both under this particular banner, and under related terms such as emotional intelligence, emotional and social competence, mental health, and emotional and social well-being. There is a good deal of debate about what these various terms mean, and some considerable suspicion and scepticism about the whole area within education. This book will try to define terms and outline concepts in ways that make sense to those who work in education, outline the scientific evidence behind them, explore ways in which schools can become more emotionally literate, and demonstrate the many benefits that can accrue when they do.

Emotional literacy may be a new, and to some a rather trendy, term, but the concept and the practice it generates have deep roots in some very long-standing work. It does not involve creating whole new structures – to be effective it has to be embedded in the familiar areas of school life that constitute the daily work and experience of all who work and learn in schools. This book will therefore examine the themes that permeate the everyday life of schools, such as understanding and managing pupil behaviour, and organizing and delivering teaching and learning – concentrating as it does so on the role emotion and emotional education play, and suggesting what may be for some readers new ways of thinking about familiar issues. This is not to say that we will just be going over old ground: there has been an explosion of work on emotional aspects of education in recent years and this book will summarize considerable new and significant thinking and research on the emotions and learning, on how we can best work with the emotions for positive gain, and on the kind of schools and classrooms that encourage emotional growth.

The approach to emotional literacy will be a wide and inclusive one. Emotional literacy is as relevant to mainstream education as it is to special needs education, and this book will focus particularly on mainstream schools. It is as relevant in secondary as it is in primary schools, and is as important for adults as it is for children, so the book will look not only at students but at staff and parents too. The book will take a broad view of what is meant by emotional literacy which will include looking at how individuals can understand and manage their own emotions. It will also examine how we can learn to relate more effectively to the emotions and motivations of other people – 'social literacy' if you like. Emotional and social literacy cannot be developed in a vacuum, and this book will focus on ways in which a wide range of aspects of school life can help develop emotional literacy and promote emotional and social well-being in children and adults. The book will argue strongly that all aspects of school life are potentially involved in emotional literacy, so this book will touch on many facets, from management, behaviour and relationships to the curriculum.

Given this broad view of what emotional literacy can mean in a school context, there will not be space to go into detail on any one issue, and the book cannot hope to tell readers everything they need to know to develop an emotionally literate school, nor can it describe the many useful projects available. The goal is to help those who work in, and with, schools to see the bigger picture and how it all fits together, to provide a framework for thinking about a complex issue, and an overview that identifies and brings together the key principles, practical strategies and approaches that have been shown to work when trying to make the school as a whole more emotionally literate. As a result of working their way through the book and seeing the broad picture, I hope that readers will be inspired to look further into the detailed aspects of emotional literacy that are of particular interest to them, and the chapters and appendices will provide suggestions for follow-up activities, contacts, websites and reading.

I have already written a book (*Promoting Mental, Emotional and Social Health: A Whole School Approach* – Weare, 2000) that focuses on the kind of whole-school climates, organization and actions that promote emotional and social well-being. This book will necessarily touch briefly and in places on some of the key themes of that book, updating the evidence as it does so. This book will, however, be very different in that it will not be so 'academic' in style, but focus more on what schools can actually do to promote emotional literacy. It will also go into much more detail on issues specifically to do with promoting emotional literacy: these will include how we define emotional literacy; the evidence for its importance; its relation to special needs work; its centrality to the management of behaviour; how to teach it so pupils can learn it, and how to help teachers acquire and practise it. The book will also look in some detail at three newer areas within emotional literacy. It will link work on emotional literacy with new work on the process of learning, on the way the brain processes information, the central place of the emotions in thinking and learning, on accelerated learning and on learning styles. To date both emotional literacy and accelerated learning have been operating on parallel pathways, when, this book will argue, they have much to gain from one another. It will focus on two other issues on which I and my colleagues at various universities have particularly fresh and relevant information. I have recently been involved in a project for the English Department for Education and Skills (DfES) (Weare and Gray, 2002) which has looked at what five English Local Education Authorities, known to be leaders in the field, are doing to develop work on emotional literacy, and what helps and what hinders that development. Chapter 7 will look at how schools can link to broader approaches, and what the key agencies that work with schools can do to support and promote schools' work in emotional literacy. Meanwhile researchers at the University of Oxford have carried out a parallel project for the DfES which looked at how emotional competency might be assessed, and Chapter 6 will explore this issue in some detail, using evidence from their research as well as from the other sources.

Working with colleagues from my University and elsewhere, I have carried out a good deal of work in Europe, including Russia, in developing whole-school approaches to health education, focusing particularly on emotional, social and mental well-being and emotional literacy, so this book will inevitably have a European, and within that an English, bias when it comes to discussing specific contexts and case studies. However the evidence on which this book is based comes from the international research and experience, especially in the USA and in Australia, and it is intended that its key messages will be applicable across a range of countries and cultures.

A word on terminology. Throughout the book the terms 'child' and 'children' will be used to refer to everyone of school age because, although this term may be accused of infantalizing the young, using the more accurate 'children and young people' is simply too cumbersome. The term 'student/s' will be used to refer to children when they are in school because it is more widely used across the world than the term which is more popular in the UK, 'pupil'. The term 'parent' will be used to cover anyone who has care of the child, regardless of their relationship with the child. The term 'staff' will be used rather than 'teachers' (except where only teachers are meant) to remind us that many other staff work in and around schools – classroom assistants, counsellors, educational psychologists, school nurses, school secretaries, lunchtime supervisors, caretakers and local authority advisers to name but a few - and all are actually or potentially involved in developing work on emotional literacy.

When asked 'How can a school promote emotional literacy?', a group of those who work in schools from Essex in England and who were just starting to think about this issue answered:

- through everything – philosophy, values – *all* who work and learn in schools, including support staff
- leadership
- example
- continuing professional development
- integrating emotional literacy with target-setting
- valuing everyone in the school and promoting high self-esteem
- by avoiding staff overload
- by being creative.

At this stage in reading the book, what would you say?

CHAPTER ONE

What Is Emotional Literacy and Why Is It Important to Schools?

GOALS OF THIS CHAPTER

By the end of this chapter you will:

- be clearer about what is meant by 'emotional literacy'
- be clearer about what is meant by other commonly used terms in this field (such as 'emotional intelligence') and how these terms, and the work they cover, relate to emotional literacy
- be more aware of what you already know, and are working on, which relates to emotional literacy
- have explored some of the current reasons why many feel emotional literacy is increasingly important in education
- have gained a broad idea of the benefits of working on emotional literacy, for students, school staff, schools and communities.

SOME KEY CONCEPTS AND TERMS

Before we launch into a book on emotional literacy it may be helpful to clarify what exactly we are talking about. The whole area of work on emotional and social issues has developed with enormous rapidity over the last decade or so, and some of the words now being used to describe such work can seem off-putting and opaque to those who work in education. This section will explore some key terms often used in this area, and look at their advantages and disadvantages. The area is something of a linguistic minefield.

■ WHAT DO WE MEAN BY 'EMOTIONAL LITERACY?'

'Emotional literacy' is the key term that will be used in this book, although there are many others that mean more or less the same thing or overlap with it considerably, as we shall shortly see. The term 'emotional literacy' is usually attributed to Steiner (Steiner and Perry, 1997) and was popularized by various 'movers and shakers' in the 1990s.

This book will define emotional literacy for the individual as the *ability to understand ourselves and other people, and in particular to be aware of, understand, and use information about the emotional states of ourselves and others with competence. It includes the ability to understand, express and manage our own emotions, and respond to the emotions of others, in ways that are helpful to ourselves and others.*

Organizations, such as schools and local education authorities clearly have a key role in promoting the emotional literacy of their members and helping them to become more emotionally literate. There is also at least a metapho-

TABLE 1.1 USING THE TERM 'EMOTIONAL LITERACY'

Advantages	Disadvantages
Popular especially in the UK: has produced a wealth of publications, projects, work in schools, conferences, etc.	Not so well known or used outside the UK
The term is meaningful in an educational context, and is now very popular with educational psychologists, schools and local education authorities	The metaphor implied in the word 'literacy' can be confusing for some people, and feel like jargon to those outside the educational sector
For those familiar with the concept of literacy (for example, teachers in primary schools and teachers of English) it can readily bring to mind ideas on how emotional and social competences can be broken down, defined, taught and encouraged, in the same ways as verbal literacy can	'Literacy' can have negative connotations for some who have negative feelings about the word, for example, some in UK schools who have experienced the 'literacy hour' (an hour a day which primary schools are required to spend on literacy, working within some very tight parameters) and who fear the onset of the 'emotional literacy hour'
It reminds us that emotional literacy can be learned rather than being a fixed, innate quality, that we all have degrees of literacy, and that the pursuit of literacy is a journey, not an end point	It can focus attention on the individual and their capacities, and make us forget to also look at the surrounding context and underlying determinants of emotional and social well-being
	It can make it sound as if we are looking at 'one thing' rather than the loose cluster of competences many think it is in practice
	It does not, in the minds of some, include social competences, but focuses only on emotional aspects.

ical sense in which an organization itself can be said to be more or less 'emotionally literate'. The level of emotional literacy in an organization might be defined as *the extent to which the organization takes into account the role of emotion in dealing with the people who are its members, and in planning, making and implementing decisions, and takes positive steps to promote the emotional and social well-being of its members.* This book will have a good deal to say about how schools, and also those who support them such as local authorities and voluntary agencies, can become more emotionally literate organizations.

No term is perfect, and at this point we will briefly explore the advantages and disadvantages of using the term 'emotional literacy', outlined in Table 1.1. We will make the same exploration for the other key terms that we will discuss as we go.

This book will generally use the term 'emotional literacy', but there are others that it will use from time to time, and others that perhaps could have been used. None of the terms are perfect, and all have advantages and disadvantages. The book will draw heavily on work that has taken place under a variety of other terms which will be discussed in this chapter.

WHAT COMPETENCES DOES EMOTIONAL LITERACY INCLUDE?

To clarify what we mean by emotional literacy, at least at an individual level, we will next outline some of key emotional and social competences: they will be discussed in detail in Chapter 2.

SELF-UNDERSTANDING

- Having an accurate and positive view of ourselves.
- Having a sense of optimism about the world and ourselves.
- Having a coherent and continuous life story.

UNDERSTANDING AND MANAGING EMOTIONS

- Experiencing the whole range of emotions.
- Understanding the causes of our emotions.
- Expressing our emotions appropriately.
- Managing our responses to our emotions effectively, for example managing our anger, controlling our impulses.
- Knowing how to feel good more often and for longer.
- Using information about the emotions to plan and solve problems.

- Resilience – processing, and bouncing back from, difficult experiences.

UNDERSTANDING SOCIAL SITUATIONS AND MAKING RELATIONSHIPS

- Forming attachments to other people.
- Experiencing empathy for others.
- Communicating and responding effectively to others.
- Managing our relationships effectively.
- Being autonomous: independent and self-reliant.

'EMOTIONAL INTELLIGENCE'

'Emotional Intelligence' is a term that is used particularly in the USA to describe more or less the same competences as emotional literacy. The popularity of the word 'intelligence' is partly due to the influence of Gardner, Kornhaber and Wake, (1995) who have worked on the whole concept of intelligence. Gardner sees intelligence as being much wider than is generally supposed, and as plural 'intelligences' rather than just one, all of which cover rather difference capacities. His precise categorization of the various intelligences is constantly evolving, but basically he sees them as including what he calls 'conventional intelligence', the logical, rational, mathematical and linguistic capacities that are familiar to us through intelligence tests. He has added a further group of what he called 'specialist intelligences' such as musical, spatial and kinaesthetic intelligences. Most relevant to our purposes here, he suggests that there are also two types of what he terms 'personal intelligences' – 'intra-personal intelligence', or self-understanding, and 'inter-personal intelligence', or understanding other people.

The umbrella term, which brings together these two intelligences, 'emotional intelligence', was supposedly coined by Mayer and Salovey, who defined it as:

> the ability to perceive accurately, appraise and express emotion; the ability to access and/or generate feelings which facilitate thought; the ability to understand emotion and emotional knowledge; the ability to regulate emotions to promote emotional and intellectual growth. (Mayer and Salovey, 1997: 10)

Goleman (1996) popularized the term 'emotional intelligence' in his book of the same name. This book brought together a wealth of data, and concluded that what he called 'emotional intelligence' is more influential than conventional intelligence for all kinds of personal, career and scholastic success. It has been suggested that Goleman overstated the case, and that if we look at the population as a whole, conventional intelligence is still very influential (Sternberg, 2001). However, it appears to be true that, if we look at those who do well educationally, the differences in work outcomes and personal success are more dependent on their emotional and social abilities than on their IQ: emotional intelligence gives them an 'edge' over their equally conventionally intelligent but less emotionally intelligent counterparts. So to this extent there is no doubt about how influential emotional intelligence is.

The idea of 'emotional intelligence' triggered an explosion of interest in scientific work on how the brain works and in particular on the central role that the emotional side of the brain plays in the process. It focused attention on links between social and emotional intelligence and educational outcomes, such as learning, cognitive development, school attendance and job success. It helped emotional and social education to be seen as important for all students, including bright ones and older ones. It meant that emotional education was no longer 'touchy-feely'; there was a new emphasis on hard-edged aspects, and an increased focus on the development of techniques and instruments to measure of emotional and social competences (although the latter aspect is seen by many as a mixed blessing as we shall see in Chapter 6). See Table 1.2.

■ 'COMPETENCE'/'LEARNING'

Rather than use the specialist and, to some, rather jargon-laden terms 'literacy' or 'intelligence', some use the term 'competence', usually with the words 'emotional' and/or 'social' attached. The phrases are often turned into the acronyms 'SEC' or 'ESC'. Some also use the broad 'social and emotional learning' instead or in addition, and use the acronym 'SEL'. A powerful example is the major US network CASEL (the Collaborative for Academic, Social and Emotional Learning) which brings together a large number of practitioners and researchers under this heading: this group tends to use the terms 'competence' and 'learning'.

In practice, definitions of social and emotional competence and learning again overlap with emotional literacy:

> Social and emotional competence is the ability to understand, manage and express the social and emotional aspects of one's life in ways that enable the successful management of life tasks such as learning, forming relationships, solving everyday problems, and adapting to the complex demands of growth and development. (Elias et al., 1997: 2)

TABLE 1.2 USING THE IDEA OF 'EMOTIONAL INTELLIGENCE'

Advantages	Disadvantages
Very popular in the USA, and in business contexts	Not so popular outside the USA, and in educational contexts
It has produced a wealth of useful and inspiring work on how emotional intelligence may best be developed, especially in business, and to a lesser extent in education, the family and the community	Using the term tends to focus the attention on measurement rather than on teaching and learning
It has provoked serious work on analysing whether there is such a thing as emotional and social intelligence. The findings are promising in terms of distinct and measurable attributes, and their effects on social behaviour, life chances and learning	The scientific connotations and expectations raised by the word 'intelligence' have aroused a great deal of controversy and some hostility, for example among some psychologists who dispute whether there is really such a thing as 'emotional intelligence' or 'social intelligence' in the strict sense of the word. These debates can undermine the credibility of all work on emotional and social development, whether or not it uses the term 'intelligence', and use up a good deal of energy and resource Calling emotional and social capacities 'intelligence' can suggest they are innate and fixed, not teachable
Using this term has linked work in the field with research on hard science, for example with work on the physiology of the brain, the neurological development of young children, and learning styles	If we use the term in a looser way, we overcome some of these problems, but then it comes to mean the same as other softer terms such as 'literacy' and 'competence', and ceases to have any precise or specialist meaning, or to add anything particular to the debate

TABLE 1.3 USING THE IDEAS OF 'COMPETENCE' AND 'LEARNING'

Advantages	Disadvantages
Used in the USA, and to some extent elsewhere	Not so popular outside the USA
Familiar terms to those who work in education	Not so inviting to those who come to this area from other sectors than education, such as the health service
They are straightforward, non-specialist and loosely used terms that feel like 'common sense' and are non-threatening in most contexts	The word 'competence' can alienate some, including those from education, who object to the logical corollary that people can be 'emotionally incompetent'
Emotional literacy and emotional intelligence are usually defined in terms of specific competences anyway in practice, to make the very general overall definitions more specific, teachable and assessable	Looking at separate competences can fragment a holistic concept
Learning is absolutely central to the whole area, both in terms of specific learning and teaching programmes on emotional competences, and in terms of the impact on learning in general – there is, as we will see in Chapter 2, a highly beneficial link between emotional literacy and all types of learning	Like 'literacy' and 'intelligence' the terms 'competence' and 'learning' can focus attention on the individual and their capacities and not on the surrounding context and underlying determinants of emotional and social competence and well-being

This book will use the term 'emotional and social competence' when look-ing at the skills, attitudes and behaviours that make up an emotionally lit-erate person, and the term 'emotional and social learning' when referring to how those competences are learned, through the taught curriculum and the whole-school experience. It will make considerable use of work that has used those terms.

◼ 'MENTAL HEALTH'

Many are uneasy with the term 'mental health', seeing it as a euphemism for mental illness, but modern definitions of mental health have taken it a long way from its traditional highly medicalized, individual focus, and now very much overlap with definitions of emotional well-being and liter-acy. Mental health as it is now commonly defined includes the ability to grow and develop emotionally, intellectually and spiritually; to make rela-tionships with others, including peers and adults; to participate fully in education and other social activities; to have positive self-esteem; and to cope, adjust and be resilient in the face of difficulties (Weare, 2000; Hartley-Brewer, 2001). There is a major push within mental health at pres-ent to make more links with work in mainstream schools (Batten, 2001; Weare, 2001). However, as Table 1.4 shows, this has not always permeated the popular, or the educational, consciousness, and the term again has disadvantages as well as advantages.

Mental health work is often emotional literacy and well-being under another name. Most countries are carrying out a great deal of useful and interesting research, publications and good practice on mental health and young people that can be drawn on by schools attempting to develop emotional literacy. The large number of mental health websites listed for the UK, the USA and Australia at the end of the book demonstrate the richness of this resource. In the UK, the Child and Adolescent Mental Health Services (CAMHS) are actively involved in developing work on emotional well-being. In Australia a major national mental health project, 'Mind Matters', has been disseminated across the country in mainstream schools for mainstream children.

◼ 'WELL-BEING'

Well-being has been described thus:

> A holistic, subjective state which is present when a range of feelings, among them energy, confidence, openness, enjoyment, happiness, calm, and caring, are combined and balanced. (Stewart-Brown, 2000: 32)

See Table 1.5.

TABLE 1.4 USING THE IDEA OF 'MENTAL HEALTH'

Advantages	Disadvantages
Meaningful term to those who work in the health service, who can be put off by educational terms	Many who work in education have an antipathy to the term. Schools tend only to think of children in 'mental health' terms if the children have some kind of defined condition, such as depression, schizophrenia or autism, and tend to see their role in these cases as restricted to helping identification of mental health problems that then need specialist help. Teachers have themselves steered clear of defining their own stress-related problems as 'mental health' issues, fearing the stigma that still attaches to the term
Modern definitions of mental health are broad and positive – overlap considerably with emotional literacy	Often used as a pseudonym for mental illness, and a label for services that deal only with the diagnosis, management and treatment of mental illness and problems in individuals
Focuses on the determinants and contexts of emotional well-being	May not bring to mind work on competence-building in individuals
Much excellent work is going on under the 'mental health' banner that is emotional literacy by another name	

TABLE 1.5 USING THE IDEA OF 'WELL-BEING'

Advantages	Disadvantages
The term 'well-being' can remove some of the anxieties aroused by the term 'mental health' while retaining many of its advantages	May not bring to mind work on competence-building in individuals
It is often put alongside 'mental health' (as in 'mental, emotional and social health') to 'unpack' the term and help it lose some of its medicalized and negative connotations	The term is rather vague and woolly, and often needs defining more closely to be of practical use
This term is widely used in both educational and health contexts. It is a generic, broad and all-encompassing term which is, on the whole, uncontroversial and acceptable to a wide range of educational, social care and health related environments, and which can help bring disparate groups together	
Has produced a great deal of useful work, e.g. The Health Promoting/Healthy School networks and focus on the importance of using the whole school as the setting for its development	
It is a positive, salutogenic and non-medicalized term and thus clearly the 'business' of everyone from parents to professionals, not just doctors	
Using broader terms such as 'health' and 'well-being' reminds us to include consideration of the contexts and environments which make emotional literacy possible and on the risk and resilience factors that undermine or support it	
It implies a focus on whole populations, not just those with problems	

Emotional well-being is in practice inseparable from the development of emotional and social competence, and is thus an integral part of emotional literacy. We have defined emotionally literate organizations as those that take positive steps to promote the emotional and social well-being of their members. So this book will make considerable use of the term 'emotional well-being' as well as the massive body of work that has contributed to our understanding of how emotional well-being, and mental health, can be developed and promoted.

■ SUMMARY OF THE USE OF TERMS IN THIS BOOK

In the light of the above discussion, this book will make use of the following key terms. It will mainly use the term *'emotional literacy'*, which it will see as being partly concerned with the learning and practice of *'emotional and social competences'*, in other words the learning and development of knowledge, attitudes and skills, which takes place partly through the organized curriculum and classroom lessons, and partly through the wider experience in schools and other contexts. Emotional literacy is an integral part of *'emotional and social well-being'* which is shaped by the environments and underlying determinants that enable emotional literacy and its constituent competences to be developed.

The book will also draw freely on work from adjacent and overlapping fields, including *'emotional intelligence'*, and *'mental health'*, as well as many others we will be examining as the chapters unfold, such as the management of behaviour and special needs work. This eclecticism is based on the belief that it is best not to be 'precious' in our use of language or bodies of knowledge but use what 'works' and speaks to people in the range of contexts in which we find ourselves. Work on emotional literacy can usefully make links and build on work from many related fields.

EMOTIONAL LITERACY IS NOT A NEW IDEA
■

■ EXISTING WORK IN EDUCATION THAT RELATES TO EMOTIONAL LITERACY

Work on emotional literacy is by no means a twenty-first century fad. Aristotle clearly understood the importance of anger management:

> Anyone can be angry – that is easy. But to be angry with the right person, to the right degree, at the right time, for the right purpose and in the right way – that is not easy.

Work in this area has a long pedigree, and many antecedents – we have already mentioned some of them, for example work on *emotional intelligence*, and *mental health*. We will here look at a few of the other most obvious sources of previous work, to remind readers of areas with which they may already be familiar and on which they can draw.

Since the 1970s, in many parts of the world, *school health education* activity has moved away from its traditional emphasis on physical health to place mental, emotional and social health at the heart of health education, and from an emphasis on health problems to more positive approaches. Many school health education projects and programmes have included specific materials on teaching emotional and social competences in areas such as building self-esteem, decision-making and resisting peer group pressure. Similar work on *'Lifeskills'* approaches have produced teaching programmes on a wide range of emotional and social competences and have been very influential in parts of Europe and Africa, for example through the World Health Organization's mental health programme. In UK schools the whole area is now most often called *'Personal, Social and Health Education'* (PHSE), recently joined by a newly invigorated *'Citizenship'*, both of which also have a central concern for emotional and social issues.

The *'Healthy School/Health Promoting School'* approach can now be found in many parts of the world, most especially Europe, the Western Pacific, Africa and Latin America. This approach grew from school health education and continues its emphasis on social and emotional issues. It has added a 'whole-school' approach that focuses on the environments that foster health and well-being, including, in many cases, mental, emotional and social health and well-being. A further emphasis of this approach has been the identification of indicators to allow for clear and reliable evaluation. We will give an example in Chapter 7 of how Healthy/Health Promoting School approaches can form a bedrock for work on emotional and social competence.

A concern with emotional and social matters is by no means confined to those who work in health and related areas: many others who work on a wide range of educational issues have long taken an interest in this field and produced a wealth of work. *Special needs* work has, of course, long included a concern for those with emotional and behavioural problems. There has also been extensive work on areas of educational research such as *school effectiveness, school improvement* and *school management* which have inevitably focused on the human side of education, for example the part that feelings such as connectedness and commitment play in producing positive educational outcomes, and what makes for effective school leadership. Since the 1960s there has been extensive work on what kind of *school climates* are most effective, which has shown how important social and emotional features of school life are to learning. Schools are invariably interested in behaviour, and work on *behaviour management and support* usually includes a concern with its emotional and social outcomes, and more rarely, its emotional and social determinants. Work on *how the brain works*, on *the process of learning*, on *learning styles* and on *accelerated learning* has undergone an explosion of research and interest in the last 15 years: it is demonstrating that the emotions are not only a necessary condition for learning but are built into the very structure of learning and the way we think.

■ WORK OUTSIDE SCHOOLS THAT RELATES TO EMOTIONAL LITERACY

Of course work in schools is in turn based on work that comes from wider disciplines. It is basic *psychology* to reflect that the world we experience is largely a product of our perceptions and beliefs, which are heavily coloured by our emotions. There is a long tradition of psychological theory and research on the emotions, and although work on the emotions has for some while been the 'Cinderella' of psychology, a concern with them is now coming to the fore, again partly inspired by work on emotional intelligence. All kinds of *child and adult therapy and counselling* have links with work on the emotions. For example, the more psychoanalytical approaches focus on the effect of our early experiences, the more cognitive approaches focus on the influence of our current thinking patterns, and behavioural approaches focus on the influence of habitual behaviours and on shaping the conditions that create them. All of these approaches can be very useful for those who would develop emotional literacy in schools, as they give valuable pointers as to what factors to tackle in trying to help people to understand and manage their emotions more effectively.

Personal development work with children and adults, in education, social and occupational settings has developed a wealth of approaches to key issues in emotional and social education, such as relationships, communication, stress reduction, the management of change, and assertion. *Parenthood education* has been a growth area, and there is considerable work on what makes for effective parenthood education, both targeted at 'at risk' parents and, increasingly, for all parents.

Work on *spirituality and the development of spiritual values* has strong parallels with work on emotional literacy, and could hardly have a longer tradition. Much of the work on emotional control parallels aspects of some eastern religions, such as Buddhism, with its emphasis on gaining control of the mind and empathizing with others.

BENEFITS OF EMOTIONAL LITERACY

This section briefly reviews some of the key benefits of work on emotional literacy and related areas, issues which will be picked up and discussed further in later chapters. For those who want immediately to see more concrete evidence, Chapter 4 contains a table of programmes that list some typical large-scale projects which aim at developing emotional and social competence and well-being, and outlines the wide range of demonstrated positive outcomes of such programmes, including higher school attainments, greater emotional awareness, improved conduct, less aggression and conflict, better relations with others, improved problem-solving and less risky behaviour.

However, a word of warning. Those who want to know more about work in this area, particular those who are sceptical about it, often call for 'hard evidence'. This call is not easy to answer, not because there is no evidence but because there is so much, but all of it presented in such different ways it is hard to bring it together or compare it. The evidence is that holistic approaches to the development of emotional literacy are more effective, but they are a nightmare to evaluate, and comparing the evaluations of different holistic interventions is even more difficult. Holistic approaches by definition look at a vast number of aspects of the situation: in the case of schools this can include the organization, its climate, its ethos and all its personnel, relations with parents and with the community. They therefore bring with them a distinct lack of consensus about what is being aimed at, what kind of actions should be taken, and what is included and what is excluded. If we look across a range of interventions we find a distinct lack of any standardized measures or agreed indicators to assess all of this. What we have is a plethora of programmes and approaches, all with slightly different but overlapping goals, a vast array of tools for assessing individuals' attitudes, beliefs, behaviours, various checklists and inventories to assess a wide range of features of organizations, and almost as many ways of assessing the impact of interventions as there are interventions. This kaleidoscope of research and development makes anything other than impressionistic comparisons between studies difficult. However, the fact that there is so much going on, using such a wealth of different methods is not a reason to fail to value or recommend work on the development of emotional literacy: just because something is complex, various and hard to measure does mean it is not worth doing.

The following subsection will give a flavour of the kind of evidence that suggests that emotional literacy can be beneficial on a range of fronts.

▨ IMPROVING STANDARDS

Many large-scale reviews of research in the area have concluded that programmes that teach social and emotional competences can result in gains that are absolutely central to the goals of all schools. Gains include improved school atmospheres, more effective learning, better behaviour, higher school attendance, higher motivation, higher morale of students and teachers, and better results for students and schools (Durlak, 1995; US General Accounting Office, 1995; Durlak and Wells, 1997; Catalano et al., 2002; Wells, Barlow and Stewart-Brown, 2003). Recent initiatives in the development of emotional literacy by local education authorities in England have all set targets in terms of improvements in academic standards, and seem to be meeting with success. An example of this is Cotham Community School in Bristol which reported, a year after writing emotional literacy into its strategic aims, significant increases in its students' grades in public examinations (Antidote, 2001).

▨ IMPROVEMENTS IN BEHAVIOUR LEADING TO MORE INCLUSION

The links between emotional literacy and improved behaviour are very much supported by the research evidence, and large-scale reviews of programmes that attempt to improve emotional and social competences and well-being have reported clear improvements in behaviour (Catalano et al., 2002; Wells, Barlow and Stewart-Brown, 2003). These reviews have been useful in giving more detailed clues as to what kind of programmes are the most successful: they suggest, for example, that the most effective programmes both teach emotional and social competences explicitly and focus on the whole-school environment.

Expectations of mainstream schools are now much higher; they are expected to help all children succeed and behave well, not give up on problem students, nor send them on to other providers. This means that all schools have to find ways to work with slow, disruptive and disaffected students without undermining the education of the other children in the schools, a requirement that most schools are finding a major challenge. Emotional literacy has been shown to be one of the tools that can help make the inclusion of difficult children easier. For example, Southampton City Local Education Authority which is among those leading the field in developing this work in the UK, set a target of no exclusions for its schools. Since making emotional literacy what they term 'the heart of the process' their exclusions have reduced steadily year on year, from 113 in 1997 to 22 in 2000. In the USA two projects which taught 'difficult' students the kind of skills that help them to fit into classrooms more easily and control their own behaviour, while helping their classmates both to tolerate their behaviour more easily and positively support their efforts to become part of the mainstream, were shown to be very effective in helping the difficult students stay in the classroom, and without undermining the learning of other students (Rogers, 1994; Epstein and Elias, 1996).

■ BENEFITS IN THE WORKPLACE

Much of the thrust of work on emotional literacy and emotional intelligence has come from the world of work, from studies of management and leadership, where it is proving to be enormously beneficial (Weisinger, 1998; Cherniss and Goleman, 2001). The nature of work in the twenty-first century is changing: there is an increasing focus on relationships, teamwork, communication and management skills. Work is also more stressful now, with rapid technological change producing more pressure and the need for us all to be resilient, flexible and adaptable, and to manage the uncertainty that comes from changing direction several times in a working career. Some companies are seeking new employees with high levels of emotional intelligence, or using profiles to assess their existing employees' styles of thinking and acting in order to place them in the most appropriate roles in the organization. Many companies are trying to raise their staff's emotional literacy and coping skills through training. The school is of course also a workplace, and school staff can themselves benefit from working on their own emotional literacy, which has been shown to enable them to relate more effectively to children, manage the classroom better and teach more effectively (Sharp and Faupel, 2002; DfES, 2003). Work on emotional literacy can bring gains for them personally too, increasing their ability to manage stress and respond to change.

■ IMPROVEMENTS TO MENTAL HEALTH

Emotional literacy has direct links with mental health. Children suffer from a surprisingly high level of mental health problems, many more than has previously been suspected, and the idea of innocent and untroubled childhood is largely a myth. It is not clear whether there are now more mental health problems among children or not; some think it is a matter of better detection (Hartley-Brewer, 2001). There are, however, some specific real increases, such as suicides in young men and self-harm in young women. Longitudinal studies show that children with emotional and behavioural problems are prone to mental health problems in later life: they have increased likelihood of school exclusion, offending, anti-social behaviour, marital breakdown, drug misuse, alcoholism and mental illness in adolescence and adulthood (Buchanan, 2000). Conversely, those with high levels of emotional and social competence do better in terms of such indicators as success at school, at work and in personal life (ibid.). The development of emotional and social competence and well-being can reduce mental health problems, such as depression, anxiety, suicide, eating disorders and stress: systematic reviews of work in schools have shown that school-based specific interventions to improve mental health can be very successful, especially if they use whole-school approaches (Wells, Barlow and Stewart-Brown, 2003).

■ BENEFITS TO SOCIETY

There is strong evidence that work on emotional literacy can result in benefits to society and to the community. There is an increasing recognition of emotion as an important part of public and private life, and an acceptance of the idea that we need to become more skilled in this area if we are to be effective in our personal lives and in our communities. Changes in society and social expectations mean that the increasingly complex challenges posed by the modern world increasingly demand emotional and social competence to cope with the waves of initiatives and continuous change that now bombard us from every side.

The breakdown of traditional social structures has removed many of the old certainties and supports, and resulted in an increasingly fragmented and individualized society in which all of us need to learn to be self sufficient and flexible. Bringing up children is harder than ever, without the transmitted knowledge and support that used to be offered by the extended family and the surrounding community. This decrease in traditional support is being exacerbated by the higher rates of divorce and subsequent one-parent families. We can no longer assume (indeed if we ever could) that it is safe to leave everything to do with the emotional and social development of children to parents: other agencies, including and especially schools, are getting involved to help children receive proper care and guidance.

From the parents' point of view, work on emotional literacy in schools can produce happier, calmer and more successful children and improved family relationships, while specific work with parents themselves to improve their parenting techniques has been shown to have significant gains for their ability to parent successfully (Sharp and Faupel, 2002).

The ultimate aim for much emotional literacy work is to help produce more socially minded citizens, who see the benefit of participating in social and community processes, increased levels of social capital (a feeling of belonging to a community), a more flexible, resilient and effective workforce, and a reduction in violence and crime. Ultimately emotional literacy should also make communities better places to live, with higher levels of tolerance, understanding, care, compassion and citizenship.

To consider as a result of reading this chapter

- What terminology do you feel comfortable with using when thinking about working in this area?
- What do you see as the advantages and disadvantages of using your chosen terminology?
- Can you identify work you and your school/organization are already doing that relates to emotional literacy? Can you identify areas in which you need to make changes?
- Consider the extent to which you and your colleagues agree with some of the reasons commonly put forward for why emotional literacy is increasingly important in education, and add any other reasons you may have, including some that may relate directly to your school/organization.
- Now you have read the section on evidence are you more convinced than you were that this is an important area to work in? If so, what bits of evidence did you find especially compelling? What further evidence would you need to take action? (You can think this through for other groups around you who may need convincing, for example parents, students, local education authorities, funding bodies.)

CHAPTER TWO

What Are We Aiming At? What Competences Are We Trying to Develop? In What Key Ways Can Schools Help Develop These Competences?

GOALS OF THIS CHAPTER

By the end of this chapter you will:

- have explored what is meant by 'emotional literacy' for individuals, in terms of the specific competences that might constitute it
- understand what these competences mean and why they are important to learning, and to shaping behaviour
- identified some key ways in which schools can develop these competences in their students and staff.

INTRODUCTION

WHY CLARIFYING THE COMPETENCES WE WANT TO DEVELOP IS IMPORTANT

It is important to start from a clear idea of what we are trying to achieve when developing emotional literacy in schools, as without clear aims in mind we cannot know when we have achieved them. Chapter 1 presented a broad definition of emotional literacy. However, definitions at this level of generality are necessarily vague: in order to operationalize emotional literacy we need to 'unpack' what we meant by it. The usual way in which this has been tackled is to draw up a list or a taxonomy of competences which is then the basis for practical and concrete action, and this chapter will suggest one such taxonomy.

Uses a school might make of the idea of 'competences'

- Consider what skills, beliefs and attitudes the school thinks are important, which they already focus on, and which they would like focus on more, with their staff and students.
- Compare their first effort with an existing list or taxonomy (such as the one in this chapter) and consider whether they would like to add or adapt any.
- Consult students, parents and staff to gain their views.
- Consider profiling the chosen competences to provide a baseline against which to assess any changes, using their own instrument or an existing one (see Chapter 6).
- Develop classroom experiences to help students learn the competences, and/or select an existing learning and teaching programme (see Chapter 4).
- Organize training courses for staff to build their competences, both for the sake of the staff's own well-being and so they may model them more effectively and create the kind of environments that foster them.
- Consider how the whole-school environment fosters these competences (see Chapter 5).
- Carry out changes and monitor them over time, using an existing tool or developing their own (see Chapter 6).
- The list of competences will of course change, being added to and refined as work develops.

◾ WHERE THE COMPETENCES OUTLINED IN THIS CHAPTER COME FROM

This chapter contains suggestions for some clusters of key competences for emotional literacy. It draws on several of the best known efforts in the field (for example, Goleman, 1996; Elias et al., 1997; Sharp and Faupel, 2002) including those that underpin the programmes of teaching and learning described in Chapter 3, and the best available instruments for assessing the competences, which will be discussed in Chapter 6. This chapter is not simply reproducing an available list because, in the author's opinion, none are yet adequate. However, the list drawn up in this chapter is only one person's stab at clarifying some of the key competences that constitute emotional literacy and are a starting point for schools to use for reflection and discussion, certainly not an attempt to provide the last word on the matter. Schools will want to have considerable debate themselves about what they think is important, and which competences they think are appropriate for the age, stage and cultural composition of their group of students and for their staff.

SOME ISSUES TO CONSIDER WHEN LOOKING AT COMPETENCE

Before we look at specific competences we will sound a few words of warning.

COMPETENCES ARE RELATIVE

Lists of competences can give a false impression of incontrovertibility. In fact there is a great deal of controversy, and cultural variation, on what might be thought to be 'desirable features' in a person. Deciding what goes in a list of emotional and social competences cannot be a value-free, culture-free or an apolitical exercise.

Some ways in which different contexts/societies may vary in their notion of what it is to be emotionally 'competent'

- The extent to which the focus is on the needs of the individual or on the group: is the emphasis on responsibility or duty?
- The extent to which individuals are encouraged to be autonomous and independent or to follow rules, authority and tradition: is the emphasis on taking a critical perspective or on obedience?
- The levels of respect due between different groups, e g., young and old; men and women; social groups, classes and hierarchies; teachers and students; and how that respect is expressed.
- The extent to which difference is tolerated.
- How (or, indeed, whether) the society thinks it appropriate to express the emotions, which emotions it is 'OK' to express, and how it is appropriate to express them

What other differences would you add?

▓ LIMITATIONS OF THE 'RATIONAL CORPORATE MAN' MODEL

Many lists that are currently in popular usage across the world have been developed in the USA, mostly because the USA has put a good deal of effort into work on emotional and social competences. These lists are often used elsewhere without much reflection. However, we cannot assume such ideas will translate and be appropriate in different contexts. Much work on what the USA tends to call 'emotional intelligence' has been developed in the context of business and management, so the definition of desirable competence is often driven by corporate interests. The competences that tend to be valued within this corporate approach are designed to help companies gain the winning edge through innovation, drive, competitiveness, teamwork and so on. It tends to be taken for granted that to be emotionally and socially intelligent or literate is essentially to be an economically active producer and consumer, motivated by the long-term need to succeed on the promotion ladder and gain materially, by following direction, working steadily and avoiding impulsive behaviour. The associated competences that are thought to be appropriate for children tend to focus on conformity, 'good behaviours', co-operation, and positive thinking, usually adult defined.

Corporate models, of course, have their uses in a business context, but some who work in schools will not be comfortable with simply lifting them and applying them in an educational context, either to students or to staff, without reflection on their appropriateness. They are in any case not the only ones in use, even for adults. For example, in Europe there is more emphasis on social and environmental goals, such as equity, sustainability, altruism, social cohesion and high levels of 'social capital' (the extent to which people feel supported and part of their local community). Certain European-based approaches, inspired particularly by the school system in Denmark and the work of the World Health Organization (WHO) Health Promotion Division (Bruun Jensen, 1997; WHO, 1997) also emphasize more challenging goals, such as autonomy, critical awareness, empowerment, the building of ecologically sustainable and democratic communities, and radical action for social change.

▓ THE LIMITATIONS OF WESTERN MODELS

We also need to beware of imposing so-called 'Western' models on other cultures. In some Eastern contexts there is greater emphasis on values such as the group rather than the individual, on obedience and respect for tradition and for people in authority, on social co-operation and on spiritual values. Indeed, spiritual values are increasingly seen as attractive to some in the West as an alternative to the Western emphasis on material gain and individualism, and are starting to underpin some newer work on the nature of intelligence (Zohar and Marshall, 2000). It is important that a plurality of concepts of emotional literacy remains, not least because teachers will find themselves working with all kinds of children from all kinds of cultures, and come from a range of backgrounds themselves, so we do not want to try to impose one template of emotional literacy on all.

COMPETENCES ARE DEVELOPMENTAL

Lists of competences can make it appear that they exist all at one level, when in fact they are fundamentally developmental over time. Children start by being capable of only a basic performance of some competences, and become capable of more complex levels of attainment, as they get older. In the case of some competences the ability to even begin to master them cannot begin until a certain stage is reached, for example empathy appears not to show itself until at least age 7, and the ability to think independently of the peer group is a tough one for most teenagers. Unfortunately lists of desirable competences are often based on a model of a 'rational adult', with standards which few adults in fact live up to, let alone children and young people for whom what is being proposed may not be appropriate at that moment.

We also need to remember that behaviours and attitudes adults tend to identify as problems in young people are those that they themselves often find threatening or difficult: the behaviours and attitudes may well not be problematic from the point of view of the young people themselves. Ideally we need to include consideration of the emotional and social competences valued by young people, but unfortunately not much is known about this and we need more research on this issue – meanwhile staff need to listen carefully to what the young people they work with are telling them. We will be discussing some efforts to get at the priorities of children and young people when we look at a variety of tools and instruments in Chapter 6.

WE NEED TO RECOGNIZE AND VALUE VARIATIONS BETWEEN PEOPLE

Lists can make it appear there is one set of competences that make up the 'perfect person', when in fact valuing and celebrating diversity and difference is both more realistic and more desirable.

■ POSSIBLE DIFFERENCES BETWEEN MEN AND WOMEN

Girls/women	Boys/men
Strengths/characteristics:	Strengths/characteristics:
<ul><li>More sensitive to feelings</li><li>More volatile emotionally</li><li>More sensitive about and in relationships</li><li>More empathic</li><li>More verbal and articulate about their feelings</li><li>More able to see connections between things</li><li>More likely to see happiness as coming from themselves and other people rather than from possessions or achievements</li></ul>	<ul><li>Focus on things and actions</li><li>Better at grasping abstractions and detail</li><li>More competitive in relations with others</li><li>More likely to see happiness as coming from what people do and achieve, such as sporting success or failure</li><li>See the world as more within their own control</li></ul>
Limitations and vulnerabilities:	Limitations and vulnerabilities:
<ul><li>Lower self-esteem and less confidence</li><li>More likely to see things as outside their control</li><li>More likely to suffer from anxiety, depression and self-harm (but not suicide)</li><li>More passive and anxious when faced with difficulties</li></ul>	<ul><li>Tendency to become angry when faced with difficulties</li><li>Problems with talking about and recognizing feelings in themselves and others</li><li>Greater tendency to suicide</li></ul>
Need to work on …	Need to work on …
<ul><li>Feeling and expressing anger including through tone, expression and action</li><li>Self-confidence and self-esteem</li><li>Assertion rather than passivity</li><li>Ability to rationalize and see the detail</li></ul>	<ul><li>Perceiving and understanding relationships, including human relationships</li><li>Developing empathy and sensitivity to their own and others' emotional needs</li><li>Ability to express sadness and anxiety</li><li>Assertion rather than aggression</li><li>Ability to see the total picture</li></ul>

Some key ways in which people tend to differ in terms of emotional style

- Whether we think and learn through pictures, words or feelings.
- Whether we think holistically in terms of the 'big picture' or sequentially and logically in terms of detail.
- The ability to handle pressure.
- The pace at which we like to live.
- Our attraction to risk or security.
- Our need for self-direction or direction by others.
- Our sociability or independence of mind.

What other differences might you add?

THE NEED TO FIND A DYNAMIC BALANCE BETWEEN THE COMPETENCES

Lists can also be misleading as they can suggest that a quality is in itself unequivocally 'good', when in practice few are wholly beneficial when viewed in isolation. Some competences are indeed directly contradictory and we often need to find a balance between them, for example between optimism and realism, or self-confidence and empathy. Therefore this chapter will suggest some of the drawbacks that can occur if we overemphasize a particular competence, and suggest some of the dynamic balances that need to be struck.

SOME KEY COMPETENCES THAT MAKE UP EMOTIONAL LITERACY

This section will explore some of the key competences that make up emotional literacy. For manageability and ease of thinking it will divide them into three basic groups: self-understanding; understanding, expressing and managing our emotions; and understanding and making relationships. This is a rather artificial distinction: in reality the competences overlap, support and flow into one another, a fact we need to bear in mind as we read. It is also only one way of organizing our thinking about competences: other categorizations of the same competences are possible. For example, a recent large-scale review in the USA by Catalano et al., (2002) used the term 'cognitive competence' to include positive self-talk, reading social cues, problem-solving and self-awareness, 'behavioural competence' to include communication and taking action, and 'moral competence' to include empathy, all of which are discussed in this chapter under different headings.

Focusing on competences is, of course, only one part of the picture and does not have to lead to 'blaming the victim' for their attitudes and behaviours which they may hold for, what is for them, a good, or at least a very deep-seated, reason, and which are often reinforced by the context they are in. However, it is a basic tenet of this book that competences are at least partially learnable and can be developed throughout childhood and adulthood, so, in order to ground the account of competences in learning and in the life of the school, the discussion that follows will give a brief indication of some key ways in which schools can encourage each competence through organizing the whole-school environment, including, but by no means exclusively, its programme of explicit learning and teaching. Later chapters will look in more detail at the role of teaching and learning and the whole environment in developing these competences.

SELF-UNDERSTANDING

■ A CLEAR, POSITIVE AND REALISTIC SELF-CONCEPT

Having a clear, positive and realistic self-concept includes:

- liking myself (although not always liking my behaviour)
- valuing and respecting myself as a unique individual
- being able to identify and feel positive about my own strengths
- being able to identify my own limitations and vulnerabilities, and accepting them without undue self-blame or guilt
- seeing myself as separate from others, with the right to be treated with respect and kindness by others
- not being harder on myself than I am on others
- understanding aspects of myself, such as my personality, preferences and needs
- having an accurate and realistic assessment of how I compare with others at the moment.

The ability to be emotionally literate, to make sound relationships, and to learn effectively is firmly based on having a clear, positive and realistic self-concept. It is a lifelong process of developing a sense of ourselves in relation to others, and involves getting a balance between feeling good about ourselves and learning that we are not, and do not have to be, perfect or better than everyone else.

We can help children build a positive self-concept by helping them to focus on themselves, their characteristics, their uniqueness, and their own talents, strengths and weaknesses. They can do this through talking about themselves, what they are proud of and what they would like to change, through depicting themselves and the things that matter to them in art, writing, through physical expression, through measuring themselves and things concerned with them in mathematics, and through testing their own reactions, in science. More generally, schools can help children by ensuring each child feels uniquely known, recognized, nurtured and valued by the school, experiences success and reward, and is protected from hurt by others. Doing well at school can in itself induce high self-esteem: in a large survey in the UK, young people claimed that doing well at school affected their own sense of well-being, levels of happiness, and self-esteem (Gordon and Grant, 1997).

It is important to note that the way this competence is conceptualized is not quite the same as simple self-esteem: it contains the key words 'clear' and 'realistic' as well as the vital 'positive'. For many years self-esteem, in other words high self-regard, was usually seen unequivocally as a universal good. It was assumed that young people with problems, including those who found it difficult to learn or who had anti-social behaviour, invariably had low self-esteem, and that all children benefit from efforts to raise their self-esteem. However, this has been found to be too simplistic. Although depression in young people is indeed associated with low self-esteem, problem behaviour is in fact often connected with high self-esteem, and young people who bully others, take drugs and use alcohol are more likely to have high self-esteem (Salimi and Callias, 1996; Balding, 1998). So self-esteem may be slightly too limited a concept, and it is nowadays often suggested that it may be more helpful to think of helping people develop a realistic self-concept.

We can help staff build a positive and realistic self-concept mainly by the way we organize and run schools and the kinds of climates we create. We need to ensure that there is open communication at all levels, with the opinions and needs of every member of staff taken into account, not just those at the top of the hierarchy. We can do this by ensuring that the way that decisions are made allows plenty of opportunity for 'bottom-up' consultation, and decisions based on that consultation. Staff need to have as much control as possible over their own work, within a supportive structure that makes sure everyone has the right degree of help and knows what is expected of them.

Schools can help develop a sense of realism by giving students and staff sensitive feedback that is realistic as well as affirming. Feedback for students and staff needs to be positive and constructive, taking into account where the person is and what they are capable of responding to at that moment. In giving feedback about emotional and social competences, some of the instruments of assessment that are described in Chapter 6 may be helpful, but there are many informal ways to give feedback, which can be carried out by staff, close friends and peers. Over time the giving and receiving of feedback can lead on to the development of self-reflection and self-assessment, so that each of us becomes our own 'critical friend' (with an equal emphasis on both words!) and a reflective learner.

We need however to be very cautious in giving feedback, as it is easy to do harm. Feedback needs to be paced carefully at the right level for the child or member of staff's development, and not attempt to take them too far, or be too much for them to handle at once, given their own levels of confidence. Children, and staff, who feel bad about themselves or are very new and inexperienced will need a great deal of bolstering and 'cannot take too much reality' until they are more confident. Children who are very different to the norm, for example who have significantly lower abilities than their classmates, or a disability that makes them seem very different, may also need a certain amount of protection while they build up a sense of their own strengths and positive characteristics.

■ A SENSE OF OPTIMISM

One way to resolve the apparently difficult balance between high self-regard and realism is through the concept of optimism. If we have a sense of optimism we can face our own current shortcomings and the immediate difficulties in our lives without being floored by them, because we have a sense that we and our lives can and will change for the better in the future (Seligman, 1998).

This competence is a variation on what is often called 'self-efficacy', the belief that you can achieve what you want to through your own action (Bandura, 1989), which is in turn influenced by your view of the 'locus con-

> **Having a sense of optimism includes believing …**
>
> - life can go right for me
> - the problems and difficulties I am experiencing are a challenge not a barrier
> - I have the potential to succeed in the things I want to achieve and be an effective learner
> - my successes are mainly due to my abilities and hard work, not just luck
> - when things go wrong it is not necessarily my fault
> - I can and will change the things about myself that I do not like that are under my control.

trol' of your actions (Rotter, 1966). Locus of control refers to whether you see your actions as influenced by yourself and your own capacities (a so-called 'internal locus of control') or by forces outside yourself, such as other people, 'fate', 'luck' or 'society' (a so called 'external locus of control'). It would appear that the higher the sense of self-efficacy and the more strongly internalized the locus of control, the higher the goals we set ourselves and the firmer we commit to them, which in itself is likely to lead to greater success. The reverse is also true, and those who have low self-efficacy and an external locus of control are often low achievers, with a low self-image.

If we want children to behave well and learn effectively it is helpful that they have a sense of optimism about their abilities as learners: the single best predictor of success has been shown to be students' expectancy of success (Meese, Wigfield and Eccles, 1990). Staff need to have a sense of optimism about each and every child. Schools often label a child as 'slow' or 'difficult' as if that were the end of the matter, rather than looking at how the context of the classroom or school may have helped create those problems, at why the child is being slow or difficult, and how they can help the child to tackle the problems they have and work towards something better. A teacher's gloomy assessment of the child can easily become self-fulfilling.

Work on the process of learning, including so-called 'accelerated' or 'dynamic' learning is suggesting that almost all of us could use our brains a great deal more effectively than we do and that many apparently slow learners can be helped to learn effectively if we understand the different ways they learn, and help them to 'learn to learn'. Meanwhile work on learning emotional and social competence is showing that quite anti-social and difficult children can learn to work and play co-operatively with others and become better adjusted human beings as a result. Staff can have high expectations of every child, 'keep the faith' in the power of the child to learn and to change, both in terms of their academic learning and in their emotional and social abilities, and use every device they have to help the child learn and grow. With the sense of inner optimism that comes from being believed in by others, extraordinary things are possible. Teachers can use a wide range of teaching methods, and use different types of assessment to appeal to the many different learning styles their students have. Schools can provide a climate in which every learner is respected.

Optimism can and should again be twinned with realism: there is no point in overfacing learners and causing them to fail or to freeze with anxiety. It has been found that the most motivating goals are short-term ones that are challenging but attainable, where the learners have a reasonable chance of success, and the basic skills and the supports to do it (Locke and Latham, 1990). Of course, over time these short-term, small steps can build to big achievements, and many learners find having a long-term optimistic aim helps them to keep motivated along the way.

Teachers need optimism too. The increasing problem of teacher shortages and high attrition rates from teaching are caused in part by teachers losing faith that they have the capacity to cope with the job. In some cases they may be right, and it is unwise to encourage those who are unsuited to the job to stay, for their sake or the children's. However, in many cases an easing of pressure, an increase in support and training, and the passage of time would allow many more potentially effective teachers to stay and succeed in the classroom. We need to lose the 'macho' notion that learning to teach has to be a 'baptism of fire' in which only the tough succeed – there simply are not enough potential teachers to make that attitude sustainable, and in any case we may be losing exactly the kind of sensitive people we need through a lack of sufficient support through difficult periods. We need to be careful not to overface inexperienced teachers in the early years when so many of them give up in despair, feeling they will never cope with the workload or the behavioural challenges their students present. Teachers need to be encouraged to feel they can admit to their own shortcomings without defensiveness, get the help they may need to rise to the enormous challenges of teaching, and believe that the job is 'do-able', or even, dare we say, enjoyable, in time and with the right support.

◼ A SENSE OF COHERENCE

A sense of coherence includes:

- being able to make sense of myself and what has happened to me
- having a sense of having a coherent and continuous life story
- making sense of my multiple selves
- seeing the world as meaningful, and events as comprehensible and connected together.

This competence is highly related to having a sense of optimism. 'Sense of coherence' is an enduring tendency to see the world as more or less comprehensible and meaningful (Antonovsky, 1987). Having a sense of coherence underlies our ability to learn, because it helps us to plan, and to see regularities and predictability in the world. It helps us to acquire clear, positive and accurate self-concept, to have optimism about the future and our ability to change, and to make relationships and attach to and trust others. People with a high sense of coherence are less likely to perceive stressful situations as threatening or worrying and will be more likely to see situations as manageable. It is an important educational and emotional competence for all of us to learn.

A sense of coherence about the world in general begins with a sense of coherence in your own life. Schools can encourage a sense of personal coherence by helping all children to make sense of what has happened to them, through talking, writing and drawing about themselves and their pasts. Staff need to listen to what they are told by children about their lives, in a non-judgemental and open minded way, listening to what the child is telling them and not imposing a stereotypical view of a 'nice' childhood or a 'good' family onto a child who may not have had that experience. Schools need work to build a sense of coherence in all children, but especially those for whom a sense of coherence may especially be lacking. Children who are likely to have particular needs in this area include those who have experienced contradictory or chaotic parenting, or who have been abused and who therefore both love and fear their parents, or who have experienced many moves and many relationships, perhaps because they are in care, adopted or fostered, have moved house and school many times, or are a refugee or asylum seeker.

History topics and lessons are a useful vehicle for building a sense of coherence. Children can focus on themselves, on their own life histories, on their family history and on their cultural history. They can look at individuals, groups and communities whose lives have been disrupted, and at how such people attempted to regain a sense of continuity and community. Literature is another valuable source of material about people's drive to find a sense of coherence to their lives, a strong theme of many stories and sagas.

Staff also need to be encouraged to talk about their experiences in order to build up a sense of coherence in their professional lives. Inexperienced staff in particular may find the multiple roles they need to learn to play as a teacher a challenge, and get help in moving between them while retaining their own integrity and authenticity. They may need help to make sense of the snowstorm of experience that being a teacher in a busy modern school entails.

It is possible that too much concern with coherence can lead to overcontrol, an inability to cope with ambiguity, a tendency to oversimplify complex reality, and difficulties with change, so this competence needs to be balanced with those competences that lead us to be able to cope with realistic levels of uncertainty and change. However, for most of us the desire to control everything is a symptom of a lack of security, which may in fact resolve as we feel that life is making more sense and we can allow for some degree of chaos without believing everything will fall about our ears. So, generally, a sense of coherence would seem to be a positive competence to possess.

UNDERSTANDING, EXPRESSING AND MANAGING OUR EMOTIONS

EXPERIENCING A FULL RANGE OF EMOTIONS

Experiencing a full range of emotions includes:

- experiencing, recognizing, and accepting the full range of emotions we experience, as they happen to us
- being aware of the effects of different emotions on our body, on our mood, on our behaviour, and on how others around us start to act in response
- talking openly and accurately about our emotions, including naming the full range of emotions.

Our society is gradually becoming more relaxed with the idea that emotion is important. Without emotion no animal, including a human animal, would last long: emotion has a crucial biological function in goading us to some kind of action. The most well-known reaction is the 'fight or flight' reflex, which causes an animal or person faced with threat to react swiftly, and often with amazing vigour, by retaliating or by running away. It is often said that, now we no longer face threats to our physical safety, such emotional reflexes are no longer useful for most of us most of the time. However, as we will see in Chapter 4, the reptilian brain in which our automatic responses reside is still very much alive and well in all of us, and its needs have to be met if we are to learn effectively. All emotions have vital and healthy biological and psychological functions. They are an indicator of what matters, for psychological, and sometimes still for physical survival, by telling us what or who to avoid, and what to move towards. Fear can help us to avoid violent and abusive people. Sadness encourages us to grieve, which in turn can help us value what we have lost and what we have left, and what people and events really mean to us. Anger encourages us to fight for what we feel is right, for what matters to us and for what we want to protect. Happiness and joy give us a guide as to what is good for our mental and physical health, such as fulfilling work, relaxation, laughter and good relationships.

Our emotions are then an indicator of how we can best assess what is happening to us, and we mistrust them at our peril. It is important to pay attention to an emotion as we experience it, to accept its presence and its validity rather than deny it. However, many of us learn to deny our basic emotions. For example, girls in some cultures are encouraged to be 'nice' and 'not angry', while boys are encouraged to be 'tough' and 'not get upset'. Such denial can lead to blocks to emotional, and indeed cognitive, development.

It is important to recognize that being emotionally literate is not about always being happy. All of us feel anger and frustration, and experience a range of, sometimes difficult, feelings, due to the many stresses we experience. It is often highly appropriate to feel frustrated, annoyed, distressed, sad or angry. Adolescents in particular will have a lot of challenging emotions to deal with, due to their developmental stage of rapid transition and hormonal changes. New teachers almost invariably find the job difficult in the early years. It is usually helpful to talk about difficult feelings, to process them, to feel better, to reach out, to realize others have such feelings too, and to feel accepted when we are down or angry. This can be very therapeutic, or at least affirming, making us feel less alone and allowing us to 'place' the experience and the emotions it generates, and move on from there. So schools are unwise to try to protect young people or staff, from difficult emotions: it is more realistic and empowering to help people recognize and accept the reality and validity of the full range of emotions, which is the first step to managing them well (Greenhalgh, 1994).

The techniques to help children and staff experience their emotions will include talk, organized formally and informally, in class, in circles, in groups and one to one. Children can also write about feelings in various ways, imaginatively and through keeping logs or diaries of feelings. However, it is best not to overly rely on talk and writing, as some children and some adults may not be effective in these media. If we want to appeal to all the learning styles, we need to use a range of methods. We can explore children's emotional reactions through pictures and other visual representations, through music, art, dance, drama and movement. We can take care to observe what the person's body language or behaviour may be telling us about how they are feeling. In learning to recognize emotion, younger children may find it helpful to look at pictures of people in various mood states and think how they would know the emotion they were experiencing from their facial expression or body posture. Older children can study the biology of emotion, and reflect on the effects of emotion on the body and on behaviour, in humans and in animals.

An overload of emotional awareness can lead to paralysing introspection, self-centredness, and/or dwelling on or getting stuck in a difficult mood rather than trying to deal with it. Emotional awareness needs then to be balanced by other competences, such as emotional management and resilience, which will be discussed a little later.

■ UNDERSTANDING THE CAUSES OF OUR EMOTIONS

Understanding the causes of our emotions includes:

- being aware of the previous events, circumstances, thoughts and past experiences that may have triggered an emotion
- being aware of what it is about the current context that may have triggered an emotion
- being aware of the extent to which our emotions are triggered by factors 'out there' or 'in here'.

Becoming more emotionally competent includes 'getting a handle on' our emotions, through becoming more aware of what causes them. There is much debate within psychology as to whether emotional states are triggered by the immediate context (crudely speaking, the behavioural view) or by our earlier experiences (crudely speaking, the psycho-therapeutic view). It is probably most helpful to cut through the debate by employing the kind of cognitive approaches that say that both can be true, and are mediated by the beliefs we have about the situation. In practice both the past and the present tend to work together in generating an emotion. Understanding where our emotions are coming from is, indeed, partly a matter of identifying what it is about the current context we are in that is triggering an emotion. However, although the causes of our emotions may sometimes appear to come solely from the immediate situation, for example what someone has said to us, this is in fact always mediated by our own beliefs and expectations which are a product of our earlier, often very early childhood, experiences. What 'pushes our buttons' in the present often depends on our past. So we need to become aware of the part our own past experiences and consequent mindsets play in shaping our emotions. Once we are aware of this we can then use this knowledge to help us rethink our reactions to, and beliefs about, what is happening in the present.

Key ways in which schools can help students and staff get in touch with the causes of emotions include encouraging people to focus on the immediate context, to explore what it is that is generating emotion in the here and now. They can think about their own past and how they felt at certain stages of their lives or when certain things happened to them, and how that might be affecting their interpretation of the present situation. Staff may find the creation of an 'emotional literacy interest group' a useful forum to talk about their feelings and 'get a handle' on why they may be behaving as they are, why a certain type of child 'winds them up' and so on.

Students can also be invited to look at causes of emotion in others. They can speculate on the underlying longer-term causes of what people do by looking at current and past biographical and social examples from history and politics, or fictional examples through books and film. Hitler, *David Copperfield* and *Citizen Kane* spring to mind as three obvious examples.

■ EXPRESSING EMOTION

> **Expressing emotion includes:**
>
> • expressing our emotions to ourselves, feeling the anger or the sadness, crying, letting off steam in a safe way, and realizing that we are not necessarily going to be completely overwhelmed by an emotion
> • expressing our emotions clearly to others, through facial expression, gesture, body language, verbal language and tone
> • developing a complex language of the emotions, with a wide and precise vocabulary and range of expression
> • expressing our emotions clearly through writing, and other forms such as drama, dance, art and physical action.

It is important to know how to express an emotion if and when we want to – clearly, appropriately and at the time – including emotions others or we may see as 'difficult'. Emotional literacy is, as we have seen, not all about being 'nice' all the time: it is about being authentic and appropriate. We all need to learn to express our emotions, because expressing an emotion is an integral part of experiencing it. As with all learning, we learn about our own emotions partly through interaction with other people. The reactions of others to our behaviour can help us more deeply experience, appreciate, understand, name, and develop the depth and breadth of our emotional experience. Furthermore, we often need others to know how we feel, for our own or other people's benefit. It can help us, for example, understand that others feel the same way as we do, get help with feelings we are finding difficult, and encourage and allow others to share our feelings.

Expressing emotion in a school context can take many forms. The key medium is often talk, but a wide range of other media, such as art, drama, dance and writing can be used to help children and adults open up and tell others how they feel. Using a range of media may help people who are not predominantly verbal in their learning style to express themselves. Staff need to remember that children and young people do not have all the defences and repertoires that adults possess, and that to a certain extent adults need to tolerate the expression of emotions they may find difficult in children, such as anger. (This does not mean that children should be allowed to hurt themselves or other people or things in the process!)

Taken to extremes, emotional expression can lead to: overimpulsivity (in other words acting too quickly and thoughtlessly on the basis of an emotion); acting inappropriately; and ignoring of feelings of others in favour of our own (for example, venting anger without thought for the other person, or crowing happily at our own achievements). There is evidence that just expressing certain emotions such as anger over and over again is not helpful: it can make us wallow in our feelings, and can in fact fan the flames of aggression. This returns us to the need for emotional management, an issue we move on to next.

◼ MANAGING OUR RESPONSES TO OUR EMOTIONS

It has been suggested many times in the previous section that the competences which are concerned with experiencing, locating and expressing our emotions need to be balanced by those of emotional management. Once we get out of infancy it is important that we realize that other people are on the receiving end of our self-expression, and that we need to make this expression appropriate to the social context we are in. We therefore need to master a cluster of competences which involve us in being able to manage our emotions, and not necessarily respond immediately or directly to them, but instead to take charge of how we express, or indeed decide not to express, them.

Managing our responses to our emotions includes being able to:

- observe our own emotions, in some sense dispassionately
- think rationally when in the throes of powerful emotion
- resist acting on impulse, particularly dangerous ones such as anger
- express our difficult emotions appropriately, including safe expression of anger or sorrow
- manage our own body states, for example by soothing ourselves when anxious, calming ourselves when angry, not sulking or withdrawing when frustrated, containing our excitement when it is unhelpful, knowing how to relax when agitated
- talk positively to ourselves when things go wrong
- distract ourselves by thinking of, or doing, something else that is incompatible with the emotion.

Some useful things to learn to do to manage our own difficult emotions

- Be aware of what sensations and signals from our body, or reactions of others, are telling us about our emotional state, for example raised pulse and flushed face/people moving away or becoming placatory means we are becoming angry.
- If possible remove ourselves temporarily from what is causing the problem – take our own 'time out'.
- Express our difficult emotions appropriately, including safe expression of anger or sorrow, through physical exercise, screaming in a place where we cannot be heard, hitting a cushion, crying and so on.
- Use 'positive self talk' to get in touch with our rational mind – this can help us realize we do not have to react, but have options.
- Consider the longer-term outcomes of acting on emotion, for example impulsive choice may be regretted later, sharp words to a friend may result in loss of friendship.
- Practice breathing and relaxation techniques.

We all need to learn to manage our emotional responses because it is not always appropriate to act on our emotions directly, at the time, or in relation to other people. Our feelings may be excessive, distorted or inappropriate, as is often the case with chronically angry people. Often it is not right to vent our feelings on the nearest person, as our feeling about what is happening now may have been be triggered by feelings that come from a previous experience. Even if our emotions are 'justified' it is not always a good idea to express them directly. The other person may not be in the right mood to hear them, for example they may be too upset or angry, or it may not be fair to vent these emotions on them, for example on a child who cannot help the irritation they cause. Sometimes it is simply not in our own best interests to express ourselves there and then, for example if the boss or playground bully is annoying us but is more powerful than we are!

To see the need to manage our emotions effectively we need to be aware of the impact our expression of emotion has on other people, and to see the world from the point of view of others. This involves the key competence of empathy, which is discussed a little later in this chapter.

Schools can do a great deal to help children and staff learn to manage their emotions appropriately. There are many programmes that teach emotional management, which will be explored in Chapter 4 on teaching and learning, and there is strong evidence that it helps to improve learning and behaviour to have such a programme in place. Opportunities for reinforcing the teaching of emotional management, and for practising it in real life, abound in the course of a normal school day. In class teachers can help children who become anxious or angry when faced with a challenge they cannot meet to use 'positive self-talk' to convince themselves they can succeed if they calm down, take it step by step, concentrate on what they know and ask for help if stuck. Senior staff can do the same by helping staff they are mentoring talk about a difficulty they may be having in dealing with a challenging class or student.

In helping children deal effectively with social situations, staff can take advantage of the myriad natural incidents and events that occur, from flamboyant fights, conflicts and bullying, to more low-key squabbles, fallings out and group exclusions. Staff may also find it helpful to discuss their own handling of difficult situations and think of ways they could manage them more effectively. Children and adults can talk through the reactions that make things worse for themselves and others, and identify and practise more helpful alternatives. In class or in a staff group they can be presented with, or think up, typical scenarios that involve people in difficult situations, then brainstorm and/or role-play, alternative responses and ways of thinking. They can practise distracting themselves, through humour, relaxation or exercise.

Children can be invited to interview someone whose self-control they admire, and report on it to the rest of the class. They can examine the results of a lack of emotional regulation by looking at current and past examples in the political and social world around them, in history, and through literature and film. They can explore the lives of those who managed their emotions effectively, including some great figures such as Gandhi and Nelson Mandela. The study of many religions, including Buddhism and aspects of Christianity will demonstrate the centrality of emotional control to spirituality.

Alone or taken to extremes, too much managing of the emotions can lead to us getting out of touch with our emotions, and to an overconcern for others at the expense of our own needs, so it needs to be balanced with the emotional sensitivity and expression we discussed earlier.

■ INCREASING EMOTIONAL PLEASURE

> **Increasing emotional pleasure includes:**
>
> - being aware of what aspects of our lives generate pleasurable emotions
> - identifying those pleasurable experiences in which we can safely indulge, without harming ourselves and others
> - organizing our time and our lives to engage in safe pleasurable experiences as often as possible
> - becoming so skilled at an activity so we can experience a sense of 'flow'.

Emotional literacy is not all about management, control and denial, although some programmes on emotional and social education might make one believe it was. Well-balanced emotional literacy emphasizes the enhancement of emotional pleasure and satisfaction, through developing the ability to increase the frequency and intensity of emotions and inner states that we find pleasurable. Some emotions and inner states that most people find pleasurable include: happiness; a feeling of optimism; amusement, fun and laughter; joy; love; 'losing yourself in the moment'; a sense of being in the here and now; engagement with a task, sometimes known as 'flow'; rapture; calmness and inner peace; and relaxation.

Schools could do a great deal more to foster these generally pleasant emotions which, as we will see in the next chapter, are highly conducive to effective learning. Many schools and members of staff would do well to take themselves a little less seriously and work harder at playing harder. We need to take care to maximize the positive, fun side of school. We need to encourage children to talk about what it is like to feel happy, so they learn to identify and keep the feeling. Children can spend time doing what they like as well as what they must, sometimes pick the bit of the task they like best without having to do the whole thing, spend time getting really good at something as well as being the 'all rounders' we expect, and be allowed to do something at a level they do well without constantly being challenged to do better. We need to allow staff the same leeway, and encourage them to take time to celebrate their achievements – or simply the fact it is the end of term – with a staff outing or staffroom celebration.

Taken to extremes, too much emphasis on pleasure-seeking can lead to the denial of difficult emotions, to problems in accepting disappointment or the more unpleasant or mundane parts of life, to a wish for constant fun and novelty, to a tendency to be easily bored, to naive optimism and to a lack of realism. We need to balance the search for the positive with work on the competences that help us accept the tougher realities of human existence.

■ USING INFORMATION ABOUT THE EMOTIONS TO PLAN AND SOLVE PROBLEMS

Using information about the emotions to plan and solve problems includes:

- looking to long-term not short-term benefits through being able to delay gratification (for example, working hard for an examination now to ensure entry to college later)
- taking emotional factors into account when planning future actions (for example, 'given what I already enjoy doing, what kind of exercise would suit me best to kick off my new fitness campaign?')
- generating effective solutions to interpersonal problems (for example, 'given the messages my friend usually responds to best, how might I make up this quarrel?')
- being creative and seeing several ways through and round a problem (for example 'what are some things we might all do as a class to make ourselves feel better after the death of poor Brownie, the class hamster?')
- reality testing ('given my own antipathy to planning, targets and paperwork, how realistic is this promotion to headteacher I claim to be working for – is there any other way forward for me that fits my personality better?').

Emotions are not only important in terms of how people feel in the here and now, they are also a building block for all aspects of our lives and learning, a tool to help us plan for the future and for all kinds of success – personal, social, educational and in our career. We can use information about our own emotions and those of others to plan ahead, to organize the emotions in pursuit of a goal and to solve problems.

The ability to use the emotions to help plan and to solve problems is a cluster of significant competences that have been called by Goleman (1996) the 'master aptitude'. It leads to the development of some personal competences that are linked with success in life, such as the tolerance of stress, resilience, the ability to persist through difficulties, to commit to a task and to show intentionality.

Again, the many programmes that teach children and adults emotional and social competences include looking at ways of helping learners use their emotions to plan and solve problems. There is a multitude of opportunities for reinforcing this teaching by helping children, and staff, to develop the ability to use the emotions to plan and to solve problems in everyday life. In class and in staff meetings we can help children and staff to get involved in their own learning and professional development, and set themselves short-, medium- and long-term goals, which they also become involved in monitoring. We can help individuals think about how to solve their personal problems in the immediate or longer-term futures. Children can explore how others solved problems in ways that either considered the emotional implications of a decision or ignored them: such examples might come from history, politics, fiction or film.

Taken to extremes, too much emphasis on using the emotions to plan and to solve problems can lead to a need for overcontrol, overanxiety about the future, a lack of flexibility and not living in the moment, so we again need to remember the importance of emotional sensitivity and expression.

■ RESILIENCE AND DETERMINATION

Resilience and determination involve the ability to:

- 'bounce back' after an experience of upset or failure
- be flexible and adaptive in our response to a problem
- process and learn from a difficult experience, and use it to aid our own development and learning
- move on rather than be immobilized by upset or failure
- stick at a task when the going gets tough.

Resilience is key feature of an effective learner. However hard the teacher tries to select the tasks to fit the learner there will be times when this does not work, and the learner has to pick him or herself up and try again.

However realistic a school tries to make its targets there will be times when individual teachers, or the whole school, do not meet them. In any case, real life does not usually present opportunities for learning that are finely tuned to our existing needs and abilities, and if we want to make progress in the real world we have to learn to be challenged, or challenge ourselves, to take risks and reach farther than we can currently grasp. In these circumstances it does not help if we are devastated if the initial result is less than perfect success.

As we said earlier, we all invariably have emotionally difficult experiences, and we cannot completely protect children, or staff, from them, nor should we always try. We have discussed the need to recognize and experience the full range of emotions, but this is only one step in the process, and we need to learn not to get permanently overwhelmed or dragged down by our emotions. For example, natural sadness at a death does not have to become long-term depression, righteous indignation at how we have been treated does not have to turn into chronic anger or irritation, natural anxiety about meeting new people does not have to become crippling social shyness, and disappointment in our own performance on a classroom task does not have to be followed by petulant rejection of the subject, teacher or school. We need to realize that the going will not always be easy, and that we often have to stick at a task if we are to succeed.

Schools need to allow children and staff to be 'in' their painful experiences, to process rather than deny them, and then also encourage them to learn from them and move on. Older children and adults will find it helpful to learn about the grieving process, and the stages a person goes through in coming to terms with a loss. Schools also need to help their members to bounce back over time, to be an 'emotional warrior' rather than a victim, so we need to encourage and reward resilience as well as nurturing those in pain. There are many opportunities for schools to help children and staff work through this cycle of pain and recovery. Children and staff can be helped to process events that happen in school, such as disappointing examination or inspection results, sporting failures, breakdown of friendships, or the death or moving away of friends, classmates or colleagues. Children and staff may also wish to talk about difficult events that happen to them outside school, such as bereavement, divorce, or a parent, sibling or spouse's imprisonment or redundancy from work. Children may find it helpful to write about such experiences. To help foster resilience and determination, children could explore stories of 'survivors', in writing and real life, or interview a 'survivor' and report how the survivor managed to come back from their difficult experience. All of this will help foster the inner sense of optimism that we have suggested can help people believe that they can learn and change.

UNDERSTANDING SOCIAL SITUATIONS AND MAKING RELATIONSHIPS

■ ATTACHMENT/BONDING

> **Attachment/bonding involves the ability to …**
>
> • love and care about others
> • trust others to – meet your needs, love and care about you, keep you safe, organize the environment so you can learn.

Attachment/bonding is the basis for forming connections with others, the basis on which all social competences are based. Without the motivation to attach and bond the person will have no cause to gain empathy, and no wish to communicate effectively or form relationships in any real sense, other than out of pure survival and self-interest. Attachment is the basis for self-regard, because unless we feel others care about us it is hard to care about ourselves. It is also the basis for success in learning. Research has shown clearly that a child's emotional attachment to schools and teachers is important for academic success, and a teacher's attachment to school is important for professional commitment and success (Hawkins and Catalano, 1992; Solomon et al., 1992; Battistich et al., 1997).

In recent years the concept of attachment has become central in much work in child mental health. Based on the work of John Bowlby (1969, 1973, 1980), attachment theory suggests that all normal babies naturally engage in behaviour that is designed to result in them attaching to their carers, and their carers bonding to them. Through the process known as 'attachment cycle' a baby is normally soothed by its carers when distressed. This builds the neural pathways in their developing brain that make them capable of forming loving attachments to others, based on the pleasure they experience through the process, the development of trust that their needs will be met, and belief in the consistency and reliability of other people. But in some cases this benign cycle does not happen. Inconsistent or punishing attention can lead to what Bowlby calls 'anxious resistant attachment', children who are clingy and more dependent, ever looking for signs that they are loved and wanted. Neglect is worse: neglected babies experience their carer as absent, either literally, through death or illness, or emotionally absent, perhaps through depression, or being 'out of it' on drugs or drink, or being preoccupied with other concerns. The neglected baby cries on for a while, often becoming hysterical, but eventually stops, not through being soothed, but through exhaustion and a sense of despair. After a while they do not bother to show the distress, but simply internalize it, along with a sense of being completely alone, with themselves as the only sure thing in the world. The neural pathways in the brain that could have made the baby capable of making attachments never form, and the developing child never becomes capable of love, concern, sociability or empathy.

Unattached children are hard to reach: they are mistrusting, suspicious, self-reliant and do not care what others think about their behaviour. They have to be in control in order to feel safe, and project their own bad feelings onto others: in the process they often cause bad things to happen because those are the known conditions under which they feel safe. They slip easily from feeling omnipotent to feeling completely worthless if things to do not go their way and they are not able to protect themselves. If nothing is done about this lack of attachment it can become deep seated and lead to anti-social, self-destructive, self-hating behaviour. This so called 'attachment disorder' is often found in children who are, or who have been, in the care system, who may have been emotionally neglected or abused as infants and passed around many subsequent foster homes without ever becoming attached to anyone. However, difficulties in attachment are widespread, including among children who remain with birth parents, and can be experienced to varying degrees.

Fortunately there is now a considerable body of work on what can be done to help children to learn to attach, which is highly relevant to schools as well as to parents, but not much known outside the narrow world or work on adoption and fostering. The basis of helping children form attachments is often the same as normal relationship-building: giving time and attention, giving approval and the experience of success, showing affection to the child and setting clear boundaries in a positive manner. Teachers need to ensure that all children are building healthy attachments, to friends, to staff and to the school itself. They need to take care to identify children who have attachment difficulties and ensure that these students have reliable and trustworthy people to whom they can attach, including adults, and older students, perhaps through 'buddy systems'.

Schools might like to consider recent work on building attachment that suggests that we sometimes need to go beyond this common sense 'love is enough' approach to treat unattached children slightly differently from the norm (Fahlberg, 1996; Hughes, 2000). Newer research suggests that schools need to look for opportunities when the child is aroused and open to new feelings, for example when they are excited by an achievement or when they are hurt or feeling ill, and take special care to show affection and caring at this time, to 'kick-start' the attachment process. There is evidence to suggest that the way in which adults deal with tantrums and outbursts can be particularly significant. The tantrum or outburst is thought to be one of the keys that starts to unlock the door, because it takes the child back to the time when they were acting out their distress, and gives the adults the opportunity to replay the experience, this time with a positive end. For attached children withdrawal of attention, such as 'time out', is often recommended for those who are throwing tantrums. However, 'time out' may be counterproductive for the unattached child, as it can reinforce his or her core belief that no one cares. There is evidence (Hughes, 2000) that it is better not to send the unattached child who is 'acting out' away, but to keep them near, and safe, while the tantrum is happening. The golden moment is when the tantrum is dying away, and the child, still in an aroused state, is open to being soothed and comforted – this can start to build the neural pathways that allow for attachment. So schools may wish to consider their 'time out' policies for children they suspect have attachment difficulties.

Children can explore the importance of attachment, from the study of animal parenting and bonding to the role of attachment in building human communities. Again examples from literature are legion.

Chapter 5 will have a great deal to say about the kind of warm and participative school climates and organization that help students and staff care for and believe in the organization, and believe the organization cares for and about them.

EMPATHY

Empathy is the building block for all social competences. It is about being able to see the world from the point of view of another person and give them the same regard as we (ideally) give ourselves.

Empathy includes …

- recognizing emotions in others
- seeing the world from another's point of view, putting ourself in their shoes
- having compassion for others
- refraining from harming others
- sensitivity – being able to intuit how people are feeling from their tone and body language
- giving people the same concern and respect as we give ourselves
- accepting others and tolerating difference.

All of us need to be able to feel and express empathy. Children need to develop this competence, as they start life naturally egocentric and, in fact, cannot start to have much of a concept of empathy much before the age of about 7. Teachers need to have it aplenty, to get behind the often baffling behaviour that children can confront them with, and start to work out what it may mean.

Some of us need to work harder at empathy than others. There is evidence that people who are chronically angry often have problems with empathy, not recognizing that others have the same range and intensity of feelings they themselves do. Bullies have been shown to underestimate the amount of unhappiness their victims suffer, suggesting an underlying lack of empathy, or possibly self-esteem and lack of awareness of their own significance for others. Shy and withdrawn people may also not be good at empathy; wrapped up in themselves they assume that others are totally confident and only they are frightened by social encounters (Morgan, 1983).

Schools can take advantage of the many daily opportunities to build empathy. Conflicts and fallings out can be used as an opportunity to encourage children and staff to say how their adversary sees the problem, and to keep trying until the other person agrees that this is accurate. New students and staff can be 'buddied' until confident. Staff can be encouraged to talk about students and parents they may be finding it hard to understand and attempt to try to see the situation from their point of view, and be helped to find the motive or pay-off in apparently irrational and purposeless behaviour. In the classroom, caring for classroom pets can awaken caring in children who are otherwise difficult to reach. Stories – from literature, film and history – are a goldmine of possibilities for helping children to see the world through another's eyes and increase their tolerance and understanding; role plays are another.

An overemphasis on empathy can lead to a denial of our own needs and an overconcern for others: it very much needs to be balanced with an appropriate degree of self-regard.

■ COMMUNICATING EFFECTIVELY

The twin cornerstones of emotional literacy, positive self-regard and empathy, are in many ways only real if they are demonstrated through practical action. The key means by which this is carried out is through communicating effectively with others, in ways that give the other person due respect while retaining respect for ourselves.

> **Some key communicative competences include:**
>
> - choosing our own response, rather than acting on impulse, so that it is one that we and others find helpful
> - listening actively to others in ways that encourage them to talk and to feel understood
> - responding effectively in ways that help the other person feel good about themselves while retaining our own authenticity and self-respect
> - being aware of our non-verbal communication: getting control of it and using it effectively.

Staff need to be effective models for children in all the competences discussed here, but above all in terms of effective communication. The most crucial area in which many schools need to improve is the ability to listen to children – what most children need is 'a jolly good listening to'. Teachers spend most of the day talking to, and often at, children, and many children get little opportunity to experience the glorious sensation of having someone really pay them attention and take time to let them talk without constant interruptions and judgements. There is nothing so certain to build the attributes of a positive self-concept and a sense of attachment, which we have seen to be central to learning and emotional literacy, as this sense of being listened to constructively. Listening carefully to children is also a diagnostic tool for uncovering the vital things teachers need to know about them – what stage they are at, how they think, what they are learning, what they are having difficulties with, what is getting in the way, what is bothering them and so on.

Children are often not good listeners themselves, being naturally egocentric, and need to learn the skills of active listening, which encourage them to stop talking themselves and find ways to help others open up at length and feel understood and cared for. Some teachers also seem to have gone into the profession in order to hear their own voice. So everyone in schools can benefit from learning listening skills.

Communication is one of the cornerstones of the emotionally effective schools, and will be discussed in more detail in Chapter 5.

MANAGING RELATIONSHIPS, INCLUDING FRIENDSHIPS AND DIFFICULT RELATIONSHIPS

Some useful competences that help us to manage our relationships in ways that help us to make good friends, and without 'losing ourselves' in the process, include:

- giving others respect, and expecting them to respect us
- being assertive (as opposed to aggressive, a very different style) which involves balancing the needs of others and ourselves, and looking for 'win-win' solutions to conflict, and ways to co-operate with others
- establishing appropriate levels of trust with others, for example by being authentic and reliable, knowing how much to disclose and to whom about ourselves, and how to keep confidences about others
- setting clear boundaries so others know how far to go with us, what they can expect from us and what they cannot
- establishing rapport: knowing how to join in with what is happening first, before attempting to change a group or person's behaviour
- managing difficulties in relationships: expecting that there will sometimes be problems and disagreements, and dealing with them in ways that can allow the relationship to continue
- breaking and ending relationships where necessary in an appropriate and positive way so that both parties leave with dignity and as positive feelings as possible.

Good relationships are essential for emotional and social well-being, and learning the competences that help us form relationships is a key priority for all of us, including and especially children. All schools can benefit from working in this area, and particularly those where student violence and aggression or staff conflicts have got out of hand: we will be discussing the management of problem behaviour in some detail in the following chapters. We also need to help withdrawn and lonely children. A percentage of children find relationship-building so difficult that they have been called 'dyssemic', in other words they have a disabling blindness to the skills that help them get along with others (Macklem, 1987). Fortunately, relationship skills can be learnt like any other, and there is considerable experience in successfully helping both violent and withdrawn children to get along with others.

Social competence is not just important for a person's personal happiness and relationships, it is important for effective learning and career success. Although the history of ideas tends to promote the idea of the 'lone genius', individual brilliance has a limited role in overall human progress, where most scientific breakthroughs and technological gains are in fact the product of teamwork. Even a genius can only be effective if he or she can persuade others to work with him or her, or at least take up and apply his or her ideas. So understanding how others work, being able to empathize with their needs and goals, motivate them and work effectively with them is an important skill for those who want to succeed and have an impact on the world. We need to enable students to learn how to work effectively with others if they are going to be effective learners now and effective workers later in life. We also need to encourage staff to work co-operatively to allow them to be effective professionals, as school staff needs to be first and foremost a team.

There is a wealth of work on how to teach relationship skills, and many of the taught programmes on emotional and social competence that are discussed in Chapter 4 have the development of relationship skills among their key goals. Relationship skills include being sensitive to others, taking turns, and finding positive solutions rather than respond aggressively to conflicts.

There is a wealth of ways in which schools can encourage the development of good relationships, and Chapter 5 will discuss this in some detail.

It is important to balance out the making of relationships with a sense of our own needs, including the need to have time on our own, to be alone but not lonely, and to be autonomous, in other words to make our own decisions, and sometimes take a stand against the crowd. These skills of self belief and self-actualization are quite sophisticated and children will need quite a bit of experience and encouragement before they learn to 'be their own people': ironically, they will probably make much better friends as a result, as 'needy' people are sadly rarely popular. We will look at the key competence of autonomy next.

Assertiveness

Assertiveness is generally seen as the most emotionally literate way to communicate with others in normal circumstances (although not necessarily with someone who has a gun to your head or is your emotionally illiterate boss). Some key assertiveness attitudes and skills are to:

- see ourself and the other person as equally important, with the same rights and responsibilities
- enter every interaction in a spirit of goodwill and co-operation: the goal is win-win, with everyone winding up feeling good
- take responsibility for your own behaviour and feelings – not blame others or try to expect other people to 'guess what you want'
- be explicit about what you want and ask for it clearly and persistently
- say 'no' clearly and in the face of opposition when you believe what you are being asked is not reasonable or appropriate
- listen carefully to feedback – accept what is fair and learn from it; hand what is not fair back to the other person.

Key ways to learn assertion: role play, simulations, rehearsal.

AUTONOMY

Many lists of competence include the competences we have looked at so far, but not so many feature autonomy, or as some would call it, self-determination. However, there is strong evidence to suggest that this competence is a central one for emotional literacy, and can balance out an overfocus on the needs of others, and an unhealthy level of social conformity (Elias and Kress, 1994).

Autonomy includes being able to:

- think for yourself and take action consistent with your beliefs and principles
- have an appropriate level of independence from others
- think critically
- resist pressure from others
- stand up for yourself and your beliefs
- chart your own course.

Children and teachers need to be encouraged to think for themselves in relation to their peers and colleagues, and to find ways to have their own opinions within the group, ideally in ways that do not involve falling out with others. This competence has to be very much context and age related. The degree of self-determination that is appropriate for older children and adults in such matters would not be appropriate with younger ones, but even quite young children can be encouraged to express their opinions and make some genuine choices and decisions that are safe for them to make, and which give them a sense of personal empowerment.

The encouragement of autonomy can permeate all aspects of school life. We need to allow children and staff at all levels to make their own decisions and contribute wider decision-making, both in the everyday world of the classroom, through larger structures such as schools' councils and staff meetings, and through special exercises such as consultations about an aspect of school development or change. Ways in which this important competence can be fostered at a whole-organization level is discussed in more detail in Chapter 5.

Self-determination is also centrally related to how we expect people to learn. As we will see in Chapter 4, schools are starting to work on the process rather than the content of learning, on 'dynamic' or 'accelerated' learning, in which the focus moves from teaching facts and known proce- dures to a focus on the outcomes of learning, thinking skills, learning how to learn and associative thinking.

Too much emphasis on autonomy can lead to risky behaviour, being criti- cal rather than constructive, and to difficulties in working with others and in taking direction. It needs to be balanced, for example with a sense of realism, an understanding of the norms of the context, an accurate assess-ment of our own abilities, an acceptance of the need to allow others to have appropriate levels of control and an awareness of the needs of others.

To consider as a result of reading this chapter

- What competences do you as an individual or as a group think are core or of priority in the context you are in?
- What competences relate to the various age groups represented by your school, including teachers and other staff?
- How might your school foster these competences?

See also the box 'uses a school might make of the idea of "competences"' at the start of this chapter.

CHAPTER THREE

Some Key Principles for Developing Emotional Literacy in Schools

Having looked at the competences that constitute emotional literacy for individuals, and touched on ways in which schools can develop them, we will now move on to look in more detail at actions schools can take. In developing emotional literacy in schools it is important not to get lost in detail, but to clarify the basic principles that need to drive the work. Once the principles are clear, more detailed approaches and programmes can be derived from them, in accordance with the specific conditions of the school in question.

GOALS OF THIS CHAPTER

By the end of this chapter you will have explored three interrelated principles that are basic to the development of emotional literacy in schools. They are:

- to embed emotional literacy within a genuinely whole-school approach
- to address the issue of behaviour in emotionally literate ways
- to target special attention to those with emotional and behavioural problems, using a low-key, non-stigmatizing, flexible approach, which keeps the child in the mainstream school wherever possible.

TAKING A WHOLE-SCHOOL APPROACH

THE GROWING EVIDENCE FOR HOLISTIC APPROACHES

Whole-school approaches are indicated as the most appropriate approach to any issue on which we hope to make a real impact, including and especially emotional literacy, but by no means restricted to it. The call for holistic thinking is based on a growing realization across a vast range of social, health and educational challenges, which is that the analyses and solutions that work in practice are usually holistic ones. It was not always thus: in educational research in the 1970s and 1980s, attempts to tackle emotional and social issues in schools tended to focus on individuals, on single problems, on the search for single causes and on proposals for single solutions. However, in recent years the emphasis has changed, and across all types of educational research there is a growing tendency to look at environments rather than individuals, both as the focus for concern and as the solution to problems, at the relationships between problems rather than at single problems, at clusters of risk factors rather than single causes, and at positive capacities rather than problems and deficits. In arguing why a whole-school approach is to be preferred we are therefore able to draw on work from a massive range of research that uses a wide range of terms. Terms commonly used to describe holistic approaches include 'settings', 'universal', 'ecological', 'environmental', 'comprehensive', 'multi-systemic' and 'multi-dimensional'.

Some well-known educational movements that use a whole-school approach include those known as 'healthy schools/health promoting schools' in Europe, Africa and the Western Pacific, 'safe schools' in the USA and the Netherlands and 'the environmental schools movement' in Sweden and Denmark. Research foci which look at schools as a whole include 'school effectiveness', 'school improvement' and 'positive youth development'. The evidence that will be cited in this section draws on work that uses all these terms, initiatives and foci.

EVIDENCE FOR A WHOLE-SCHOOL APPROACH

There have recently been several large-scale systematic reviews of the research evidence (Lister-Sharpe et al., 2000; Catalano et al., 2002; Wells, Barlow and Stewart-Brown, 2003), which have concluded unequivocally that whole-school approaches are essential when attempting to tackle emotional and social issues in schools. Wells, Barlow and Stewart-Brown (2003:2), who reviewed programmes designed to promote mental health

concluded 'the most robustly positive evidence was obtained for programmes that adopted a whole-school approach'. Whole-school approaches
have been shown to be much more likely to make long-term changes to students' attitudes and behaviour across a wide range of social, emotional and
behavioural issues than are specific, one-dimensional programmes, which
focus only on limited issues, such as curriculum interventions or behaviour
(Durlak, 1995; US General Accounting Office, 1995; Durlak and Wells,
1997). It is important too that holistic approaches are wider than the
school: in a recent review of US progammes designed to promote 'positive
youth development', of the studies that were deemed to be effective, two-
thirds of them included not only the school but at least one other setting,
usually the family and the community (Catalano et al., 2002).

■ WHAT IS MEANT BY A WHOLE-SCHOOL APPROACH

It is worth taking a moment to say clearly what this book means by a
'whole-school' approach as, although teachers and others are often
exhorted to take a 'whole-school' approach to a wide range of educational
issues, there is considerable variation in the way the term is used in practice. The term is sometimes used in a very partial way to describe a situation that is not very different to a traditional approach. For example, it is
often used to refer to working with all students rather than just those with
special needs and difficulties and/or working through the taught curriculum to teach emotional and social competences. These approaches are
indeed important, and later chapters will look at them in some detail.
However, the evidence suggests that we need a 'whole-school' approach to
emotional literacy that goes a great deal further than special needs, and the
curriculum alone if it is to be really effective.

Table 3.1 sets out the contrast between three approaches – a traditional
'special needs' approach, which focuses on emotional and behavioural
problems, an approach which teaches emotional and social competences
to all, and a genuinely 'whole-school' approach.

In the sections that follow we will unpack the elements of, and the implications of taking, a genuinely whole-school approach.

■ A POSITIVE PERSPECTIVE

Traditionally most work on emotional and social issues in schools has
been targeted on troubled and troublesome students, those with special
needs and emotional problems, and those whose behaviour disrupts the
school community. However, recently the focus has moved to a more

positive approach, which emphasizes strengths, capacities and competences as the overall framework. Again the shift in thinking that this reflects is part of a much wider movement: right across society we are moving from problem-focused approaches to more positive ones. We suggested in Chapter 1 that work on mental health, for example, has undergone a radical shift, and is now starting to use strategies for promoting mental health

TABLE 3.1 THE THREE APPROACHES

Aspect of school life	Traditional 'special needs' approach to work on emotional and behavioural problems	Teaching emotional competences through the taught curriculum	'Whole-school' approach to the promotion of emotional literacy and emotional well-being
Focus of concern	Focus on individuals with problems and 'special needs' procedures and responses, e.g. identification, referral to outside agencies, support for students in school	Focus on teaching and learning for all students, as well as special needs procedures	Focus on the totality of the school as an organization in its community, including all aspects of school life, e.g. ethos, relationships, communication, management, physical environment, learning strategies, curriculum, special needs procedures and responses, relationships with parents and the surrounding community.
What constitutes 'quality'	Emphasis on getting the procedures and responses right for children with 'special needs'	Emphasis on getting the taught curriculum right for all students	Emphasis on a ensuring an embedded, coherent, congruent and co-ordinated approach across all parts of the school
Goal	Goal is to overcome negative problems and difficulties in a minority of students, those with 'special needs'	Goal is to promote the learning of competences for all students, and prevent and overcome problems and difficulties for students	Goal is to promote positive emotional literacy and well-being, including the learning of emotional competences, and prevent problems and difficulties for all school members, e.g. staff, students, parents, etc.
Timing of the response	Short-term response to events, often 'crisis management'	Long-term, developmental approach which starts early, for all children, includes promotion of competence and prevention of problems	Long-term, developmental approach which starts early, for all children, and which includes teacher and parental development, includes the development of emotional literacy and well-being, the learning of competences and the prevention of problems
Theory of causes of the problem	Focus on 'difficult' behaviour	Focus on the emotions, beliefs, attitudes, and skills that underlie behaviour	Focus on the emotional and social contexts that shape behaviour as well as the emotions, beliefs, attitudes and skills that underlie it
Role of parents and community	In school focus: parents and community asked to 'support' the school		Parents and the wider community actively involved, e.g. in school decision-making
Relations with outside agencies	Outside agencies used for referral of children with problems and difficulties		Outside agencies are involved with whole-school work, in school, as well as being used for referral

which are not just about illness and problems, but are about increasing peoples' levels of positive wellness, including their sense of fulfilment, concern for others, joy, humour, laughter energy levels, self- esteem, sense of engagement and feeling of being valued. Meanwhile work on organizations is beginning to consider the social contexts that foster productive and pleasant relationships such as teamwork, co-operation, bonding and attachments, and sense of mutual responsibility and delight in the company of others. In a health context work that starts from a positive premise is often called the 'salutogenic' or wellness model (Antonovsky, 1987).

■ TAKING A WHOLE-SCHOOL APPROACH HELPS CHILDREN WITH PROBLEMS

One of the implications of taking a positive approach is that work on emotional literacy starts to be seen as necessary for able, well-adjusted children as well as for those with special needs and problems. This is not to say that we must never target those with problems, and this chapter goes on to discuss targeting in some detail later, but there is strong evidence that targeting is much more effective if it takes place within a whole-school approach, which both help the majority and is actually more effective in meeting the needs of the troubled and troublesome than targeted approaches on their own. For example, in their systematic review, Wells, Barlow and Stewart-Brown (2003) showed that whole-school approaches were more effective in influencing what they called the 'mental health' of children than those that were limited to classroom approaches alone: this increase in effectiveness included meeting the needs of students with emotional and behavioural problems.

■ WHY WHOLE-SCHOOL APPROACHES ARE MORE EFFECTIVE IN DEALING WITH PROBLEMS THAN TARGETING ALONE

Even if our main concern is to help those with problems, we still do better to use a whole-school approach, for the following reasons:

- Emotional, behavioural and social problems are extremely widespread – they are by no means minority problems.
- The same risk and protective factors predict more or less the whole range of problems in children and adolescents, from teenage pregnancy to school failure.
- Problem behaviours tend to cluster together, and reinforce one another (Catalano et al., 2002).
- Most behaviour and emotional problems exist on a

continuum and affect a very high percentage, sometimes the majority of, the population, so where we decide to have the cut off (for example, '20 per cent have problems') is arbitrary. If we target an arbitrary percentage, the very many people who suffer from a problem to some extent will be ignored.

- If we have an overall school climate that supports emotional literacy it is less likely that children will have problems in the first place, so a whole-school approach has a preventive function.

- Those with problems will be spotted early. Staff will be more confident of their assessment because they have a clearer yardstick of relative 'normality'.

- The basic processes that help some help all. The principles and strategies advocated in this book, such as starting early, being clear about what is needed to be learned, active listening, counselling, building warm relationships, setting clear boundaries, and participation, have been shown to be especially helpful in helping those with emotional and behavioural problems (McMillan, 1992; Cohen, 1993; Rutter, Hagel and Giller, 1998). Children with special needs may need more of certain approaches, but they do not need different approaches.

- It is less stigmatizing to work with everyone, as it means that those with problems are more likely to use the services offered and feel positive about them than if they feel they are being singled out.

- The principle of 'herd immunity' means that the more people in a community, such as a school, who are emotionally and socially competent, the easier it will be to help those with more acute problems. The critical mass of people has the capacity to help those with problems (Stewart-Brown, 2000).

- Those who are given extra help will be able to return to mainstream school more easily, as the way they are dealt with in terms of special help is then congruent with the school to which they return and they are not so likely to get into difficulties in future.

■ TAKING A SUSTAINABLE, LONG-TERM, DEVELOPMENTAL APPROACH

There is a danger that work on emotional literacy can be seen as a fad and a fashion, something in which schools engage in for a while with some students, and then drop in favour of the next initiative. However, to work like this would be largely a waste of time.

There is a strong consensus in the literature that work in emotional and social competences has to be high profile, not tucked in between other matters and topics that the school perceives as more important. The approach and strategy need to be explicit, with all involved. Staff, governors, students and parents need to be made aware that work on emotional and social competence is a key priority and an integral part of helping all students learn and be made clear about why and how they and the rest of the school are setting about it. Every teacher needs to believe that they and their subject have an active part to play in the total enterprise, whatever their specialism, and themselves receive education and support to make this a reality. All other members of staff, such as classroom assistants, counsellors, educational psychologists, school nurses, school secretaries, lunchtime supervisors and caretakers, need to see where their part of the jigsaw fits into the whole.

Any educational approach needs to be developmentally appropriate to the age and stage of the learner. Whatever they are learning, younger children mainly need very concrete experiences of demonstration and some rote learning. As students get older they are increasingly able to reflect consciously on the processes and use more complex and abstract ideas and principles. Adults require an approach that uses the principles of adult learning, for example challenging entrenched attitudes and building on the considerable prior experience that they are bringing to the situation.

If the need to take a developmental perspective holds true for learning as a whole, the imperative to do so is even stronger when we are considering education to develop emotional and social competences. The kind and level of competences children are capable of is fundamentally affected by their developmental stage. One of the most demonstrably successful projects, the 'Child Development Project' (Battistich et al., 1989; Battistich et al., 1996) now to be found in schools across the USA, which has been shown to be highly effective in developing a wide range of emotional and social competences, is, as its name suggests, based on a strongly developmental approach, which is carefully tailored to meet the stage-specific needs of the child.

The implication of taking a long-term, developmental approach is that we need to begin work on emotional literacy early and continue it throughout the school life of the child, from nursery school to sixth form. Reviews of interventions, including recent reviews (Marshall and Watt, 1999; Shonkoff and Philips, 2000; Carr, 2002) have invariably shown that programmes which start early and with the youngest children, and are developmentally sensitive to the age and stage of the students, are best able to promote improvements in emotional and social behaviour, for all children. The systematic review of approaches designed to promote mental well-being in schools by Wells, Barlow and Stewart-Brown (2003:2) concluded 'the most robustly positive evidence was obtained for programmes that … were implemented continuously for more than a year'. A major review of 'positive youth development programmes' in the USA (Catalano et al, 2002: 6) agreed: 'effective programs … require sufficient time for evidence of behaviour change to occur and to be measured … 80% (of effective programs) provided their services for nine months or more'. There is clear evidence that programmes that aim at developing emotional and social competences are more effective the longer they are in place, and most take years really to establish (Durlak, 1995; Lantieri and Patti, 1996). Programmes which are based on a long-term commitment have been shown to be more successful in changing behaviour than are approaches which are short-term, 'one-offs', triggered by particular 'crises', restricted to a particular age or other target group, or had long gaps in between (Elias, 1995). Education for those who work in schools needs to take a similar, long-term, drip-feed approach, not just be delivered in the form of a single 'one-off' short course.

■ HAVING A MODEL IN MIND OF THE TOTAL ORGANIZATION OF THE SCHOOL

We have seen that, within a whole-school approach, the total focus is wider than the individual, and includes the whole social organization of the school. Modern approaches to educational research have demonstrated that there are no simple causes or solutions in relation to learning or behaviour, and the influences on any aspect of student achievement or behaviour will be plural, the coming together of a vast range of aspects of the child's immediate context and the wider locality. It follows that several aspects of the school organization need to be taken into account, not just one or two. Aspects of the school that have been shown to be very important in the promotion of emotional literacy include not only the curriculum, but also the way the school is managed, its ethos, the quality of the relationships and communication across the school, the physical environment, and relationships with parents and the surrounding community.

Chapter 5 will be exploring many of these features, and examining how they can work together to promote emotional literacy.

It is the author's experience in working with schools that it is helpful for schools engaged with work on emotional literacy to decide at the outset what aspects of school life they wish to tackle and in what order, and devise a model of how these aspects relate to one another. A simple model, which outlines some key aspects that need to be taken into account within the whole-school approach, is given in Figure 3.1.

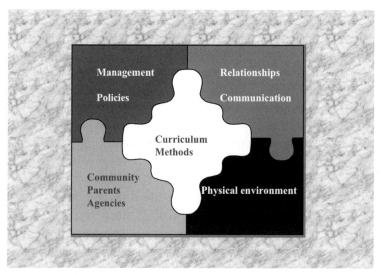

FIGURE 3.1   SOME KEY AREAS FOR A WHOLE-SCHOOL APPROACH TO EMOTIONAL LITERACY

Hampshire Local Education Authority in England have evolved what they call the 'doughnut model' which they find is helping to organize their thinking about how to develop emotional literacy. This model suggests three concentric circles, with 'sugary bits' on the outside, then 'dough' and then 'jam' in the middle. Under 'sugary bits' they include the rewards system, 'buddies' schemes, school councils, sanctions, privilege time, school counsellor, tutor system, mentor scheme, circle time and bubble time. The 'dough' includes the school behaviour policy, PSHE programme, appraisal, community involvement, bullying policy and teaching for lunchtime staff. The 'jam' is the values, vision and emotional life of the school.

Other schools and education authorities will of course evolve models of their own, both to conceptualize the issues they need to examine and to guide their proposed solutions. It is probably the case that the process of jointly deciding on a workable model is at least as valuable the end result.

■ ENSURING CONGRUENCE

Within a whole-school approach, the success of initiatives cannot be left to chance. In promoting emotional literacy it is important that schools use ideas, strategies and materials in co-ordinated ways, that make sure that the whole is greater than the sum of the parts, and that there is no undermining of messages from one part by contradictory messages from another. For example, we need to ensure that the techniques children learn in the classroom for communicating effectively in respectful, empathic and assertive ways are also used by all staff when dealing with children, and noted and praised by staff when they see the children attempting to practise them around the school. If we want children to be independent learners in the classroom, we have to solicit and respect their views about wider aspects of school life, such as discipline, rewards and the physical environment.

Real-life example: emotional literacy helps coherence

Emotional literacy work can itself be a powerful force to bring about coherence within a school. Southampton City Council have found that it can help schools to sort out the tensions that may exist between its various policies, such as equal opportunities, which encourage respect for difference and behaviour policies which regulate the expression of difference. 'An emotionally literate school recognizes such dilemmas and takes steps to explore safe ways to deal with the issues in a consensual manner' said the Chief Educational Psychologist who ran the initiative (Sharp and Faupel, 2002: 10).

ADDRESSING BEHAVIOUR IN EMOTIONALLY LITERATE WAYS
■

■ THE PROBLEM OF BEHAVIOUR IN SCHOOLS

Students' problem behaviour has always been a major issue, often the major issue, of concern to schools. This is understandable as problem behaviour invariably undermines everything schools are set up to do and, alongside workload, student problem behaviour is probably the largest cause of stress and attrition rates in the teaching profession. Aggressive, violent and disruptive behaviour creates fear, anger and unrest in all students, those who are its victims and who witness it as well as those who engage in it, and sabotages learning across the whole-school community. Once it becomes an entrenched part of the culture of a school or classroom it is highly contagious, drawing in many students who would be keen to learn in other circumstances but who nevertheless join in the aggression and disruption because they wish to be part of the peer group or because it seems the 'only game in town'.

Unsurprisingly then, in many parts of the world student problem behaviour has become an educational issue of national concern, and one in which many agencies, including governments, take a strong interest. In the USA, programmes which aim to help students learn emotional and social competences are often prompted by the desire to tackle the growing problem of violence in schools (US General Accounting Office, 1995; Aber et al., 1998). In the UK, the Department of Education and Skills has developed a 'comprehensive strategy for improving behaviour' that is attempting to address the problem of a reported rise in the rate both of low-level disruption classrooms and in the number of children with more challenging and long-term behavioural problems, by co-ordinating action across a vast range of activities and fronts. In Australia attempts are being made to prevent crime by working in schools (Marshall, 2000).

THE NEED TO LINK RESPONSES TO BEHAVIOUR WITH EMOTIONAL LITERACY

Schools obviously need to find ways to address difficult behaviour, and it is by no means the purpose of work on emotional literacy to suggest that schools ignore or condone it. Children need firm boundaries and clear guidance and rules about what is acceptable, including clear sanctions for what happens when they break the rules: we will be discussing how schools can achieve this kind of clarity in Chapter 5. But strategies for addressing behaviour need to go well beyond punishment, management or even the establishment of clarity, if they are to be effective. Work on emotional literacy is an integral part of any attempt to address student behaviour, and vice versa. This section will explore some of the fundamental principles involved in addressing behaviour in emotionally literate ways.

THE POINTLESSNESS OF FOCUSING ON 'BAD' BEHAVIOUR AND USING PUNISHMENT ALONE

Although unsupported by any educational or psychological theory, or research evidence, many schools, and many teachers within otherwise more enlightened schools, still attempt to tackle what they see as 'bad' behaviour by the age-old responses of identification, punishment, containment and exclusion. This may well be the only method the teachers have themselves known, and therefore the only strategy they can imagine.

A punitive approach may appear to work in situations where students are basically willing to learn, believe they can succeed at school, already know how to behave in ways teachers like because they have learned it at home, and identify with their teachers and share the goals of the school. Such students have much to lose by misbehaving: they therefore will generally not misbehave for long, or very severely, or with most teachers. In these cases punishment can be an unusual and rare event and, even though more positive measures would almost certainly work better, it can appear that punishment is effective, or at least not doing much harm.

However, generally a punitive approach tends to worsen or sometimes even create the very problems it is intended to eradicate. In the many contexts where it does not work swiftly and cleanly but no other strategies are tried, it can become the normal, routinized experience for some children, or even sometimes, disastrously, for the whole school. Once it becomes chronic, a punitive approach is poison: unfortunately this happens often and in many schools.

Punishment does not work cleanly and quickly with the many children who do not fit in easily with the behavioural demands of the school, and there are a whole host of reasons why children may not fit. Children may be slow at learning and therefore fall behind in class and misbehave to mask their shame, or may be too clever for what is being offered and become bored. They may find it difficult to behave in ways the schools demands, perhaps because they have not learned an appropriate repertoire of behaviours at home, or indeed have come from homes or cultures where the kind of loud, lively and aggressive behaviours schools do not like are the norm, especially for boys. They may have short-term emotional problems that are distracting them, such as bereavement or divorce, or long-term emotional problems, perhaps stemming from abuse or neglect. They may not learn easily in ways that schools tend to use to teach: we are discovering that many children, boys in particular, are 'kinaesthetic' learners who learn by action and doing, which schools, generally geared to visual and aural learning, do not recognize or support.

Punishment alienates children from their teachers and does nothing to build up trust that is the bedrock of relationships and, thus, learning. It helps create a climate of violence, aggression and fear, which frightens more timid children and feeds the aggression of children who are already so inclined. It can become normalized for children, especially those that come from backgrounds where punishment and negativity are all they have experienced and thus actively seek to make them feel comfortable and, sometimes literally, 'at home'. In any case, for most people any attention is better than none: where children conclude that realistically the only attention they are likely to get is for being difficult, those that have the 'bottle' will generally opt for that as better than being ignored.

◼ EXCLUSION IS NO LONGER USUALLY AN OPTION

Some schools hope to avoid the problem by excluding those who misbehave, either temporarily, to be dealt with and 'fixed' by experts outside the school, or permanently so they become someone else's problem. However, increasingly this is not an option. The sheer, and growing, numbers of students who behave in ways schools do not like makes the exclusion of all of those who are a problem impossible. Even if we restrict our concern to students whose behaviour is extremely disturbing and disruptive, it is increasingly accepted that, as far as possible, students with special needs, including disturbed and disruptive students, should be accommodated in mainstream schools (Elton, 1989). Schools are being asked to cater for diversity, and address the needs of children across the whole community they serve. In some countries governments discourage exclusion: in the UK inclusion is at the heart of the current government's efforts to deal with the problem of widespread disaffection and underachievement in education (New Policy Institute, 1998). Internationally the need to reduce exclusion has been heavily backed by organizations such as the United Nations Educational, Scientific and Cultural Organization (UNESCO) as a way to promote social justice and equity.

There is a wealth of evidence that school exclusion contributes forcibly to educational failure and social marginalization (Parsons, 1999). Exclusions tend to be strongly associated with all kinds of educational and social deprivation, being more common in schools with higher levels of illiteracy, poor results and poor discipline, and in neighbourhoods with high unemployment, high crime rates, poor health, poor housing and high rates of family breakdown. Some groups, in particular boys, ethnic students, those with special needs and looked-after children, are more likely to be excluded than others, exacerbating the tendency of these groups to become socially marginalized. Those excluded from school tend to become much more vulnerable to the use of illegal drugs and the crime that often accompanies it, as well as being disadvantaged educationally, and thus more likely to be unemployed. Exclusion de-skills school staff, who have no opportunity to learn how to manage the full range of cultures, behaviours, and cognitive and physical abilities in the community they serve. In any case, students have to be educated somewhere, and if one school excludes, another agency has to take up the challenge.

■ UNDERSTAND TEACHERS' EMOTIONS IN DEALING WITH CHILDREN WITH PROBLEMS AND WHY THEY WANT TO EXCLUDE

However desirable inclusion is in theory, in practice there is a growing tendency for schools to exclude special needs and difficult students, in the UK at least (Hayden, 1997). Many more schools would like to increase exclusions if they were allowed, and do not feel at all positive about the drive to reduce exclusions. If we are to address this and move towards improved figures for inclusion, a greater acceptance of the need for inclusion, and teachers who can manage inclusion without undue stress, we need to understand why schools exclude. Understanding this includes looking at the role of teachers' emotions in the process.

The simple reason why teachers exclude is that that they feel they cannot cope with the students who they wish to exclude, either in terms of personal stress or in terms of their ability to then meet the needs of less troublesome students. The research evidence suggests that teachers are highly affected by troubled or troublesome students and need help with their feelings, and often practical help too, to cope with violence and aggression. Many find it hard to admit to others that they are having difficulties for fear of being thought inadequate. Teachers in mainstream schools tend to report that they do not feel competent to work with difficult students (Cheney and Barringer, 1995) and that they feel they have not received enough training. Many schools feel beleaguered by having to cope with children with special needs in mainstream classes, especially children with emotional and behavioural difficulties who can be violent, disruptive and threatening.

If they are to cope, teachers, and especially young and novice teachers, need a great deal more support. They need to have their concerns taken seriously so they do not feel that admitting to finding it hard to cope with difficult students will be seen as a weakness on their part. They need education in the skills of coping with difficult students. They need smaller classes and classroom support so they can divide their attention appropriately between different types of child. They need appropriate in school provision for students with problems, such as short-term withdrawal units for violent, disruptive or disturbed students (Munn et al., 1999). They need expert advice and support to be immediately, easily and flexibly available.

■ USING ELEMENTS OF THE BEHAVIOURIST APPROACH

One approach, which has formed a useful antidote to the traditional punitive reflex, is the behaviourist approach. Early work on emotional and behavioural problems was dominated by behaviourist theory, which, by definition, focuses on behavioural outcomes rather than on underlying causes or reasons for that behaviour. Considerable work on emotional and social education still falls within the behaviourist approach, particularly in the USA. A great many initiatives that have attempted to teach social and affective competences use a behavioural approach, concentrating on the teaching of skills and routines, as examination of any database of such pro- grammes in the USA (CASEL, 2002) and Europe (Hendren, Birell Weisen and Orlay, 1994) will immediately show. It is still a very popular perspec- tive on the best way to tackle the issue of promoting children's social and emotional competence, and many of the books written from a behaviourist point of view have some very useful advice to offer (for example, Webster- Stratton, 1999).

■ EVIDENCE FOR THE LIMITATIONS OF THE BEHAVIOURIST APPROACH

Many who work on emotional literacy and related areas believe that behav- iourism may have useful insights but is an inadequate total theory to account for what people are like, or to understand and change behaviour. New work on the structure of the brain, which we will look at in Chapter 4, is supporting the established intuitive belief that there is far more to the brain, let alone to the mind and the person, than behaviour, and that we need to understand the entirety of a person, their attitudes, values, emo- tions, beliefs, and indeed their subconscious, as well as their behaviour.

In terms of classroom research there has not been much empirical research that tests the effects of behaviourist approaches against others, but Morgan (1983) concluded that, in the rare studies which do compare behavioural approaches with those that emphasize understanding and emotion when teaching of social and affective competences, behavioural approaches do not stand up well. Without grounding in deeper attitudes and values, behaviour can be empty, shallow and easily changed. There is some evi- dence that using behavioural approaches with younger children to engage them in practising healthy behaviour achieves compliance in the short term, but can backfire as children get older and more knowledgeable, and lose trust in the truthfulness of their teachers as a result of feeling coerced (Stewart-Brown, 1998b). It would appear that the behavioural approach can be effective initially, but that, used on its own, it has few long-term benefits, being ineffective in helping children and young people internal- ize their learning and generalizing from it (Palardy, 1992; 1995).

■ BEHAVIOUR HAS MEANING

A key contribution of work that goes under the heading of 'emotional literacy' is the assertion that behaviour has a meaning, or at least a pay-off, and that we need to work to uncover and understand the meanings or rewards that are stemming from that behaviour, and in particular its emotional origins and outcomes, as well as trying to shape the behaviour. Cognitive approaches are helpful here: they emphasize the important mediating role that beliefs play in the process, and suggest that if we work on uncovering a person's beliefs and help them reframe unhelpful beliefs, different and more helpful behaviour may then follow (Hains, 1992). Again, new work on the structure of the brain is emphasizing the need to engage the parts of the brain that govern rational thought in processing emotional experience, as we will see in Chapter 4.

Work on emotional literacy work is central in assisting schools to take a holistic view of children, to see the links between behaviour, learning and emotion, and shifting from seeing children's problems as primarily cognitive and behavioural to include a concern with their emotional components (Greenhalgh, 1994; Sharp, 2001). It has been helpful in making us aware that difficult children are not always simply being 'naughty' when they misbehave – there are sometimes underlying emotional and contextual reasons for their behaviour that need to be addressed. It has helped in developing an understanding of the two-way link between the emotions and learning difficulties, and realizing that emotional problems can lead to learning difficulties, while learning difficulties lead in turn to emotional problems, such as lack of self-esteem and alienation from school. So those who work on emotional literacy are keen to encourage schools and agencies to think through how their work on student behaviour would be strengthened by a greater and more explicit focus on emotional and social competence. They suggest that approaches to student behaviour need to deal with the underlying emotional, social and contextual causes of behaviour in the school environment, and positively teach the skills of emotional and social management that can help improve behaviour, rather than focus just on the behaviour itself.

Behaviour, beliefs and emotions all have an important part to play in the development of emotional literacy, and indeed the relative importance of each will vary from child to child and situation to situation. Behaviour, emotion and belief are fundamentally interrelated, and we need to understand and tackle all three aspects together. It is perfectly possible both to work with the underlying emotional 'causes' of behaviour and also to recognize that the behaviour and beliefs that are the outcome of the emotion can persist as a mental habit after the 'cause' has gone. The thought processes and habits may need to be changed, and the person helped to gain recognition by acting in new ways. So, for example, we can attempt to get to the underlying emotional reasons why a child is angry enough to behave aggressively, teach them to reframe their thoughts about those 'causes', and also teach them to express their anger in ways that are not damaging to themselves and others.

■ BEHAVIOUR IS LEARNED

A fundamental principle that can help us manage behaviour more effectively is the recognition that behaviour is generally learned. This means that schools have the task of helping students to learn helpful behaviours and unlearn unhelpful ones. This realization immediately takes the debate away from the pointless moralizing in which some schools engage about children being 'good' or 'bad', or, even more alarmingly, 'evil'. It locates the problem in the behaviour, not the child, and enables schools to work with the vital distinction that we can dislike a child's behaviour without having to dislike the child. It induces a sense of optimism and possibility for change in teachers and students which, as we saw in Chapter 2, is a key emotional and educational competence.

■ LOOK AT THE CONTEXT WHICH SHAPES THE BEHAVIOUR

Schools often focus their attention on the problem child rather than on the context, blaming the child and/or the homes they come from, for all aspects of that child's behaviour. They often do not appreciate that the problems they are facing may be at least partially created, and will certainly be shaped, by the school context they have created and by their own responses to the child. The most classic conundrum, to which we have already alluded, is created by schools paying most attention to the kind of behaviour they claim not to want and thus unwittingly fostering more of this behaviour, both among those students who are inclined to it anyway and see the attention as the only recognition they are likely to get, and those who might not be particularly so inclined but who find that other types of behaviour merely result in them being ignored. It is a useful maxim to remember that 'what you pay attention to you get more of', whether it is wanted or unwanted behaviour. Chapter 5 will have a great deal to say about the kind of warm, supportive, clear and participative environments that tend to reduce problem behaviour and induce learning.

▓ RECOGNIZE POSITIVE BEHAVIOUR

We have long known that reward is far more motivating than punishment in inducing wanted behaviour. This does not necessarily mean we have to use 'extrinsic' reward systems, in which students accumulate certificates, stickers or stars for good behaviour that are then exchanged for wanted 'goodies' such as activities, sweets or treats. Although at one time often presented as a simple panacea for almost all problem behaviours, the effectiveness of extrinsic reward has recently been shown to be questionable: it can lead to shallow behaviours that are easily set aside, and in some cases is no better than no attention at all (Jensen, 1995). However all schools of thought agree that it is enormously beneficial to pay attention to the kind of behaviour we want. The emphasis on 'paying attention to the positive' has had a massively beneficial impact on the management of difficult behaviour, redirecting attention from the negative feedback and punishment that so often dominate a school's reaction to difficult behaviour. The advice to find opportunities to praise children for wanted behaviour, to 'catch 'em being good' rather than punish unwanted behaviour, is immensely effective and practical. Teachers have been shown to be quick to praise good academic performance and criticize bad social behaviour but not often praise good social behaviour. Schools need to be encouraged to base their communication, discipline and classroom management on positive techniques. These include being clear about what is wanted, focusing on and paying attention to positive behaviour rather than bad behaviour, keeping any punishments very short, and having high expectations of students.

▓ START WHERE PEOPLE ARE

Even schools that take care to have a differentiated curriculum for learning that is responsive to the varied knowledge and abilities of their students often have a 'one size fits all' attitude when it comes to behaviour, and teachers can fail to appreciate the radical extent to which children of the same age can differ in this respect. Children will vary in their capacity to behave well, for example the extent to which they can concentrate, sit still, resist impulses, keep quiet, show empathy and concern, and control aggression. They will differ in terms of what they value as rewards, with some being content with verbal praise, others needing more tangible signs of appreciation. They will vary, too, in the speed with which they can change their behaviour and for how long they can sustain new behaviour without further input. So we need to take all these differences into account when thinking about how to help them develop from where they are to where we would like them to be. Chapter 6 will have a good deal to say about techniques for finding out where people are.

There is then a whole range of ways in which schools can manage behaviour in more emotionally literate ways. These techniques are often particularly helpful when dealing with children with problems, an issue we will examine next.

TARGETING WITHIN A WHOLE-SCHOOL APPROACH

A HOLISTIC APPROACH DOES NOT PRECLUDE TARGETING

Key principles for working with those with special needs on emotional literacy

- Provide a foundation of work with all children within a whole-school approach.
- Take special care that children with emotional and behavioural problems learn the competences of emotional literacy.
- Understand the emotional and social causes of behaviour rather than just focus on the behaviour in isolation.
- Understand teachers' emotional reactions to working with children with problems.
- Identify those who are having problems early and tackle them straight away.
- Provide any special help in as low-key a way as possible, concentrating on alleviating the problem, not labelling or stigmatizing the person.
- Provide the special help within mainstream schools wherever possible.
- If a child is out of mainstream class/school, see it as a short-term highly focused intervention which aims to return them to the mainstream as quickly as possible.
- Ensure the special unit and the mainstream class/school use the same clear, positive approaches, so that the child can return to class/school easily and not then go round the loop again.
- Meet the needs of troubled as well as troublesome children.
- Take special care to work in a co-ordinated, coherent way when dealing with vulnerable children, who need help quickly and efficiently, including liaising effectively with outside agencies, and with parents.

We have said that schools need to take a 'whole-school' approach to work on emotional literacy and on the management of behaviour. Taking a whole-school approach does not mean we fail to take into account the needs of those with emotional or behavioural problems or fail to give them extra help. We can continue to target time, attention and resources to give appropriately differentiated provision, but against a backdrop of adequate overall provision for everyone, which is, as we have seen, much more likely to be effective than targeting alone. The original impetus for working on emotional literacy came largely from work with children with problems, and the long tradition of work on special needs and emotional and behavioural disturbance has a great deal to contribute to whole-school approaches to emotional literacy.

We have looked at the first four principles (outlined in the box on the previous page) already: the rest of this chapter will be spent exploring the others.

■ THE IMPORTANCE OF EARLY IDENTIFICATION

Research consistently demonstrates that all children need to be taught in environments that foster emotional and social well-being right from the start, that they need to learn emotional and social competences at a very early age, and that any targeting needs to start early too. Many emotional and social problems are best tackled in primary school, when children are most open to help (McGinnis, 1990). There is overwhelming evidence that the ability to change negative behaviour decreases with age (Loeber, 1990), and that signs of difficulty can be seen very early and are best tackled when they still are mild (Rutter, Hager and Giller, 1998). Most children who become near impossible to deal with in secondary school, when they are large and their behaviour flamboyantly difficult, have been showing clear signs of behaviour problems from early primary school, but because they were smaller and their behaviour less threatening they tended to be left without help, as staff thought they would 'grow out of it'. In the light of this there is now a considerable drive to encourage schools to intervene early (Coram Family, 2002).

Chapter 6 will suggest some approaches and instruments that may be useful in identifying those with emotional and behavioural problems at an early age and which can help ensure that schools are tackling early identification in a systematic manner.

■ TAKE A LOW-KEY, NON-LABELLING APPROACH

Many parents, and some teachers, are reluctant to obtain help for children with problems for fear of labelling them irretrievably as 'difficult' or 'disturbed'. There is therefore a tendency to leave referral too long in the hope that the problem will solve itself: usually it does not, and professionals are later called in to help a child whose problems are now deep-seated. However, parents' and teachers' fears do have foundation: there has been copious work on how damaging such labelling can be, and how it can become a self-fulfilling prophecy. Furthermore, the large and complex bureaucratic procedures that often surround getting help for children with problems not only tend to label but also often preclude getting the kind of immediate, short-term help that might actually address effectively a large number of children's mild problems, because the procedures are too time-consuming to be entered into lightly or very often.

More effective responses to special needs involve teams of specialists working in a routine way with schools, wherever possible to plan approaches that prevent problems, and, where a problem is getting established, to deal with it in a solution-focused way, swiftly, flexibly, with a maximum of positive action and a minimum of paperwork and procedures. Dealt with in this way many minor problems can rapidly resolve, particularly if schools and parents are left with clear strategies to use when problems recur and have open lines of communication back to the specialist team to call on again if needed. In the UK, the Department for Education and Skills is setting up 'Behaviour and Educational Support Teams' (BESTs) which are multi-agency teams (including social workers, health professionals and others) that intervene early, and work very closely with a defined group of schools to support teachers, to work directly with students who have problems, and to involve and support their families. Chapter 7 will look at the responses of five local education authorities (LEAs) in England who are taking such a low-key, non-labelling approach to the support of children with difficulties.

■ TARGETING DIFFERENT KINDS OF GROUPS

Special interventions in schools do not have to be targeted at those who would be officially labelled as having 'special needs' – any who are causing concern to themselves or others might benefit from targeting, and many recent initiatives have been aimed at groups of students who would not usually be officially categorized as having special needs. The box below gives an example.

> **Real-life examples of low-key interventions**
>
> Southampton Local Education Authority has encouraged schools to develop targeted approaches to emotional literacy for all kinds of groups with problems, including both troublesome and troubled children:
>
> - Sixty-five schools have worked on anger management, to help address the common problem of routinized violence, aggression, disaffection and impulsive behaviour among what is often a large percentage of students.
> - Kanes Hill Primary School has a very successful and carefully evaluated intervention focused on encouraging friendship skills among a small group of unpopular children,
> - Woodlands Community School in the same city taught assertiveness skills to children in danger of being bullied (Sharp and Faupel, 2002).

■ PROVIDE IN SCHOOL SUPPORT

Now schools are increasingly expected to deal with troublesome students 'in house' they may find it helpful to know that work on emotional literacy has been shown to play an active part in making the inclusion of difficult children easier. For example, two projects which taught 'difficult' students the kind of skills they need to fit into classrooms more easily and control their own behaviour, while helping their classmates both tolerate their behaviour more easily and positively support their efforts to become part of the mainstream, were shown to be very effective in helping the difficult students stay in the classroom, without detriment to the learning of other students (Rogers, 1994; Epstein and Elias, 1996).

Some schools offer in school programmes of student support (Munn et al., 1999), including the recently introduced learning support units and nurture groups. There is strong evidence that well-planned school-based programmes of this type can be very effective (Rogers, 1994; Epstein and Elias, 1996). Some who have had considerable experience of such programmes claim that they are a great deal more effective than those that are based in the community, because they encourage the school to take the issue seriously, and to own its problems and solutions (Surber, 1999). Such units within mainstream schools can be effective in giving help and support to young people with behavioural and emotional problems. They need to be seen not as long-term containment devices, but as short-term and highly focused bridges back to the mainstream classrooms, which tackle the problems students have in proactive and clear ways. The in-school support and the mainstream classrooms to which students return need to use the same calm and clear strategies for managing classroom behaviour, so that students experience consistent messages, expectations and boundaries (Elton, 1989; Briggs, MacKay and Miller, 1995). The same need for a short-term, highly focused and coherent approach applies if students are helped in units outside the school.

■ USE PEER GROUP TEACHING

It is important to involve the students themselves so they feel a sense of ownership of any programme in which they take part, and start to take responsibility for their own behaviour. Peer group teaching can play a significant part in this. Children's being troublesome is rarely just about individuals; it is usually about group behaviour, especially among older children. Children with behavioural problems such as violence, aggression, disruption and low levels of co-operation, tend to cluster together in groups (Farmer and Hollowell, 1994). Fortunately, there is some evidence that we can reverse this equation by using the peer group itself. Students with emotional and behaviour problems have been shown to be very effective teachers of emotional literacy, and the effects of such peer teaching are beneficial both for those doing the teaching and those on the receiving end: both parties have been shown to gain in emotional and social competence, as well as improving their learning and attitudes to school (Lazerson, 1980).

■ FOCUS ON TROUBLED AS WELL AS TROUBLESOME CHILDREN

At present the main focus of most of the funding, energy and interventions in this area is on 'troublesome' children, in other words those with behavioural problems and conduct disorders, who 'act out' by being violent, aggressive, rude and destructive. However, as we have suggested, this can be counterproductive, as the effort that goes into these students, the extra attention, lessons and special classes they receive can reinforce problem behaviour – it can become a vicious circle of schools creating what they claim not to want.

It has been thought in the past by those keen not to simply punish troublesome behaviour (a strategy which we have suggested is rarely effective), that troublesome behaviour invariably masks unhappiness and disturbance, and that all troublesome children are at root unhappy, have low self-esteem and need understanding. In many cases this may well be true. Troublesome students may well come from troubled backgrounds, for example with a struggling single parent or violence in the family. They may start as unhappy, and when no one notices or cares, become troublesome as a way of avoiding thinking about what is bothering them. So it is wise for schools first to investigate whether there are underlying emotional difficulties behind a child's troublesome behaviour. However, we now know it is simplistic to see all troublesome children as unhappy. Many children who are troublesome have normal or even high self-esteem and no history of trauma in their background (Salimi and Callias, 1996). Some have simply learned to misbehave because this is the behaviour they have seen around them, for example from parents and in their neighbourhoods, because it has brought them pay-offs, because no one has ever set them proper boundaries, or because they have been 'spoiled' by overindulgent parents who fail to set proper boundaries and rules. They have learnt to get their own way and that making life difficult for others can be rewarding and fun. Such children will need more than sympathetic understanding, although this is important. They need to learn that their behaviour is unacceptable, and that they can, and need to, find other ways to feel confident and have a good time. They need very clear boundaries, clear feedback, and skills programmes to improve behaviour. They need to learn empathy, as this is often what such children lack.

In contrast to the 'troublesome' children we have been discussing and who mop up so much professional time and attention, 'troubled' children might be thought of as anxious, unhappy and/or withdrawn. They often have low self-esteem, and are the target for bullying, or inflict self harm (Salimi and Callias, 1996). Troubled children are often overlooked, especially in large, busy secondary schools. They are not so obvious as the troublesome: no one takes the time to listen to their difficulties, or spot the signs. Often staff are so busy 'crisis managing' the troublesome they are simply grateful not to need to spend time on those who do not overtly annoy. Some staff are not particularly sympathetic to unhappy children's needs, finding them to be irritating, whiney, wet or wimps. But, however busy they are, staff do need to pay attention to all students, both in order not to add to the problems they are attempting to address by rewarding the troublesome and ignoring quiet children, and because all students have the right to have their needs met. Troubled children may need one-to-one attention, to work in smaller groups and, possibly, counselling to help them talk about their problems and feelings. Troubled children also need more than sympathetic understanding; they too need to learn skills, such as how to overcome shyness, communicate effectively, make friends, be assertive and think positively about themselves and their lives.

USE A CO-ORDINATED, COHERENT APPROACH

We have emphasized the importance of a coherent approach to emotional literacy in schools: such an approach is especially necessary for helping students with emotional and behavioural problems. Walker (1995) looked at what schools can do to prevent anti-social behaviour, and concluded that schools need to: have a coherent plan, which includes a school-wide discipline plan; manage the classroom environment effectively; explicitly teach social skills; manage violent, aggressive and anti-social behaviour in the playground; and involve parents and the community. All parts of the school experience need to reinforce one another, so students experience consistent messages, a principle, which we have seen, is helpful for everyone, but is particularly important for those who are having difficulties.

LINK WITH PARENTS

Whatever actions are taken with individual students, their parents need to be consulted, involved and kept fully informed. Educational interventions with students with all kinds of behavioural and emotional problems have consistently emphasized the importance of involving families (Kamps and Tankersley, 1996), and parents of children who are receiving specific help have been shown to benefit from receiving help themselves, both by developing the parents' own skills and ensuring that the messages home and school give to young people are congruent (Middleton and Cartledge, 1995). This is an issue we shall take up in more detail in Chapter 5.

To consider as a result of reading this chapter

Whole-school approaches

- Does the school you work in, or with, use a 'whole-school' approach to any issues? If so, what do you see as the advantages and problems?
- What does that school include in a 'whole-school' approach? Having read this chapter, is there anything else you feel they might usefully add?

Approaching behaviour in emotionally literate ways

- In your school, which students are giving you the most cause for concern? What do you see as the key influences on their behaviour?

- Does your school work to understand teachers' emotions about working with children with problems?
- What kind of approaches does your school use in approaching this problem behaviour? To what extent do you focus on any of the following: punishment; positive approaches; shaping behaviour; learning skills; developing attitudes and values; shaping the context; understanding the underlying emotional causes?
  Which of the strategies you are using are working? What else might you try?

Targeting

You might like to think about whether your school is doing any of the following, if so what are the advantages and disadvantages, and if not whether they might be worth trying:

- Targeting students with special needs in terms of emotional and social learning, within a whole-school approach.
- Early identifying children who are having problems and tackling them.
- Providing special help in a low-key way, concentrating on alleviating the problem, not labelling or stigmatizing the person.
- Providing special help within your school.
- Meeting the needs of troubled as well as troublesome children.
- Working in a co-ordinated, coherent way when dealing with vulnerable children who need help quickly and efficiently, including liaising effectively with outside agencies, and with parents.

CHAPTER FOUR

Emotional Literacy and Learning

GOALS OF THIS CHAPTER

By the end of this chapter you will have explored a range of ways in which emotional literacy can be developed through a school's learning and teaching programme and the issues the various approaches raise. These issues will include:

- the place of the learning and teaching programme within the whole-school approach to emotional literacy
- the general features of successful programmes designed to help people learn emotional and social competences
- the role of a wide range of school subjects in helping people learn various aspects of emotional literacy
- links between work on emotional literacy and work on whole-brain thinking, on learning styles and on accelerated/dynamic learning.

Note: throughout this chapter we will mainly talk about *'learning'* rather than 'teaching', to remind us that it is what students learn that matters, not what teachers think they are teaching them: indeed there is often a rather large gulf between the two!

INTRODUCTION

THE NEED FOR THE WHOLE SCHOOL TO SUPPORT WHAT HAPPENS IN THE CLASSROOM

It is a basic argument of this book that learning does not only take place in a formal, classroom context – the whole-school experience is an opportunity for learning. Some (for example, Antidote, 2003) would argue that we do not need a taught programme at all, and that the necessary competences are best learned directly through the everyday experience of school organization and patterns of communication and relationships. It is certainly essential to get the organizational environment right alongside introducing any programmes for learning emotional literacy. Without an emotionally literate environment, any programme is empty and cannot hope to have an impact. The processes that happen in the wider school need to be congruent with what happens in the classroom so that what happens outside the classroom reinforces what happens in it. Attitudes, policies, learning and problem-solving strategies, routines and key competences must be known by everyone in the school and practised across the school as a whole. Congruence will not happen by chance, so successful programmes have to be planned from the outset to be part of the overall school approach, not 'bolt-on extras'. They need to be carefully co-ordinated, especially if they are to work through school subjects as well as in designated lessons, and to have the strong support and backing of the rest of the school, especially the headteacher and senior management.

■ REASONS FOR LEARNING AND TEACHING ABOUT EMOTIONAL LITERACY

Having acknowledged the need for a whole-school approach there is nevertheless an important role for a programme of learning and teaching to reinforce the values and procedures we want students to practise at the whole-school level. Given the fact that learning and teaching are centrally what schools are about, if we neglect this aspect of the total picture we may be in danger of suggesting that emotional literacy is not itself very central.

There is a range of reasons why we may want to develop learning and teaching to promote emotional literacy: they include:

1 As an end in itself, on the grounds emotional literacy is an important human competence that helps students become happier and get on better with others – schools have a role in developing their students as fully rounded, fulfilled human beings.

2 Because it improves the health of students, for example by preventing or reducing behaviours risky to health, such as drug-taking, immediately and/or in later life.

3 Because it helps students manage their own behaviour, which impacts on their behaviour in school, and thus on

learning, attendance and exclusion rates, and impacts on their behaviour out of school and in later life, and thus reduces violence, aggression and crime.

4 Because it helps students learn, for example by helping them think and solve problems more effectively.

Evidence would suggest that all these goals are achievable, at least to some extent. However not all are likely to be equally attractive to mainstream schools. Concentrating on goal (1), instrinsic worth, is probably in these instrumental days a non-starter, a goal that schools may perhaps like but will almost certainly believe they do not have the luxury to spend time on. Many programmes focus on goal (2), health, which some schools may well not see as a central concern. Goal (3), improving behaviour, is more attractive to many schools, as most are concerned to improve behaviour, and can see the links with learning. However, it still does not go far enough to ensure that emotional literacy is offered to all. Emphazing the links with behaviour tends to 'ghettoize' work on emotional literacy into schools with students with a high level of behaviour problems, and into work with problem students, and cause it to be seen as a short-term 'inoculation' process: this indeed has been the case with the pattern of the take-up of many programmes of emotional and social learning which tend to be found in low-income localities, and mostly aimed at students with problem behaviour and used for a limited time. A major step that has been taken in recent years is to work on goal (4), the linking of work on emotional literacy with work on the process of learning. Moving in this direction means that emotional literacy is clearly the concern of every school, in the interest of every student, and relevant throughout the student's learning career – which is, increasingly, a lifetime.

WAYS TO DELIVER LEARNING AND TEACHING FOR EMOTIONAL LITERACY

There are many ways in which emotional literacy can be delivered through the organization of the learning programme in schools. Table 4.1 summarizes some of them, and suggests some advantages and disadvantages.

This chapter will explore this range of strategies. We will begin by looking at the most obvious and well developed, which is the use of taught programmes purpose-designed to help people learn generic emotional and social competences.

TABLE 4.1 WAYS IN WHICH EMOTIONAL LITERACY CAN BE DELIVERED

Method of delivery	Advantages	Disadvantages
Through a taught programme, purpose designed to help people learn generic emotional and social competences	Makes sure work on emotional literacy is carried out Easy to evaluate Evaluations have shown that many programmes are very effective, especially in changing behaviour Can be motivating for those involved	Time-consuming Feels like an addition to the main curriculum May disappear when keen people leave
Through a taught programme that focuses on one aspect of emotional literacy such as anger management or assertiveness	Makes sure this aspect of work on emotional literacy is carried out Easy to evaluate Evaluations have shown that many programmes are very effective especially in changing behaviour Can be motivating for those involved Can meet specific local need Flexible, changeable, not boring to deliver	Only focuses on some of the issues involved in emotional literacy Time-consuming Feels like an addition to the main curriculum May disappear when keen people leave
Emotional literacy part of a wider taught programme, e.g. on health	Grounds emotional literacy in wider perspective. Can be motivating for those involved. May achieve wider support, e.g. funding, government backing etc., than emotional literacy programmes alone	Wider goal, e.g. health, may not seem important to those in schools Emotional literacy may be swamped by other concerns. Wider programme is still time-consuming and feels like an addition to the main curriculum Hard to evaluate the specific impact of emotional literacy component
Emotional literacy integrated into school subjects (e.g. English, Maths, Science, History, Art, Drama, PSHE and Citizenship)	Time saving compared with the methods outlined above Makes relevance of emotional literacy to range of issues clear Engages wider range of staff – not just dependent on a few keen people	Emotional literacy may be swamped by subject-oriented goals Students may not be aware of emotional literacy component May be 'bitty' – effective co-ordination across the curriculum is challenging Still takes time from other parts of the curriculum
Emotional literacy integrated with work on the process of learning, e.g. on how the brain works, learning styles, accelerated/dynamic learning/whole-brain learning	Goal – improved learning – highly central to schools The two ways of thinking (process of learning and emotional literacy) share the same theoretical base, and often share methods and strategies	Some versions of work on the process of learning have an 'intellectualized' view of students as 'learners', forgetting in practice the emotional and social side Not many schools are as yet working on the process of learning – new and 'trendy' area

PROGRAMMES DESIGNED TO HELP PEOPLE LEARN EMOTIONAL AND SOCIAL COMPETENCES THROUGH A TAUGHT CURRICULUM

■ THE ROLE OF TAUGHT PROGRAMMES

There is currently a plethora of programmes, projects and teaching materials that attempt to help people learn emotional and social competence (few use the actual term 'emotional literacy'): most of these are to be found in the USA. Many of these have been evaluated, some very rigorously. For example, a recent review of a wide range of school, community and family programmes that aimed to promote 'positive youth development' found 77 with 'evaluated interventions', and designated 25 of them 'effective' (Catalano et al., 2002) by some very rigorous evaluation criteria. A similar review of 'universal' programmes, which were in practice largely the same as those reviewed by Catalano, which looked at how effectively they appeared to be in 'promoting mental health' found 70 that were evaluated, of which 17 stood up to its rigorous criteria (Wells, Barlow and Stewart-Brown, 2003).

All the studies in the Wells review included a curriculum or taught programme. In the Catalano review, not all of the 75 'evaluated' programmes included a structured curriculum, but those that did were more likely to be among the 'effective' 25. 'Twenty-four (96%) of the well evaluated effective programmes incorporated a curriculum or programme of activities … Far fewer (20, or 50%) of the excluded programmes incorporated a curriculum or structured programme' (Catalano et al., 2002: 71). This review also found that the most effective programmes used structured programme guidelines or manuals which helped those who were attempting to deliver the programmes to do so consistently. So there is a strong case for saying that if we want to help people learn emotional and social competences we need to include a clear, well-planned, central curriculum.

■ EVALUATED PROGRAMMES FROM THE USA

Table 4.2 contains some examples of the programmes included in these two recent reviews: the examples are meant to be illustrative rather than exhaustive. The programmes in this table have been chosen from the many available and that the researchers reviewed because:

- they have passed the systematic review process and can be found in either the Catalano et al. (2002) review or the Wells, Barlow and Stewart-Brown (2003) review. This means they have carried out rigorous evaluations, which include the use of controls, which have demonstrated that they are effective in certain specific ways, outlined in Table 4.2

- all the programmes are ongoing and currently in use
- the programmes listed here are typical of the many programmes in use, and so illustrate the kind of work that is being attempted across the USA, and in a few other places
- the programmes all attempt to develop social and emotional competences, and some of them also attempt to promote emotional well-being
- all the programmes are aimed at children in a mainstream school setting, not at those only with special needs
- all the programmes include a taught curriculum
- the programmes are illustrative of the wide range of settings that can be used, some being school only, some including the community and/or families.

PROGRAMMES DEVELOPED OUTSIDE THE USA

Almost all the evaluated curriculum-based programmes are to be found in the USA, and there are almost none that have originated in other countries, although schools in other parts of the world have made use of evaluated US programmes such as the PATHS curriculum. However, although evaluation is generally lacking outside the USA, energy and commitment are not. In the UK, for example, there is at present a great deal of activity around the development of specific programmes for emotional literacy, and there is a vast range of programmes and materials being produced to teach it. So, there are a great many published programmes designed to help people learn about emotional literacy, inside and outside the USA. (Some of the key programmes and materials, the organizations that deliver them and details of how they can be contacted, are described in the list of contacts at the end of the book.)

SHOULD SCHOOLS JUST USE AN EXISTING PROGRAMME?

The development of many successful projects has included a collaborative approach, and they have often piloted and trialled materials in different locations, so many of these programmes have

TABLE 4.2   TABLE OF PROGRAMMES

Programme name, references and website (if known)	Setting	Aims/content	Main methods of delivery	People involved in evaluated programme	Duration, continuity of programme, timing of evaluation	Areas in which intervention children showed significant change
PATHS Curriculum (Greenberg et al., 1995) http://www.prevention.psu.edu/PAT HS/	Schools (elementary) Seattle, USA	Improvement of children's ability to discuss, understand, express and regulate emotions	Didactic instruction, role play, class discussion, modelling by teachers and peers, social and self-reinforcement, worksheets, generalization techniques	Teachers 4 schools, 30 classrooms, 286 children	3 terms 60 sessions – 3 times a week, 20–30 minute sessions Evaluation after a year	Better able to: name different feelings; recognize emotional cues in others; be aware that people can hide feelings; be aware that feelings can change; resolve conflict; tolerate frustration; be assertive; be empathic; get along with peers; control aggression
Resolving Conflict Creatively (Aber et al, 1998) www.esrnational.org/about-rccp.html	Schools (elementary) and Community New York City, USA	Conflict resolution, curriculum (listening, assertiveness, negotiation, problem-solving) Peer mediation	Training of teachers (self-selected) in curriculum Curriculum using role play, discussion, brain storming Selected children trained as peer mediator Classroom visits by project staff	Teachers and project staff 16 schools 288 teachers 5,053 children	Ongoing up to 3 years Up to 55 curriculum sessions a year Evaluation up to 5 years from the start	Decrease in aggressive beliefs Decrease in children attributing hostile intentions to people Better interpersonal negotiating strategies Less self-reported problem behaviour
Metropolitan Area Child Study (Eron et al, 1997)	Schools (elementary and high) and Family 'High risk' areas of Chicago Work with whole population Also work for at risk pupils	Preventing violence through treating cognitive reasons (e.g. low self-esteem) and social/ ecological reasons (e.g. family conflict, poor communication, peer conflict)	Whole school: – Teacher education – Collaborative support from project staff – Curriculum – Teacher manuals – Student work books At risk students: – Intensive small-group work for students – Family training: family management, family cohesiveness strategies, positive communication	16 schools, 1,673 pupils	40 x 1 hour lessons taught over 2A years Evaluation 2.5 years from start of project	Increased pro-social behaviour Decrease in aggression Prevention of growth of aggression (growth that was found in control group over time)

Programme	Setting	Theory/Aim	Components	Sample/Measures	Timing	Outcomes
Seattle Social Development Project (Hawkins and Catalano, 1992; Hawkins et al., 1999) http://depts.washington.edu/ssdp	Schools (elementary) and Family	Reducing childhood risk factors for school failure, drug abuse and delinquency. Teaching teachers and parents how to actively engage children in learning, strengthen family bonding and encourage positive behaviours	Teacher education – 5 days a year on classroom management, interactive teaching and co-operative learning. Parents taught positive behaviour management, and how to help your child succeed at school and drug prevention. Children taught 4 hours of training on resisting social influences and staying out of trouble	643 fifth grade students identified – 593 students tracked and interviewed at age 18. Questionnaires to parents, students and teachers. Data on delinquency charges, achievement test results, grade point averages, school disciplinary reports	Started in 1981, followed and interviewed same 800 youths annually.	Stronger attachment to school: improvement in self-reported achievement; less involvement in school misbehaviour; less violent acts; less heavy alcohol use; less risky sexual behaviour
Child Development Project (Battistich et al., 1989; Battistich et al., 1996) www.prevention.psu.edu/CDP.htm	Schools (elementary) Family and Community Across the USA	Based on the theory of the central importance meeting children's developmental needs as the basis for: - encouraging co-operation - developing an attachment to the school - developing pro-social norms. Improving connections between parents, schools and community	Training of teachers. Co-operative learning, values based reading and language arts programme, developmental discipline techniques. Children used as peer mediators. School community-building activities	Outsiders to train teachers. Teachers. 24 elementary schools in 6 school districts	Programme is ongoing and continuous. Baseline assessment in 1992, then annual repeats	More interpersonal sensitivity. Greater ability to solve personal problems. Better strategies for dealing with social situations. Better conflict resolution strategies. Better acceptance of and acceptance by peers, less loneliness, lower social anxiety. Decline in alcohol use

TABLE 4.2 (continued)

Programme name, references and website (if known)	Setting	Aims/content	Main methods of delivery	People involved in evaluated programme	Duration, continuity of programme, timing of evaluation	Areas in which intervention children showed significant change
School Transitional Environment Project (STEP) (Felner, Ginter and Primavera, 1982; Felner et al., 1993)	Transition from elementary to middle and middle to high schools	Making the school environment supportive during a critical transition time	School structure made simpler: providing 'homerooms' for new students Creation of classmate and peer networks to provide support during lessons	Teachers 65 intervention students in 4 classes Replication study with 1965 students in 8 schools	5 year follow up	Lower levels of stress Reductions in anxiety, depression and delinquent behavior. Students in STEP schools made better academic progress
Social Competence Program for Young Adolescents (Caplan et al., 1992)	Schools (middle)	Enhancing personal and interpersonal effectiveness	Training for teachers: – 10 x 90 minute workshops – on-site consultation and coaching during teaching lessons. – 3 monthly two-hour follow-up training. Curriculum for students: – 16 highly structured, scripted 45 minute lessons – Creation of environmental supports	410 (in final sample) fifth to eighth grade students	12 week intervention	Reduction in minor delinquency, improved conduct, involvement with peers, and social acceptance, problem-solving, conflict resolution

proved to have wider acceptability and transferability. It may be that people wanting to have an explicit learning and teaching programme decide to use an existing one. However, if they do, they should bear in mind that this is not necessarily a simple and easy solution. Taking an existing programme on emotional literacy and imposing it on an unprepared or unwilling nation, region or school is unlikely to be a recipe for success, and may well be a disaster. The success of programmes that attempt to help people learn emotional literacy is highly dependent on the goodwill, understanding, attitudes, skills and levels of emotional literacy of those who teach it. An imposed package will almost certainly be rejected, or only partly used, misused and discarded, when the next fashionable approach comes along. Pre-existing programmes tend to die out more quickly than those which are generated by people who are going to use them. Where those who will use them are involved in designing and evaluating teaching materials and teaching them to one another, they tend to be more motivated and committed than when they were delivering programmes that were given to them to deliver.

Schools, or clusters of local schools working together, may indeed decide to use a published programme, but such a decision needs to be arrived at after a process of considerable thinking and discussion about their own specific needs and conditions, a process in which training and awareness-raising can help considerably. Schools will need to consider, for example, what they are trying to achieve, the nature of their students, how they currently organize the curriculum, how they are tackling related areas such as Personal, Social and Health Education and Citizenship, their staff's strengths and weaknesses, and so on. At the end of this process, schools or clusters of schools may prefer to produce their own programme, and/or use a range of materials in their own way.

In any case, no one programme has been developed that is universally used, even in the USA. Nor has any one programme emerged that is unequivocally successful. The US-based network, the 'Collaborative for Academic, Social and Emotional Learning' (CASEL), does not promote any particular programme, but concentrates on discussing the general features of all successful programmes and reporting on evaluations of a range of programmes. This chapter will follow this model, and consider the principles that have been shown to underlie successful programmes, rather than describing any individual programmes in detail. There will be no surprises, nor will we go into this in any detail, as all the principles that emerge echo those that are being put forward elsewhere in these pages as important for the development of approaches to emotional literacy.

■ LEARNING FROM THESE EVALUATED PROGRAMMES

All the programmes share the view that emotional and social competences are very much learned, and that the best way to teach them is to focus on helping learners acquire positive attitudes, behaviours, values and skills, with an emphasis on skills. In Catalano et al.'s (2002) major review of programmes to promote 'positive youth development', all 25 that were deemed to be effective included considerable teaching of skills, to students, staff and, often, parents. Other research has shown that programmes which attempt to teach attitudes and values alone have been shown consistently not to be so effective as those that also teach skills (Fertman and Chubb, 1992). Successful programmes spend considerable time on clarifying the kind of emotional and social skills that are needed, which often parallel those competences outlined in Chapter 2 of this book. They make sure students know what the skills are, and have a good deal of regular, routinized practice of them. They provide opportunities to learn the skills in a controlled and clear environment with easily remembered clues as to the steps. They provide feedback on progress in learning the skills, with feedback and coaching for individual students, and regular opportunities to practise them in real life.

The programmes all use the whole school as the context for practising competences, building in everyday, routine interactions which reinforce the messages the programme as a whole is wanting to instil, such as respect for others, self-esteem, and feeling valued. Many go further towards a whole-school approach, and look at aspects of school organization and climate. Most programmes include work on teacher education, on the grounds that teachers are key role models in this respect, and cannot in any case teach these competences unless they have them themselves. Many make links with community and families.

The programmes take a developmental approach, and attempt to tailor the programme to the stage, rather than just the age, of the learner. They are usually based on an effort to assess where the learner is starting from in order to determine what type and level of skill is appropriate. They use a range of instruments for this, including checklists, and audits and quantitative scales which have been tested for validity and reliability: these are discussed in detail in Chapter 6, together with other approaches. Successful programmes then break down complex skills into small steps which build from where the learner is to where they would like to be.

All the programmes use a range of group sizes including whole-class discussion, circle time, group work, individual work and one to one. All use a range of methods, with the emphasis on active and the experiential learning, such as discussion, games, simulations, and role-plays. Many make links to other parts of the curriculum such as information technology (IT), art, drama and language work.

■ EMOTIONAL LITERACY AS PART OF WIDER PROGRAMMES

In addition to programmes solely devoted to emotional and social learning, there is a tradition of curriculum development in related areas such as Health Education, Health Promoting Schools, Personal and Social Education, Lifeskills and, more recently in the UK, Citizenship, all of which include elements on emotional and social learning. There is also work on mental health, most notably in Australia, where 'Mind Matters', a resource pack which provides advice to schools about how to adopt a whole-school approach to mental health, includes a comprehensive set of curriculum materials, and is free to all Australian schools. At the time of writing, 'Mind Matters' is being rigorously evaluated. Work on emotional literacy has also been integrated with work on special needs and on the management of behaviour. We will be looking at examples of all these approaches in Chapter 7 when we look at the role of local education authorities and Healthy School approaches, and so will not discuss them in any more detail here. Contact details for them can be found at the end of the book.

TEACHING EMOTIONAL LITERACY THROUGH SCHOOL SUBJECTS

■ THE POTENTIAL OF THE SUBJECT-BASED CURRICULUM

A teaching and learning programme about emotional literacy does not have to be completely separate and special: the kind of subjects schools teach routinely can be a valuable vehicle. The process by which all subjects are taught, the classroom climate, the way students and teacher behave and the patterns of communication invariably have an impact on emotional literacy, for good or ill. The content subjects cover can also be mobilized to explore emotional literacy. Table 4.3 sets out some examples of aspects of emotional literacy that teaching as a whole might develop and which various subjects are particularly well suited to cover: it is meant to be illustrative rather than exhaustive.

▓ CO-ORDINATING THE SUBJECT-BASED APPROACH

Saying that normal school subjects have a part to play in helping students develop various aspects of emotional literacy is not to say that all schools are by definition already covering emotional literacy adequately. Often the aspects of emotional literacy that subjects can potentially cover are not in fact there, or emotional literacy is seen as incidental to the cognitive and technical aims of the teaching. In order to use the potential of the subject-based curriculum to promote emotional literacy effectively there needs to be a strong sense of there being an overall school programme of emotional literacy. This overall programme needs to be carefully planned, co-ordinated and monitored, in order to ensure that the competences it is trying

TABLE 4.3 EXAMPLES OF ASPECTS OF EMOTIONAL LITERACY

School subject	Examples of aspects of emotional literacy the subject is particularly well suited to cover
All subjects, in the *way* they are taught	Positive self-concept though experiencing success and mastery, a positive and warm classroom climate and positive and realistic expectations
	Sense of coherence through discerning predictable processes and outcomes
	Social skills, e.g. conflict resolution, respect for others, empathy, co-operation through group tasks and projects, teacher modelling, and rules of classroom behaviour
	Emotional sensitivity, through discussion of how you and others feel when learning
	Increasing emotional intensity through experiencing success, a sense of 'flow', laughter and having fun, celebrating learning
	Emotional control, e.g. through waiting your turn, having persistence through difficulties, self-monitoring, self-management
	Resilience – bouncing back when learning goes badly
	Autonomy through independent thinking
	Problem-solving and decision-making
Personal, Social and Health Education	Can include comprehensive work on emotional literacy, or be emotional literacy by another name
Education	Modern approaches include work on: positive self-concept; self-protection; making relationships; resisting pressure; decision-making; stress management; communication skills; negotiation
Citizenship	Can include comprehensive work on emotional literacy
	Whole area still in development. Current approaches tend to include positive self-concept; goal-setting; personal problem-solving; self-respect; social responsibility and social skills; conflict resolution; anti-racism; anti-bullying; respect for others; tolerating difference; co-operation; negotiation, assertion; autonomy
Sex Education	Modern approaches focus on: positive self-concept and self-respect; relationships including loving, caring and respect for others; social skills including negotiation, assertion; making decisions; taking responsibility

TABLE 4.3 continued

School subject	Examples of aspects of emotional literacy the subject is particularly well suited to cover
Drug Education	Modern approaches focus on: positive self-concept; self-espect and self-care; social skills including resisting pressure; assertion; making decisions; taking responsibility; finding alternative ways to meet emotional need to relax, let go, and have a good time
The Arts – dance, music, painting	Direct emotional experience – through seeing, listening or taking part Expressing own emotions – through movement, sound and pictures
Literature/stories	Empathy – through seeing world through another's eyes Experiencing emotions Broadening and deepening emotional experience, vicarious emotion, anticipatory experience Personal problem-solving including rehearsal of current or future challenges Resilience, optimism, through experiencing others coping, coming through Sense of coherence through experiencing others making sense of their lives Comfort, sense of connection, feeling understood through reading/hearing about others with same problems and experiences Understanding the causes of emotions through exploring why people do what they do
English Language/ talking/writing	Developing an emotional vocabulary Developing positive self-concept through talking and writing about the self Sense of coherence through exploring own and family life history Expressing feelings Writing stories can increase empathy
Drama and role-play	Direct emotional experience through watching or taking part Expressing emotion through movement, facial expression, tone, words Communication skills Self-confidence. Empathy through playing and discussing the part of another Co-operation through group work Can be used to teach skills directly, e.g. assertion, negotiation
Biology	Understanding physiology of emotion, including own body's reaction Understanding how the brain works, centrality of emotion to how we think, learn, behave and experience the world Exploration of the mind–body link Emotion in animals: our common ancestry
History	Empathy Understanding the causes of emotion, e.g. through study of biography Relative impact of individual action v. social forces in shaping events Sense of personal coherence through study of own and family and local history Exploring role of emotion as part of the causes that shape major events, e.g. territoriality, identification with a group, fear of 'the other' leading to nationalism, tribalism, negotiations, treaties, invasions, war, atrocities Include positive influence of emotions, e.g. desire for peace, justice, humanitarianism leading to liberations, abolition of slavery, human rights movement
Physical Education	Expressing self through movement Co-operation through group work Exploration of the mind–body link: importance of motivation, focusing, optimism, positive belief, rehearsal, visualization on performance Relaxation and stress reduction

to help people learn are clearly defined, developed through the curriculum in a systematic and developmental way, and made explicit and overt to students, staff and parents. It is highly likely that a successful programme will need to have a core of specific teaching on emotional literacy, with the subjects then developing various aspects as appropriate.

EMOTIONAL LITERACY AND THE PROCESS OF LEARNING

We will now look at a further way in which emotional literacy can be linked with learning and teaching, which is through new work on the process of learning, which is starting to have an impact in schools. This has the advantage of linking emotional literacy with a goal which is indisputably central to schools – learning. Both work on the process of learning and work on emotional literacy/intelligence share a theoretical base in recent work on how the brain works, an issue that will be explored next.

Real-life experience: whole-school scheme of work on emotional literacy

Draft scheme of work for emotional literacy proposed by Southampton City Council local education authority and as practised by Mason Moor Primary School:

- Adopt two key feelings per half term (i.e. 12 a year).
- First session to benchmark existing feelings vocabulary.
- Further sessions using drama, role-play, etc.
- Explore body language.
- Use circle time.
- Assembly themes.
- Central theme displays.
- Music/artwork.
- All adults to model, extend, rehearse new 'feelings' vocabulary.
- Fiction/library links (Southampton City Council have published a lengthy list of books for primary school children organized under emotional themes, such as anger, bravery, calmness and jealousy. It is part of their *Promoting Emotional Literacy: Guidelines for Schools, Local Authorities and Health Services* – Sharp and Faupel, 2002).

- Evaluation at end of term (Sharp and Faupel, 2002: 21).

See also the 'Record of assessment for emotional literacy checklist' used by Mason Moor, reproduced in Chapter 7.

■ NEW RESEARCH ON HOW THE BRAIN WORKS

Throughout the late 1980s and 1990s, considerable research was carried out on various structures of the brain, which showed the startling extent to which the brain is an organ governed by the emotions (MacLean, 1990; LeDoux, 1998). Table 4.4 attempts to summarize thinking about some key brain structures, and their emotional functions.

We will now go on to consider the implications of this new research.

■ PEOPLE NEED TO BE IN A POSITIVE STATE TO LEARN EFFECTIVELY

Schools, and especially secondary schools, have traditionally taken the view that students' feelings about their learning are irrelevant to how well they do at the task in hand. Some have even taken the view that students learn better when stressed, humiliated, anxious and under pressure. We can now see that the opposite is in fact the case. It is clear from the account of how the brain, and in particular the reptilian brain, works, (see Table 4.4) that a positive emotional state is a crucial prerequisite for learning. When a person is under stress – fear, anxiety, anger – the rest of the brain more or less shuts down and the brain reverts to primitive survival needs. We need therefore to pay attention to the emotional state of the learner, and ensure that they are not stressed or feeling under threat, if they want them to learn anything. We need to recognize and help prevent the emotional states that can block learning. We also need to promote the emotional states, such as calmness, a sense of well-being, and feeling safe and valued, that make it easier to learn. If learners arrive in, or get into, a stressed state it is well worth taking the time to de-stress them through relaxation techniques or a physical activity. Effects of stress can last a long time – half an hour of stress can affect the functioning of the brain for up to two weeks (Black, 1991).

The sense of stress does not necessarily come from the immediate environment, nor is it always reasonable and proportionate. A sense of stress can come from any sense of personal or emotional threat, generated from without (such as witnessing violence or being bullied) or from within (such as feeling incapable of doing a task set by a teacher). So, the wider context and long standing and seated attitudes are highly significant in shaping a person's ability to learn. For example, environments that induce a 'sense of optimism' can make a learner approach a difficult task with a 'can do' attitude and thus see it as a welcome challenge rather than a source of stress. Creating a sense of safety and 'attachment' can give the learner the sense of trust that the challenge must be a safe rather than a stressful one in which they can count on support to help them succeed. Supporting the

TABLE 4.4 KEY BRAIN STRUCTURES AND THEIR EMOTIONAL FUNCTIONS

Name of the part of the brain, where it is, what it is	General functions and emotional functions and effects
Reptilian brain Oldest part of the brain Just above the spine at the base Shared with reptiles and all higher animals	*General functions:* Works at an unconscious level. Ensures survival; stores very early memories; monitors breathing, balance and instinctive responses, has basic emotional needs, responds strongly to stress *Emotional functions and effects:* Controls semi-automatic reflexes – fight or flight, territoriality and defensiveness, attention-seeking, the need to be part of a group, ritualistic behaviours. When a person is under stress – fear, anxiety, anger – the rest of the brain more or less shuts down and this reptilian brain takes over. Learner reverts to the basic behaviours of territoriality, attention-seeking or ritual
Limbic system Middle brain Shared with all mammals	*General functions:* Works at an unconscious level. Site of long-term memory, body's maintenance functions, such as the immune system, sleeping and eating patterns, and emotional reactions *Emotional functions and effects:* Emotional gatekeeper. Sifts incoming information according to emotional significance – ignores information coded as emotionally meaningless. Responds to what it believes is emotionally valuable, true, meaningful and routes to rest of brain, including neo cortex to process, and body, including hormonal system, to respond. Particularly uses thalamus and amygdala for this sorting and routing
Thalamus A small structure in the middle brain	*General function:* Works at an unconscious level. Receives information from the senses and sends it on to other parts of the brain *Emotional function:* Codes information emotionally – sends emotionally routine information to neo cortex for processing. In 'emergency' goes straight to amygdala, causing instant reaction of 'fight or flight' before consciousness even aware
Amygdala – a small structure in the middle brain Formed very early in life	*Emotional Function:* Is purely concerned with the emotions. Works at an unconscious level. Stores emotional memories Decides on emotional significance of an experience – people whose amygdala is damaged have no emotional responses If told directly by the thalamus that an experience constitutes an 'emergency', then communicates directly with the body to fight or fly – an 'emotional hijacking' Registers and remembers most strongly experiences which are highly coloured emotionally Imprecise in its recognition systems – overgeneralizes from old experiences to new
Neo cortex Top of the brain Shared with primates but much bigger	*General functions:* Works at the conscious level. Higher-order thought, processing, making sense of incoming information, discerning relationships and patterns of meaning, problem-solving and long-term planning *Emotional functions:* Processes and generates emotional experience in more considered sense than limbic system. Regulates responses to emotion through pre-frontal lobes. Creates personal metaphors or models of understanding, which are value driven, and thus at root emotional *Corpus callosum* connects the two 'halves' of the neo cortex and enables them to communicate with one another

TABLE 4.4 continued

Name of the part of the brain, where it is, what it is	General functions and emotional functions and effects
Right neo cortex	*General functions:* Governs the left side of the body Associative – looks for relationships between things. Simultaneous processing, learns the whole first then parts. Processes in images, pictures, forms and patterns Responsible for creativity and imagination. Responds to being asked to engage in experiential learning, games, role-play, visualizing, archetypes *Emotional functions:* Through right prefrontal lobe: seat of negative emotions, e.g. fear and aggression, worry, pessimism
Left neo cortex	*General functions:* Works at a conscious level Governs right side of the body Analyses detail and parts first and builds from there to wholes, processes in a sequential, linear, logical way, responsible for language, logic and mathematical formulae. Responds to being asked to engage in processing, discussion, reflection *Emotional functions:* Through left pre-frontal lobe, regulates negative emotions of the right lobe, also seat of positive emotions, e.g. joy, optimism, calm

learner to become more 'resilient' can cause the learner to conclude that not doing well at a task is not the end of the world, and leave an unsuccessful learning experience with a sense of calmness that will allow them to return to it later. So all the emotional and social competences we examined in Chapter 2 turn out to be essential for effective learning.

This new research validates Maslow's (1970) earlier intuitive and highly influential theories which suggested that human beings have a 'hierarchy of needs', and unless basic social and emotional needs such as love and belonging and self-esteem are met, students are not going to be capable of intellectual learning, let alone what Maslow called 'self-actualization', or independent thinking.

■ SCHOOLS NEED TO MEET BASIC EMOTIONAL NEEDS – TERRITORY, RITUAL, BELONGING

Our basic survival needs, governed mainly by the most basic brain that we share with our reptilian ancestors, are not something we should fear, or attempt to suppress and ignore: they are an essential part of our brain, and thus an integral part of what it means to be human, and their demands, basically useful and healthy, are best met in positive ways. Wise schools will respect and pay positive attention to their students' basic 'survival' needs, such as the need to have their own belongings and space respected, the need for attention, and the need to be part of a group, and ensure that these needs are met in ways that are positive and productive rather than harmful. So, for example, schools can develop affirming rituals to mark and celebrate key events such as the beginning and end of lessons, weeks and terms. They can prioritize ensuring that all students feel known and recognized, feel they belong to a group and feel a sense of attachment to the school.

■ THE EMOTIONS ATTACH VALUE TO EXPERIENCE

We have seen that humans are, particularly when stressed, still at root very much primitive animals. We need to acknowledge and work with our basic survival patterns, such as the need for safety and the removal of stress, and the way we respond to a crisis or an emergency with 'fight or flight'. However, our deeper understanding of how the brain functions is showing us that there is a great deal more to the emotions than this. Work on the functions of the middle level of the brain, the limbic system, has shown that emotions, far from being merely primitive responses, are built into the very nature of how we think, how we learn, and how we attribute meaning and value (see Table 4.4). This marks a radical shift in our thinking about the emotions, and elevates them to a central place in the higher forms of thinking. If we want any learning experience to pass through the crucial 'gatekeeper' of the limbic system, and its sorting, sifting and bell-ringing thalamus and amyglada, we have to pay attention to the emotional content and connotations of the learning, or it will be ignored or rejected as valueless. If we want the brain to code experience as 'true' 'valuable' and 'meaningful', and thus pass it on for processing to the neo cortex, we have to associate it with strong emotions, and ideally pleasurable emotions, so the learner wants more of it, rather than associating it with pain or boredom. (Although stress blocks learning, this is not the same as saying that all strong emotion blocks it: we want learners to be 'aroused' but not stressed: relaxed alertness is the ideal state for learning.) We have to accept that learners have to *feel* that something is true and important before they will believe it, and certainly before they are likely to act on it (Damasio, 1994; 2000). If we want learners to respond to an experience, to remember it and to change as a result of it, we need to make the learning personally compelling, emotionally deeply felt and, vividly real.

■ THE EMOTIONS ARE PART OF 'HIGHER ORDER' THINKING

Research on the workings of the cerebral cortex has shown that emotional responses are an integral part of the highest order of thinking, and can be every bit as complex, thoughtful and reflective as any other cognitive process. We have the ability to do far more than respond blindly to feelings; we can think about them, organize them, modulate them, moderate them, and shape them through reflection and learning (LeDoux, 1998).

Ground-breaking research by Nobel Prize winner Roger Sperry (Sperry, 1968) demonstrated that the two sides of the neo cortex process information differently and Table 4.4 has summarized the differences. Research also showed that most of us tend to have a preference for one side or the other, which results in us tending to be one kind of learner or another (Riding and Rayner, 1998). Table 4.5 summarizes the key differences between the different types of learner.

When the differences in function between the two sides of the brain were discovered it had a convulsive effect on educational thinking. Traditional approaches to education and learning, with their emphasis on learning received methods, procedures and content, were seen as tending to speak mainly to the conformist, logical, sequential left brain and failing to use the innovative, creative, intuitive holistic processes of the right brain. Traditional approaches were also seen as causing 'right brain' holistic thinkers to struggle and fail: tellingly it would appear that 75 per cent of teachers are analytic learners, while 70 per cent of students are holistic learners (Blackman, 1982). As a result there was at the time a swing towards promoting creative, holistic, intuitive right thinking, through more experiential, discovery-type learning, a swing which included emotional education. It became common to assert that children need to experience life, including, emotional experience, not just read, write and talk about it. This represented a helpful rebalancing which undoubtedly opened the way for an explosion of useful work in a hitherto neglected area, which reached holistic learners better, which may have helped analytical learners become more flexible, and enriched emotional education.

Time has passed, and there are now concerns that we may have gone too far in overpromoting the importance of the right brain. The finding that the analytical, rational 'left brain' is found to be the seat of positive thoughts, such as optimism and calm, represents a major 'rehabilitation' for the much derided left brain. The left brain clearly has a vital task regulating emotional response, through the medium of logical, rational, words-based, reflection, and moderating the more gloomy gestalts of the right brain, bringing a sense of proportion and realism into the inner dialogue we have with ourselves. (This may explain incidentally why cognitive therapies, which work on helping people modify their beliefs about the meaning of their past experience, have been shown empirically to make a demonstrable difference in actually helping people feel better.) Walpole was clearly well ahead of his time when he said; 'The world is a comedy to those that think; a tragedy to those that feel'.

TABLE 4.5 KEY DIFFERENCES BETWEEN DIFFERENT TYPES OF LEARNER

Left brain/analytical learners	Right brain/holistic learners
Concentrate on details and differences and build from parts to wholes	Like to grasp the total picture, assimilating details and differences within the whole
Use deductive reasoning and focused, logical, and sequential processing	Associative – look for relationships between things Simultaneous processing
Like doing things better rather than differently	Use spontaneity and intuition
Realistic – prefer to concentrate on what is feasible	Like novelty and doing things differently
Conformist, like repetitive work that accumulates over time, like to follow rules and authority figures	Idealistic – seeing what could be rather than what is
Deliberate and reflective	Generate ideas and think for themselves
Respond to facts, evidence, logic, discussion, processing, language, logic, and mathematical formulae, being asked to engage in processing, discussion, reflection	Impulsive, creative and imaginative Respond to experiential learning, images, pictures, forms and patterns, games, role-play, visualizing

The final conclusion we can draw from this 'see saw' of interest in the left and right brain is that both are essential to effective human thought and feeling – the key is to achieve a dynamic balance between the two (De Beauport, 1996). Schools that wish to develop emotional literacy need to both engage children in emotional experience that inspires the right brain and help them process that experience in ways that engage the left brain, talking about feelings, and becoming more analytical, rational and logical about them. Schools need to help their students engage in the kind of 'positive self-talk' that can link them with their inner potential for the optimism and resilience that we have seen are so helpful for learning and behaviour change. Whole-brain learning suggests that we need to help all learners move freely and flexibly between the holistic and the specific, between the big picture and the detail, between innovation and known procedures, and to 'connect up the learning' through fusing reflection with experience.

■ LEARNING STYLES

At the same time as research on the way in which the brain works has been developing, research on learning styles has also developed rapidly and has enormous importance for those who wish to develop emotional literacy. There have been several attempts to categorize learning styles, with more or less evidence to support them. By no means all the learning styles that have been put forward, especially in the popular literature, have stood up to rigorous testing: only two survived the scrutiny of a review by Riding and Rayner (1998) who looked at a great deal of research which had tested the most widely used. One learning style which has a good evidence to back it is the 'holistic/analytical' dichotomy we have already discussed. The second is a categorization of learning style according to which 'modality' we prefer to learn – pictures, words or feelings/sensations. These two categorizations are useful because they take in many of the others that are often used, and are also the two most often used in work on emotional literacy.

This chapter has already explored one of the two categorizations of learning styles for which there is good evidence – the 'holistic–analytical' dichotomy. We will explore the other next.

■ IMAGE/VERBAL/KINAESTHETIC

There is good evidence that many of us tend to have a preferred 'modality' through which we learn: pictures, words or feeling/sensation. Table 4.6 sets out the characteristics of three types of learner according to which modality they prefer.

TABLE 4.6 LEARNER CHARACTERISTICS BY MODALITY

Auditory learners:
• Learn best through the written and spoken word, music, sound
• Enjoy linking learning with sound, such as a piece of music or a mantra or mnemonic
• Use the language of sound, e.g. 'I hear what you say', 'It sounds to me as if …'

Visual learners:
• Learn best through visual images, shapes, colour, patterns, pictures, diagrams
• Enjoy linking learning with visual images, imagined or real, e.g. mind maps, visualizations
• Use the language of sight, e.g. 'I see' or 'I'll look into it'

Kinaesthetic learners:
• Learn best through physical and emotional sensation, feelings, movement, action, body movement
• Enjoy acting out learning and linking learning with movement and action
• Use the language of feeling, e.g. 'I feel', 'I'm under pressure here' or 'I'm a bit stuck'
• Often communicate emotions and thinking through body language.

Many teachers use a limited range of teaching styles, probably the ones they like best themselves. However, limiting the range of styles can exclude and alienate a large percentage of students and cause learning difficulties which could be overcome if a wider range of styles was used. It is helpful for teachers to become more flexible in their use of the three modalities, be aware that students learn in different ways, and not be quick to judge one way as good and another bad. When teaching a whole class, teachers need to use all three modalities to construct a range of learning experiences that can meet the different learning styles of the learners in their class. When planning more individual work, teachers can work initially with the student's preferred style, particularly if the student is having problems, in order effectively to help them. There is clear evidence that students learn more quickly if they are taught in the style they prefer (Shipman and Shipman, 1983).

However we need to remain open minded about learning styles and not 'pigeon-hole' learners. All of us can, and in fact do, use all three modalities. Many schools overuse words and could do more to employ visual and kinaesthetic learning. As it would appear that 90 per cent of the brain's sensory input comes from visual sources for all learners (Fiske and Taylor, 1984), using more images, pictures, diagrams and mind maps, and less words, might in fact help everyone. Increasingly it would appear that the whole body is engaged in learning, not just the mind, so using more kinaesthetic approaches, which link learning with physical movement and bodily sensation, might also help everyone.

Once they are confident in their preferred style, students need to be encouraged to become more flexible learners, and stretch themselves by using other modalities. Too much concentration on one style, including the one they prefer, causes learners to become ever more set and inflexible in their ways, rather than encouraging a more helpful flexibility and a range of styles. Research has shown this is possible, and that students can change or enhance their learning styles by working in other styles (Torrance and Ball, 1978).

■ WHOLE-BRAIN/WHOLE-BODY THINKING

The explosion of work on how the brain works and on learning styles has resulted in a great many specific implications for learning. Recent work is emphasizing the need to find ways to help all the parts of the brain work more effectively as a whole. The brain itself may be made up of separate parts but it is essentially an organ of communication, and this is what it is designed to do, internally within itself, with the body and with the outside world. Our thinking and our learning strategies need to reflect the holistic nature of the brain and its relationships. It would appear that almost all of us could use our brains a great deal more effectively than we do (Ornstein and Thompson, 1986), and that whole-brain approaches can help us make this leap forward. So-called 'whole-brain' or 'associative' thinking involves making new associations of ideas, bringing together information in new ways, and finding new ways to look at a problem and new solutions (Sylwester, 1995; Gelb, 1998). It involves both sides of the neo cortex and all three 'layers' of the brain working powerfully together in symbiotic ways and in harmony with the body enabling people to learn, not only more quickly, efficiently and effectively, but also in more humane and ethical ways.

We are also starting to realize the extent to which learning is a 'whole body' experience, and that intelligence and learning can reside in the body as well as the mind. 'Brain Gym' (Dennison and Dennison, 1986) is a promising way forward that is becoming increasingly popular in schools. Brain Gym proposes that engaging in complex and usual whole-body movements for a few minutes, and in particular cross-lateral movements (for example, touching knees with opposite elbows) not only gets the blood and oxygen flowing to the brain but also triggers different parts of it into action, most particularly linking the right and left brain so that communication can start to flow effectively between the two. Brain Gym is a potentially useful source of ideas for 'kick starting' the brain when it is stuck, for connecting up the different parts of the brain so the whole works more effectively and for reaching the kinaesthetic learner in all of us.

CREATING REFLECTIVE LEARNERS

Interest in whole-brain thinking is linked with the dramatic rise of interest in learning strategies and is showing that many children, and indeed many adults, learn more effectively if we shift our focus from the content and outcomes of learning to the process of learning, to learning how to learn. Such approaches are being shown to help all students to achieve greater mastery over their own learning by helping them to focus on how they learn as well as what they learn (Pauley, Bradley and Pauley, 2002). These approaches can help able and average students to improve their learning. This can also help students who are struggling, or even in danger of giving up on learning, often because they do not learn easily in ways that schools tend to teach and had no insight into their own ways. Learning how to learn can induce that vital sense of optimism about their own abilities in students who are finding learning difficult, which in turn can help sort out many negative emotions about school and make a contribution to helping with any associated behaviour problems.

LINKING WORK ON EMOTIONAL LITERACY WITH ACCELERATED LEARNING

Some schools are now starting to come at emotional literacy from an interest in accelerated/dynamic learning (Dilts and Epstein, 1995; Smith, A, 1996; 1998). The theories, research and literature that underlie both schools of thought are largely common to both, and both ways of working have a good deal to gain from one another, and from coming together.

Work on emotional literacy would gain from being able to locate its work firmly, not only within a concern for health and for behaviour (which will remain important) but also within a concern for learning, which is the main goal of schools. It will also enable emotional education to become embedded into mainstream schools, and into the education of every child. An infusion of thinking and techniques from the more challenging world of accelaterated and dynamic learning approaches, with its emphasis on stimulation, challenge and achievement, would help to shake up the rather cosy world of emotional education and move it on from its sometimes rather visible roots in the world of special needs. The link would provide access to the newest thinking on teaching methods, for example on ways to use whole-brain thinking and meet a wide range of learning styles.

Work in accelerated/dynamic learning would also have a great deal to gain from linking up with work on emotional literacy. Basically, work on the process of learning has not made much connection with the experience that has come from the growing body of work on emotional literacy, and until it does it is never going to live up to its own aspirations. Accelerated/dynamic learning may emphasize the centrality of emotion in the learning process in theory, but in practice appears not to be sufficiently aware of the depth and complexity of what is needed to put this insight into operation. There is a tendency for such work to demonstrate a shallow view of what emotional and social education involve. It often views students in an intellectualized way, predominantly as 'minds' and 'learners' rather than as whole people with relationships, social lives, or any kind of spiritual dimension. It concentrates mainly on cognitive processes, especially on speedy processing and improving recall, as if the person is a computer in need of constant upgrades. It tends to operate with the naive assumption that all problem behaviours are caused by boredom and/or underachievement, and that if we help students learn effectively, all their emotional, social and behavioural problems will disappear. It focuses mainly on the classroom, both as the source of learning and emotional problems and as place where changes need to be made, rather than including the school and community context and the totality of the learner's life in its vision.

There is huge scope for the two bodies of knowledge – emotional literacy and accelerated/dynamic learning – to come together to inform one another's thinking and form a powerful combination, which can start to reach the lives of all school students and staff in a fundamental way.

To consider as a result of reading this chapter

- In what ways does your school currently make links between emotional literacy and its learning and teaching programme?
- Does the categorization of the different types of learner – holistic/analytical and visual/aural/kinaesthetic – hold water in your opinion? Which do you think you are? Can you see examples around you of the types of learner in people you know?
- Does your school work on the process as well as the content of learning? If so, is it having any benefits for learning? How might it make more links with work on emotional literacy?

CHAPTER FIVE

What Kind of Schools Promote Emotional Literacy?

GOALS OF THIS CHAPTER

By the end of this chapter you will have explored the kind of school climates and organization that promote emotional well-being, develop the competences that make up emotional literacy, and create supportive and congruent environments for classroom-based learning. The issues you will explore include:

- creating warmth, person centredness and involvement
- developing empathic communication
- encouraging autonomy and self-reliance
- creating an emotionally literate physical environment
- ensuring staff have high levels of emotional literacy and well-being
- developing emotionally literate management and leadership
- working with parents in emotionally literate ways.

THE SIGNIFICANCE OF THE WHOLE-SCHOOL ENVIRONMENT

In Chapter 1 we suggested that organizations can themselves be more or less emotionally literate, and defined the level of emotional literacy in an organization as 'the extent to which the organization takes into account the role of emotion in dealing with the people who are its members, and in planning, making and implementing decisions, and takes positive steps to promote the emotional and social well-being of its members'. This chapter will explore the kind of environments, climates and organizations we need

---

Real-life example

When asked to complete the sentence 'In an emotionally literate school …' a group of school staff from Essex in England said:

- All members of the school community are equally valued, respected, motivated and also challenged.
- There is clear and open communication.
- Teachers have high expectations of students, and vice versa.
- Opportunities to succeed are built in and celebrated.
- There are clear roles/job descriptions/action plans/steps/targets/responsibilities/accountability.
- There is consultation and dialogue.
- There is an active School Council.
- Lots of smiles seen and lots of laughter heard – staff *and* children.
- There is strong, positive discipline, based on mutual respect.
- The school is open to visitors – parents, governors, etc.
- There are clear and strong policies on bullying, which includes teaching children not to be victims.
- The school takes steps to get a picture of the emotional literacy of itself as an organization.

What would you say?

---

to promote emotional literacy, in classrooms and across the whole-school experience. As with competences for individuals, so there is no one element that on its own makes for an emotionally literate school, what is needed is a dynamic equilibrium between several different elements.

CREATING WARMTH, PERSON CENTREDNESS AND INVOLVEMENT

PUTTING EMOTION AT THE HEART OF THE SCHOOL

Schools traditionally have been concerned mainly with the intellectual and cognitive side of students and staff, plus, to a lesser extent, their technical and physical skills. However, it is now being recognized that schools need to concern themselves with their students' and staff's emotions because they are central to effective learning and professional practice. This recognition needs to happen at the organizational level as well as at the individual level, and schools need to encourage the consideration of emotional issues to enter into all aspects of school life. This is not just so that emotions do not 'get in the way' of rational planning, but because emotional considerations are at the heart of an efficient and effective school. In the same way that emotional evaluations are what give experience truth and value for individuals, so emotional values invariably govern the decisions schools make, whether or not staff are consciously aware of it. The value a school places on, for example, what subjects need to be taught and why, respect for and belief in the learning potential of every individual in the school, care and compassion for others, teamwork and co-operation, protection for the vulnerable, the promotion of equity and inclusion, the tolerance of difference and the encouragement of individuality and independence of spirit, are essentially matters of judgement, not of fact. The inclination to teach is in any case for most teachers an emotional one, often based on some version of a wish to help children to reach their full intellectual and social potential – certainly few are likely to be attracted to the profession for the money or prestige.

So schools need to be places where emotions are accepted as normal and unthreatening, discussed freely, expressed in safe ways, written about in school statements, prospectuses and policies, and generally validated and considered when considering all processes and decision-making. Everyone involved in the school, staff and parents as well as students, needs to feel that it is quite acceptable to discuss how they 'feel' about something as well as what they 'think' about it, and that they can expect to have their feelings listened to and taken into account, alongside other factors as appropriate. The consideration of the potential impact of planned changes on the emotions of those involved in the school as well as, for example, its budget, needs to be a routine matter. All feelings need to be seen as acceptable, not just the 'nice' ones (although this is by no means carte blanche for people to act out all feelings without inhibition!).

■ EMPHASIZING THE PERSON

'Person centred' education went somewhat out of fashion for a while, as schools were asked to focus on learning objectives, targets and standards. It is, however, starting to make a comeback as those involved in education discover that you cannot in fact raise standards very far unless you concern yourself with the feelings, wants and needs of the people you are so rigorously testing, especially if those people are no longer inclined to want what schools are offering. Meanwhile those who are concerned to promote person centred education occasionally grudgingly admit that the drive for standards is in some ways beneficial to their cause, in that it is requiring schools to focus on the needs of each and every child, rather than write some off as ineducable, because the school is judged by the performance of all its children, not just the brightest.

Research has shown that children need to feel attached to a school and to the staff in it if they are to behave well in school and learn effectively, while staff too need to feel attached if they are to be effective practitioners (Hawkins and Catalano, 1992; Solomon et al., 1992; Battistich et al., 1997). Schools need to make sense to every child, including those who do not find school achievement and appropriate behaviour naturally easy as well as those who get top marks, and to make sense to every teacher, including the newly qualified as well as the head. Each person needs to believe the school is there for them, to feel known, valued, respected and nurtured as an individual, to have a sense of belonging and to experience success and recognition.

Class lessons offer endless opportunities to put the learner at the heart of the process. Children can make themselves the subjects, reflecting on aspects of themselves, their physical and mental characteristics, their likes and dislikes, abilities, beliefs and so on, in art, writing, science and so on. This is fairly common practice in most primary schools, and one which secondary schools could usefully continue. The work on accelerated learning and learning styles we examined in the previous chapter can be in itself person centred, making the process by which each learner learns the main focus of concern, and expecting and encouraging a range of different learning styles and strategies.

Names are essential to our identity, and schools can prioritize making sure that everyone's name is known, spelt and pronounced properly as soon as possible after new children and teachers arrive. Named photos and self-portraits on the wall, and name games, all help speed up and consolidate this process. Large schools may like to provide sheets of class photos in the staffroom so new or supply teachers can quickly learn names. The way in which staff greet their students is very influential: a friendly, personal comment to as many as possible in a day from a teacher or head takes very little time but goes a long way to making each person feel they are known and they matter rather than being part of an anonymous 'herd', especially if the comment shows that the teacher remembers something special about the student. Wherever possible it helps if the teacher can get to the classroom ahead of the students and greet them as they arrive.

Any interaction can become a chance for people to get to know one another better. Even five minutes spent waiting in the cold with a student for their parents to turn up to collect them from a coach trip can become a valuable opportunity for the kind of chat that makes the student feel recognized as a person, and forms the basis for the network of positive social relationships that underlie the effective school.

BUILDING GOOD RELATIONSHIPS

Good relationships at school are fundamental to school effectiveness. A major review of a range of studies (Wubbels, Brekelmans and Hooymayers, 1991) showed that students did better, enjoyed learning more, were more motivated, and had better attendance if they felt that their teachers understood them, and were helpful and friendly. Reviews of the factors that improve student behaviour have invariably shown that positive staff–student relationships are a key factor (Durlak, 1995; Durlak and Wells, 1997). Surveys of what matters to students almost invariably show that students themselves perceive the quality of the relationships they experience at school with 'other people' as one of the most significant sources of both their happiness and unhappiness (Gordon and Grant, 1997).

A vivid example of how central relationships are to students emerged in the work of the voluntary organization Antidote, who are attempting to develop emotional literacy in three schools in the London Borough of Newham. They used a 'draw and write' survey with children in years 1 to 6 to look at what issues the children thought were priorities. Children were asked to depict themselves as 'feeling good' and 'feeling unhappy' at school, and these were the results:

> They made it clear that relationships with peers and with staff are of central importance in determining whether or not they are happy at school. The survey showed that:
>> the thing that made most students feel unhappy at school was the experience of being left out, lonely, insulted, hit or bullied;
>> a quarter found that being with friends or being helped by other students made them feel better at school.
>> a third said that they would feel better at school if other students were more friendly and helpful. (Antidote, 2003: 5)

The children in this Antidote survey were also aware of the importance of their own relationship skills. 'About 40 per cent suggested they could make things better for themselves and others by reaching out to other children, making sure they were not left out, or helping them with their work.' Interestingly, a survey in Eastern Europe by this author, using the same technique, found very similar things, both about the essentially interpersonal nature of the causes of happiness and unhappiness and children's awareness of their own potential for making things better (Weare and Gray, 1994).

Relationships are significant for staff effectiveness too. Poor relationships between students and staff, and between staff and their colleagues, is one of the most commonly cited sources of stress in staff (Kyriacou, 1996). Schools that are unsupportive and have poor relationships have been shown to produce absenteeism and depression in both staff and students (Moos, 1991). When we consider how many staff days are lost to schools through sickness and stress, and the extent to which staff are leaving the teaching profession, it is clear that finding ways to develop good relationships makes good economic sense. Schools and other settings need to prioritize the development of good relationships, between staff, students and parents, in the staffroom, classroom and wider community, and to make the learning of relationship skills, within the wider context of learning about emotional and social competence, a clear priority.

Primary schools often have more success in centralizing the person, building good relationships and inducing a sense of belonging than do secondary schools. Children who progress happily at primary school often experience setbacks when they enter the very different world of the secondary school. Secondary schools usually are bigger, with a large staff which can bring problems of communication, and with quite a different culture to primary schools, more focused on attainment and less on the person. Many children withdraw and become invisible in secondary schools; others conclude they have to 'act out' to survive and be noticed.

■ BUILDING ATTACHMENT THROUGH ACTIVE INVOLVEMENT

Fostering attachment involves more than 'doing things for people': one of the best ways to get people to feel attached is to engage them in the kind of involving activities that induce a sense of commitment, and a sense of having some influence on the context. Children and staff need to be involved in the process of making decisions and running the school, at a level appropriate to their age, stage and position. This can have a profound effect on standards: failing schools have been shown to be put back on the road to success, not by autocratic action but by the degree of active involvement of all staff, including support staff such as cleaners and caretakers, in the decision-making procedures of the school (Devlin, 1998).

Emotionally literate schools work to achieve a high level of consensus and agreement between participants about, for example, values, standards, what matters, how people should behave and so on. Battistich et al. (1991) who are involved in a major 'Child Development Project' across schools in the US, carried out a study of six schools and found that students with a 'high sense of community' showed significantly greater academic motivation and performance, liking for school, empathy for others, and conflict resolution skills. Schools with greater levels of shared values and a more common agenda of activities tend to have students who are more interested in school, have better achievements, and experience less school disorder, absenteeism and dropout rates. Teachers in schools with a higher level of consensus are more likely to be satisfied with their work, be seen by students as enjoying teaching, have high morale and be absent less often (Byrk and Driscoll, 1988). To obtain this consensus, schools need to take what is sometimes called a 'bottom-up' rather than a 'top-down' approach, with genuine consultation, and involvement of all, including those low down in the hierarchy of power and influence. Transparency of communication, with constant dialogue at all levels is the cornerstone of creating this sense of ownership – communication will be discussed in detail a little later in this chapter.

Involvement is achieved by doing rather than just by words, and begins in the classroom with the use of active learning methods and helping students focus on the process of learning as well as the content, including and especially when teaching and learning about emotional and social competence (Fantuzzo et al., 1988). Students who discuss material and make it their own are more likely to act on it (Jensen, 1995). It also includes the way the classroom is run: students work harder and with better results in classrooms where they have a greater say in planning and deciding both what they learn and classroom rules about behaviour (Schaps, Lewis and Watson, 1996). Involvement continues outside the classroom, with students' conferences and councils, students' parliaments, parents' councils, all with real decision-making powers and participative management strategies which encourage teamwork and participation.

The drive for active involvement in schools needs to take in all sections of the community, the whole ethnic and social mix, and of those often marginalized in education such as 'slower' and 'difficult' students and their parents, and those who have little tradition of success in school. Schools need to take care to cater for diversity of culture, social background, age, ability, personality and learning styles.

■ INVOLVING THE PEER GROUP

One useful way to get students to feel involved is to use children themselves, and throughout the discussion of the various themes explored in the book we have mentioned ways in which children themselves can help in the process of helping others learn. Many schools now use peer mentoring systems, peer induction systems for new year groups, 'buddy systems' for new students or those with specific needs, and cross-age tutoring mixed age groups, for example, for pastoral care and sports teams (Goodman, Powell and Burke, 1989; Elias et al., 1997). Using peers as tutors has proved to be particularly effective for students with behavioural and emotional problems, particularly where the subject is itself the improvement of behaviour, and particularly when the students who are acting as tutors have emotional and behavioural problems themselves (Gable, Arllen and Hendrickson, 1994). Peer tutoring has been shown to improve self-concept, behaviour, attitudes to school and learning of both the person being the tutored and the tutor, and helps both of them get along better (Lazerson, 1980).

CREATING A POSITIVE CLIMATE

Chapter 3 spent some time discussing the principle of using a positive rather than a punitive response to difficult behaviour, and paying attention to children 'doing right' rather than wrong. The whole climate and ethos of the emotionally literate school needs to be a positive one if children are to behave and learn well, and teachers practise effectively. Schools need to focus maximum attention, including in their formal assessments, on what children and staff do well in terms of learning, behaviour and professional practice, on the celebration of successes of everyone at their own level. Rutter et al. (1979) found many years ago, in their large-scale studies of what kinds of school are the most effective, that students did better in schools in which they received more praise and positive rewards and where staff had high expectations of them. Teachers also respond best to the positive expectations (Sarros and Sarros, 1992). The atmosphere needs to be a non-judgemental one, with those in difficulties helped and understood rather than criticized. This does not mean the acceptance of all kinds of behaviour, and everyone in a school needs to know that certain behaviours such as aggression, violence, bullying, sarcasm, racism and abuse will not be tolerated.

Time can be spent in engaging in activities that foster important and helpful emotions, such as celebrating success, in greeting new arrivals, staff as well as students, and saying proper goodbyes to those who are leaving. The school can build opportunities for games, laughter, jokes and relaxation into every school day, indeed ideally every lesson. Children are highly motivated by this kind of fun, and will learn all the better as a result. Not least, an upbeat, warm and sometimes lighthearted atmosphere will reduce student and staff stress and anxiety in the classroom and staffroom – stress is, as we have seen, a major block to learning.

■ SETTING CONSISTENT AND CLEAR GOALS, RULES AND BOUNDARIES

Positive climates should not be confused with those that induce an 'anything goes' sense of laissez-faire chaos, and an emotionally literate school is a great deal more than 'warm and fuzzy'. The school improvement movement in particular has emphasized the central importance of clarity in schools and classrooms (Hopkins, 2002). Effective approaches to emotional literacy in schools ensure that concerns with warmth, communication and involvement take place within a context of clear goals, rules and boundaries, a process which does not have to be negative, imposed or autocratic, but does have to be consistent and vigorous. People need to be clear about their role and place within an organization, to know what is expected of them and others, and the rules that govern their interaction, before they can feel safe and secure enough to relate to one another effectively, in open and trusting ways. Children who are troublesome particularly need the security of very predictable routines, clear boundaries, clear feedback and skills programmes to improve behaviour: they are often scared of their own power, appreciate knowing that there are limits to what they will be allowed to do and respect those who set them these limits, provided this is done with a degree of warmth and respect. Schools need clear and strongly enforced codes of polite and respectful behaviour, including staff to students. Schools that have attempted to improve behaviour have found that improving the clarity and consistency in discipline procedures helps a great deal (Gottfredson, Gottfredson and Hybl, 1993). Students achieve more and learn better in classrooms with higher levels of goal direction and less disorganization (Haertel, Walberg and Haertel, 1981). Staff are more highly motivated and more effective where goals are clear (Little, 1982). Clear feedback about the quality of their performance to students and to staff, so long as it is supportive, is strongly associated with greater satisfaction and more effective performance (Moos, 1991). Students learn more and behave better when teachers show clear leadership and are certain of what they are doing (Wubbels, Brekelmans and Hooymayers, 1991).

So, the emotionally literate school will spend considerable time working out what the school community believes is acceptable and unacceptable, disseminating the results of this consultation vigorously and enforcing them strongly and consistently. It will give empathic and positive, but nevertheless clear, feedback to students who overstep the boundaries, ensure there are robust systems for dealing with poor behaviour, and that the consequences of problem behaviour are proportionate, predictable and consistent, with non-hostile, non-physical sanctions consistently applied.

■ TAKING ACTIVE STEPS TO PREVENT BULLYING, VIOLENCE, DISCRIMINATION AND RACISM

Although it would be good to think that schools could devote all their energies solely to building positive relationships, for many schools the immediate priority is to tackle violence and aggression, discrimination and racism and bullying (which in the USA is called 'mobbing'). Schools across the world are attempting to tackle these basic and pernicious problems. For example, in the USA many programmes of emotional and social competence have their base in programmes of conflict resolution and violence reduction (US General Accounting Office, 1995; Aber et al., 1998; Catalano et al., 1998). In the UK the prevention of bullying has become a major strand of the National Healthy School Standard in England in its efforts to promote emotional well-being (DfEE, 1999), and often forms a part of emotional literacy strategies in the UK. Fortunately there is now a wealth of knowledge about what kind of approaches help with these problems.

First and foremost we need to take a preventive, whole-school, approach to emotional literacy being put forward in this book rather than thinking of the problem in a piecemeal fashion, as being isolated to certain children or as the management of specific incidents. With these general strategies in place, there are specific things schools can do to help.

Schools may first need to raise their own awareness of these problems to avoid a very common 'head in the sand' attitude towards them. Schools often benefit from carrying out their own surveys of the extent of bullying, violence, discrimination and racism, and the results often surprise and shock them. These investigations may also throw up some underlying patterns and potential influencing factors which schools can tackle, such as boredom or underachievement in the perpetrators, and give more precise information, such as when and where incidents are occurring and who is involved.

We have already commented on the need to teach the social and emotion skills which can help students to manage their own emotions better, and reduce conflict. Work on empathy is particularly helpful with this cluster of problems, especially for those who perpetrate the problem, as a great deal of research has demonstrated that violent people, bullies and racists lack empathy, and underestimate the amount of unhappiness they cause (Arenio and Fleiss, 1996). Assertiveness can help victims and bystanders to counteract bullies and racists, and some victims of bullying may benefit from learning the social skills that help them fit in with groups better, although this is not to say that we then 'blame the victim' for the problem. If we want to promote tolerance, the curriculum will also need to be examined to ensure that it provides a balanced account of different cultures, beliefs and religions, give a view of history and literature in which the pasts and traditions of the range of groups that make up society are fairly represented, and contain work on the importance of valuing difference and of tolerating a range of ways of opinions, attitudes and cultures.

Staff may need to recognize that they may be unwittingly colluding with bullying, violence, discrimination and racism, for example by themselves showing sarcasm, intolerance and prejudice towards the kind of children who are its victims, or by favouring the kind of outgoing confident children who are often the perpetrators. They need to ensure that they are not conceptualizing problem behaviours as 'high spirits', 'just a bit of fun' or 'horseplay' or seeing those who complain of it as needing to 'learn to stand up for themselves' and not 'tell tales'. Students need to know that the school will not tolerate bullying, violence, discrimination and racism, that if they report it whenever they see or experience it they will be supported and generally believed, and if they practise it they will be in serious trouble.

Schools need to look at the physical layout of the school to avoid 'no go' areas and blind spots where incidents can happen, and enlist the involvement in the overall strategy of the support staff, such as lunchtime supervisors and school transport drivers in whose 'patch' problems can happen. They need to set up energetic, transparent and reliable systems to record and manage incidents, and involve parents in both prevention and incident management. Some schools have trained children themselves to be proactive in reducing conflict, by acting as mediators when other children fall out: their role includes knowing their own limitations and seeking assistance when out of their depth.

DEVELOPING EMPATHIC COMMUNICATION

■ USING NON-VERBAL COMMUNICATION EFFECTIVELY

Warmth and good relationships do not exist in the abstract: to be real they have to be expressed through effective communication. Communication does not of course have to be verbal, indeed the evidence is that most of it is not, and that we gather about 90 per cent of what others 'tell us' about what they think and feel through their non-verbal communication. Non-verbal communication includes body posture, gestures and touch, facial expression and tone. Some people, adults and children, are not very good

Norway's 'Bullying Prevention Programme'

A whole-school approach to the prevention of bullying has been used with great success right across Norway, pioneered by Dan Olweus (1995; 2001) and developed and evaluated for almost 20 years. It is now found in schools across the world. Effective actions have been shown to include:

- creation of whole-school environments characterized by warmth, positive interest and involvement from adults/firm limits to acceptable behaviour/non-hostile, non-physical sanctions consistently applied
- questionnaire survey to discover the extent of problems – starting point for increasing awareness and involvement of all, results reviewed in a school conference day
- teacher discussion groups
- class rules against bullying
- regular class meetings with all students to discuss the issue
- monitoring system of student behaviour
- close liaison with parents
- effective supervision during breaks
- with bullies: serious talks with them and their parents, development of intervention plans
- formation of a co-ordinating committee to oversee the intervention.

Evaluation suggests this approach is highly effective in reducing bully/victim problems and broader anti-social behaviour.

at using words at all, and express themselves better through pictures or action, while most children generally tell a sensitive teacher most of what she needs to know – for example, about what they understand, what worries them, the mood they are in – through what they do, look and sound like rather than what they say.

Given how little words count in communication, and indeed in learning, it is ironic that so much of what happens in schools is based on words rather than on other media. Schools that wish to become more emotionally literate would do well to think about what the school and the staff are communicating to students in non-verbal ways. Later in this chapter we look at the role of the messages that come from the physical environment; here we will look at people's behaviour. Both students and school staff can benefit from becoming more aware of their own body posture, facial expressions, gestures and tone of voice, and make sure it is congruent with what they are trying to express, or at least with what they would like to express. They also need to become more aware of how their reactions to others are usually more about what they do than what they say, and of the 'triggers' to which they tend to respond in other people, for good or ill.

Staff who wish to practise emotionally literate responses to their students need to get control of their non-verbal communication. Simply smiling can help enormously: teachers who smile more have been shown to have students who do better in school. Giving the outward appearance of being relaxed, in a good humour and interested in students through your posture, breathing and expression can go a long way to helping children feel calm and cared for so they can settle and work effectively – particularly helpful when attempting to deal with a difficult situation or with problem behaviour. It is also important for staff to be aware of and get control of differentiated messages they may be giving through their body language: there is not a lot of point in 'talking the talk' of equal opportunities if the teacher mainly interacts with the achievers in the class while communicating less with lower achieving children. Teachers' preferences are often expressed in subtle ways of which even they may not be consciously aware, but children are highly likely to pick up on them, again possibly subconsciously.

ACTIVELY PAYING ATTENTION

It is helpful to think first of the broader category of 'actively paying attention' before we go on to consider the more narrow 'active listening', because, as we have said, 90 per cent of the way in which we show that we are paying attention to someone else is in what we do rather than in what we say, while most of the other person's communicative response is likely to be non-verbal, even when they are speaking. In any case, we often need to pay attention to other types of communication than words: children, and especially younger children, often want to show adults something they have done, such as a picture, or to demonstrate how good they are at an activity such as a game, dance or a somersault.

Both staff and children can benefit from learning and practising the skills of actively paying attention to people, and there has been a massive amount of research on this issue. We can demonstrate our attention non-verbally in the immediate sense by turning to the other person and looking at them, keeping an appropriate degree of eye contact (bearing in mind that some people find too much eye contact threatening), smiling and looking interested, and by not interrupting but making encouraging noises to help them talk or continue with the activity. We can shape our behaviour to 'mirror' and complement theirs, for example our tone of voice or our body posture, to encourage them to feel understood. In the longer term we can show we have paid attention and that they matter to us by remembering what they said or did on a later occasion and referring to and building on it.

RESPONDING EFFECTIVELY

If the other person is talking, then active listening may be all we need to do. Simply hearing ourselves speak and having the sensation of really being attended to is enormously helpful to most people. There is also some skill in responding in ways which help the other person feel understood and help them to solve their own problems as far as possible. The key is to focus on the other person and find out what they are trying to tell us, rather than focusing on our own needs or our assessment of what they are saying. It is best to say as little as possible, and to be non-judgemental in our response. The other person may find it helpful if we help them to clarify what they are saying, provided we do not put words into their mouth.

If we then feel there is a need for feedback on what the other person has said, perhaps because they ask what we think they should do next, we need first to think why we feel this is necessary and check it is really in the other person's interests. It can often be a good strategy to ask the other person what they would now advise themselves to do: the good sense they already have may well be surprising. The listener is now in the happy position of being able to affirm the speaker's good strategies, or at least build on some starting points. If we do decide to give feedback we may need to think carefully about what the other person is ready to hear: it is far better to say too little than say too much and overdo it. It is usually better to phrase suggestions tentatively, for example 'As well as what you have suggested, might it be worth trying … ?' These strategies are as important for helping students learn as they are for encouraging them to talk about personal problems.

IMPROVING COMMUNICATION IN SCHOOLS

Actively paying attention, including listening to someone, is one of the most powerful ways to help them learn, including, and especially, emotional and social competence. It is one of the best ways of promoting someone's self-esteem and sense of attachment, of helping them consolidate their learning, of helping them practise skills or sort out their thoughts, and of motivating them to continue. It also helps the listener to understand them better and so provide useful information for planning to help them more effectively.

However, some children may never enjoy the luxury of someone paying them active and positive attention. Teachers can become so obsessed with their own performance and the 'business' of teaching – which nowadays, in the UK at least, is in danger of becoming all about prepared lesson scripts, learning objectives and targets – that they have no brain space left to pay attention to children. Traditional schools, and especially secondary schools, are places where, in classrooms at least, teachers are mostly supposed to talk and students supposed to listen, apart from short answers to the teachers' questions.

Many primary schools, and some secondary schools, do of course use student talk constructively, for example through the use of group work in which students tackle a task together, sometimes with verbal feedback to the whole class. Circle time is commonly used in UK primary schools, and its regulated use of talking round the circle attempts to ensure that every child has a chance to speak. However, even this can be off-putting for some shy children, who may need more sympathetic, informal, one to one attention.

Listening enhances learning in the classroom – as every teacher knows, the root of many a child's learning problem is that they have either 'switched off' from listening to the teacher or never learnt to do it in the first place. 'Good listening' needs to be noted and encouraged whenever teachers spot it. Teachers can check carefully that students really heard what they were being asked to do before letting them go do it. Lessons can be organized so that children have to take it in turns to listen carefully to one another. Regular use of pairs and small group work is particularly useful here, with children given a task they have to discuss or a problem to solve, with one person charged with producing an output from the group such as a verbal report or a poster, and asked to check that all children in the group feel that the output reflects their contribution and point of view. Teachers might like sometimes to make the children who are the worst listeners the group spokespeople! Children and adults can learn a good deal about empathic listening though being asked to state a situation or problem as another person sees it in a way that the other person agrees is an accurate representation of what they said or felt: sometimes this can take many 'goes' until the speaker concurs with the version being put forward. This is particularly helpful when helping people to resolve conflicts.

Good listening needs to permeate the whole-school consciousness and the whole-school day. Children need to be listened to as individuals in the immediate encounters of the classroom, playground and corridor, and to have opportunities for private talk about what is concerning them. Children also need listening to collectively, and to believe that staff are paying attention to what they are telling them by responding accordingly, for example in adjusting their teaching programmes, or how the school is organized and run. Teachers also need to feel that they are listened to, and that their views count with colleagues, school management, parents and the local education authorities.

USING COUNSELLING

Counselling is a more formalized form of listening, in which two people agree to meet to talk about a specific issue, and often over several sessions. Counselling has a long and distinguished history, and has a key part to play in the emotionally literate school.

Counselling has been shown by some major reviews work in the UK (Rutter, Hagel and Giller, 1998) and in the USA (McMillan, 1992) to be very effective in helping at risk and behaviourally disturbed students. Some schools employ specialist in school counsellors, whom students can visit on a drop-in basis to discuss their problems in confidence without having to stigmatize themselves in the process. Counselling does not necessarily have to be offered by specialists, and some schools have trained their own staff to be more effective in listening to and advising students. Training selected children to be peer counsellors can be very effective, and in some studies children have been shown to be better than adults in helping young people engage in discussion (Rickert, Jay and Gottlieb, 1991). Offering parents counselling at the same time as their children can be very helpful too.

School staff themselves often need counselling to cope with the many challenges of their role. A review of 80 research studies of counselling in the workplace showed that it reduced sickness rates by up to 50 per cent, and some employers have shown their commitment to staff well-being by providing an employee counselling service (DfES, 2003).

Whatever format is used, to be effective, counselling needs to be voluntary and positive, not used in a stigmatizing, mandatory or punitive way, or as a condition for re-entry following an exclusion. It is important to check that the person being counselled is happy to talk, is clear what realistic goals are, does not expect too much from any one conversation and is clear on the ground rules of confidentiality. The counsellor can follow the guidelines for effective listening and responding we have outlined above: listen carefully, focus on the person not the problem, do not be judgemental or moralistic, stay positive, ask open-ended questions, and be as knowledgeable as they can but not pretend to have knowledge they do not have. There needs to be a set time limit for the conversation, and both parties will need to be prepared for several meetings.

■ TALKING WITH CHILDREN ABOUT DIFFICULT ISSUES

The suggestions that follow here can also largely apply to talking with staff who are experiencing difficulties.

All children are faced with difficult issues that they find worrying and upsetting and hard to understand. In their personal lives there are inevitably losses, sometimes large ones such as the loss of a parent, sometimes smaller ones such as the death of a pet or falling out with a friend. Change is difficult for children – again this includes both a huge change such as being adopted and starting again in a new town with a new family and a new school, and smaller changes such as moving house, or a new baby in the family. All children find events in the outside world upsetting, for example terrorist attacks and war, and can find tales of what happens to children, such as abductions, particularly upsetting. Many are concerned about what they hear about threats to the environment, or cruelty to animals. It may be that something difficult has happened in the school itself, such as the death of a classmate, or even a violent attack.

Staff need to know how to talk with children about difficult issues at an appropriate level for their development. We cannot hope to shield children from difficult emotions, but how we talk to them can make a big difference. This is not to say we force children to confront issues for which they may not be ready; the main thing is to pay attention to the children and take cues from them, not to push them, but to allow them the opportunity to open up an issue that is bothering them, and if they do, not to ignore it. Sometimes children may not do this directly, but how they are feeling may become evident in overheard conversation, or a game that acts out some event. Or it may become apparent in their non-verbal communication, in gestures, facial expressions and body movements. If they do not speak, we may need to just give them space until they are ready. But if we feel they do need to talk, because something is clearly bothering them, we need to know how to open up a conversation with an open question, but not a lecture. It may be helpful to tell children that we are really interested in knowing what people of their age think – then listen.

Once the listener knows what is worrying the child, he or she can try to give whatever assurances he or she can. These may include introducing a sense of proportion, for example talking about what a small percentage of children die in road accidents, or the steps the school is taking to keep people safe, or the efforts people are making to save the environment. It can be helpful to get the child themselves to say what they might say to another child who was feeling as worried as they are – children often have a surprising range of inner resources. It is important that the listener does not promise what they cannot deliver – such as world peace, or an end to children being abducted – nor try to trivialize the child's concerns. At the end of the conversation it can be helpful to thank the child for talking and being honest about their feelings.

ENCOURAGING AUTONOMY AND SELF-RELIANCE

WHAT AUTONOMY MEANS AND WHY IT IS IMPORTANT

Autonomy or self-reliance, means that people are encouraged to be independent, to think for themselves, to make their own decisions, to be self-directed, responsible for their own learning and behaviour. It involves people in being self-disciplined, questioning, reflective and critical of what is going on around them, able to take control and to take personal responsibility. Autonomy has strong links with the need for active involvement that we have discussed earlier in the chapter.

There is strong evidence that the pursuit of autonomy is fundamental both for academic and for emotional literacy. Students learn better and are happier at school if they are encouraged to be as autonomous as their stage, age, personality and attitudes allow (Wubbels, Brekelmans and Hooymayers, 1991). Although we have said that students need to feel safe, this is not the same as feeling bored, and there is evidence that learners respond better to a manageable degree of uncertainty and confusion, as it reflects the kind of real-life problems to which the brain is designed to respond (Jensen, 1995).

So autonomy is a key goal for an emotionally literate school, but one that is often neglected. There are many reasons why adults find the encouragement of autonomy in children particularly difficult. It is tempting for adults to focus on trying to keep children safe and to protect them from the world in a mistaken belief that to do so is 'caring'. Of course we need to think carefully about how we gradually expose children to the harsh realities of the world, and children do indeed need a certain amount of shielding as appropriate to their age and stage. But protection is not a viable long-term option and to use it 'past its sell by date' is to be overprotective and suffocating. It risks either alienating young people, or stifling their initiative and the ability to grow and cope with the challenges of modern life. Less confident adults often find the independent thinking and behaviour of young people threatening. But healthy young people need to move away from their teachers and parents and become able to question and to criticize. Adults need to find ways to work with young people that respect their growing need for independence while continuing to set appropriate boundaries.

■ AUTONOMY IS DEVELOPMENTAL

Autonomy is a relative, not an absolute, concept, and students respond best, including when learning about emotional, social and health related issues, where the degree of freedom is suited to their age, stage and personality (Moos, 1991). Younger, less mature and more introverted and anxious students need higher degrees of structure and organization but still benefit from being given as much autonomy as they can handle, and by being gradually encouraged to work more independently. Older, more mature and more confident students can handle higher levels of individual choice and autonomy.

All students need to be moved towards independence and autonomy, whatever their starting point: indeed learning to be autonomous is particularly important for those who come from homes where it is not so encouraged. We need to start this from an early age, and build gradually towards independence. It is a matter of working in partnership with young people, with a gradual handover of responsibility.

■ STAFF NEED AUTONOMY TOO

Staff feel better about themselves and their work, and are more effective, if they are given as much room for independent action, freedom and flexibility as possible. The level of autonomy we experience is highly influential on both teachers' professional effectiveness and for health (Tuettemann and Punch, 1992). Giving staff more freedom to make their own decisions results in better morale and better attendance, and less stress. A large-scale, long-term and now classic study of English civil servants by Marmot and colleagues (Marmot et al., 1997) found that those at the top who had more control over their work and who used their skills more were less likely to be absent from work, and even less likely to die of early heart disease than those lower down the hierarchy, even though those at the top had a faster pace of work and higher workloads which might common sensically have been considered more stressful. So stress is not just about workload and pressure, it is centrally about autonomy.

▧ AUTONOMY AND EMOTIONAL LITERACY

The need to encourage autonomy applies as much to the teaching of emotional literacy as in any other area of school life, but is often one of the weaker points of work in this area.

We have already suggested that projects that are imposed on schools sink after a short while, pre-prepared initiatives have been shown to disappear more quickly than those which are generated by the school itself, and staff who are involved in designing and evaluating teaching materials and teaching them to one another are more motivated and committed than when they were teaching programmes that were given to them to teach. Those who work with schools need to resist the temptation to provide a 'prepared package' or another highly directed approach on emotional and social competences into schools for everyone to follow, as this top-down, imposed solution is likely to undermine rather than support effective work in this area.

Sometimes teachers are under such pressure they feel they do not have time to think for themselves and claim they prefer to be told what to do. In these circumstances, rather than simply providing a pre-packaged and another disposable answer for them, it may be more helpful to examine the causes of the problem and help relieve the problem of stress and overload.

We need to be careful that, in our efforts to encourage people to become emotionally literate we are not replacing one orthodoxy with another, by imposing one model of what emotional literacy means or coercing people into conformity. This book has suggested elsewhere that some models of emotional intelligence can be highly normative and used to attempt to impose one specific set of standards on everyone. These are often those that relate to adult needs for 'well-behaved' children and the needs of business for a docile and productive workforce, motivated by individual need to be a consumer in a materialistic society. We need broader approaches, in which there is a wide range of ways to be emotionally literate, which can include a wide range of cultures and classes, both genders, all kinds of personality and learning styles, and which encourage independent and critical debate.

Successful projects that attempt to develop emotional literacy and well-being have almost invariably used approaches that work with schools to develop initiatives in partnerships. For example the director of Antidote, the Campaign for Emotional Literacy, believes that the success of his organization's work with schools and others is due to the strategy they have adopted of bringing people together to discuss issues, to engage in dialogue rather than imposing ideas from above or outside. In an interview with the author he commented, 'Schools don't need to be told what to do, but to be helped to come to their own conclusions' (Weare and Gray, 2002, p.63). The Southampton Local Education Authority's Emotional Literacy Initiative worked over many years with a network of schools on a voluntary basis to help schools come to their own conclusions, including their own curriculums and checklists for assessment (Sharp and Faupel, 2002).

CREATING AN EMOTIONALLY LITERATE PHYSICAL ENVIRONMENT

▇ THE IMPORTANCE OF THE PHYSICAL ENVIRONMENT

The physical environment of the school invariably conveys messages to those who work, learn and visit there, whether or not these are intentional. These messages tell people how much the school values them, and contribute to making them feel stressed, frightened or bored, or alternatively relaxed, safe and stimulated. The physical environment is a major component of the school's level of emotional literacy, and we need to ensure that the messages sent by the layout, quality, sight, sound, smells and sensations of the physical environment are congruent with the messages we are attempting to convey in other parts of the school's climate and ethos.

The physical environment can also be used to support specific work on emotional literacy, for example by the creation of special spaces in which to work, and through displays of materials and work devoted to emotional literacy, through the display of school statements on codes of conduct towards one another, and visual reminders, for example about processes to go through when feeling angry, stressed or in conflict.

▇ THE SCHOOL AS A WHOLE

It helps to look at the physical environment of the school from the child's point of view, sometimes literally, for example by ensuring that noticeboards are at child height. Children need to feel comfortable, and physically and emotionally safe in school. They need to have somewhere that is special to them, with their work and special things around them, with people and things with which they can identify, and with somewhere they can store their belongings safely. Children need to be and feel safe from bullying, and have play spaces that are properly supervised. Furniture needs to be comfortable, and in some places relaxing. Colour needs to be appropriate: stimulating in some areas, calming in others. Outside, the playground and gardens can be landscaped to provide opportunities for the more active to run and play, and cosier areas for those who wish to play quieter games or to get into small groups and chat. The school entrance hall is both its 'shop window' for visitors and its opening arms to staff children and parents, and it needs to be welcoming. There need to be clear instructions as to where to go when you arrive if you are strange, useful information for parents, and displays that are often changed and that represent the work of the whole school community, and make children, staff and parents feel when they arrive that they are proud of their achievements and that the school belongs to them.

> **Real-life example**
> The STEP programme in the USA, which attempted to help children make the transition involved in moving up from a smaller school to a larger, found the creation of 'Homerooms' where children spent a good deal of their time was a key component in making children feel safe and confident. Evaluations showed that children who were part of the STEP programme had lower levels of stress, reductions in anxiety, depression and delinquent behaviour and made better academic progress, compared with a control group of students not in the programme who had no 'Homeroom' (Felner, Ginter and Primavera, 1982; Felner et al., 1993).

CLASSROOMS

The emotionally literate classroom will be a well-organized, calm, attractive and stimulating setting for learning. Ideally the teacher will arrive early to greet the children, take charge of seating arrangements, attend to the wall displays, use plenty of visuals, including copious examples of all children's work and ideas, and change them often. Children will be seated in good light, at furniture that is comfortable and the right height for them, able to see the teacher and work with one another or on their own easily, and as appropriate. Children will themselves have a good deal of influence over what the classroom looks like and responsibility for keeping it as all have agreed they would like it. Teachers may like to introduce specific physical features to support emotional literacy work, for example in some schools children can put a peg on a line if they would like to request five minutes' 'bubble time' alone with a teacher to discuss any worries.

SOUND, TEMPERATURE, SMELL, LIGHT

[Much of the evidence in this section is taken from a book by Jensen (1995) who summarizes the research on these and many other issues related to learning in his very useful work on 'The Learning Brain'.]

The sound quality of any environment makes a massive difference to how we feel when we are in it. Schools are often a cacophony of loud noise, particularly secondary schools at lesson changeover times, punctuated by jangling school bells. Many children, and staff, find the nature and volume of the noise either stressful or aggression inducing. Some schools have tried to reduce the volume of unpleasant sound by staggering lesson changeover times, introduced carpeting and replacing bells with something less ear splitting: some schools just use teachers' watches! Music and other pleasant sounds have been shown to be highly effective in inducing appropriate moods and encouraging learning: calming music can create an appropriate relaxed atmosphere, for example in public spaces and at the end of lessons. Different types of music induce different types of learning, for example upbeat music puts learners in a state of readiness to learn, while certain complex classical music such as Mozart helps them to solve problems.

Other unseen but influential aspects of the physical environment include smell, temperature and lighting. Smell links directly into our reptilian and mid brains and thus our mood and our long-term memories: how many of us have bad memories of school induced by a sudden whiff of overcooked cabbage or rank boys' toilets? Certain smells, such as flowers have been shown to improve learning to a highly significant extent. Temperature is another key influence, and although it is more conducive to learning be too cold than too warm, it is best to be neither. Lighting is also key in affecting mood: some children and staff may suffer from Seasonal Affective Disorder depression induced by the lack of light on winter days: schools do well to ensure that everyone gets out as much as possible in winter, or even consider installing broad spectrum lighting which has been shown to impact significantly on this problem.

■ TIMES OF DAY

It may be helpful to think about how the way in which the school handles different times of the day impacts on children's mood. For example, at the start of the day, how are the children welcomed? How are they gentled into the start of the learning day? How are any problems, worries or exciting news they may bring with them from home dealt with? How are they let out to play or to go home – in a calm mood with a few reminders on how to 'play nicely together' or to 'have a nice evening', or in an elephantine rush with staff turning their backs in relief? How is lunchtime organized: can the children eat their meals in a civilized and peaceful setting?

> **Making special spaces to promote emotional literacy**
>
> In Leicestershire, England, some schools have created 'time out' or 'calm down' rooms where children can go if distressed and where an adult is available to supervise and support, and a 'buddy bench' where isolated or unhappy children can go and where trained peers can then go to give support (Leicester Local Education Authority, 2001). Other schools have introduced relaxation sessions, such as lunchtime 'chill out' sessions to help children undergoing examinations.

STAFF AREAS

Staff, too, need to make sure they provide themselves with an emotionally literate working environment and take the time to keep it that way. Teaching-staff rooms, and the rooms of support staff, are often dingy, untidy and uncomfortable places, crammed with assorted and ancient furniture, with nowhere for staff to store their belongings or get piles of work out of sight, and with walls that are covered with work-related notices, which are often out of date. Providing time and resources to improve such depressing environments can energize staff, and signal clearly that management care about them. With time and a little money staffrooms can become more relaxing and pleasant to work, tidy and attractive, with comfortable chairs, good working areas with good lighting, good quality decoration, water chillers and coffee and tea, and easy access to a phone, radio, television and the Internet, so staff can feel they remain part of the human race while at school.

ENSURING STAFF HAVE HIGH LEVELS OF EMOTIONAL LITERACY AND WELL-BEING

Throughout this book we have been at pains to apply the principles being suggested to staff as well as students. We will look in more detail at the issue of staff emotional literacy and well being next.

EMOTIONALLY LITERATE SCHOOLS NEED STAFF WITH A HIGH LEVEL OF EMOTIONAL LITERACY AND WELL-BEING

A highly significant factor in determining how effectively children learn emotional and social competences and experience emotional and social well-being in school is the behaviour and attitudes of the adults with whom they come into contact. It is these behaviours and attitudes that are the main means by which the competences are transmitted, through direct teaching, through the quality of the relationships and communication in the school, and through the way the school is managed and run. A recent study showed interestingly that, while teenagers do not generally see adults as role models as far as health behaviours such as smoking or exercise are concerned, they do feel strongly that school staff need to model good interpersonal behaviours, such as respect, calmness and rapport (Gordon and Turner, 2001).

Barriers to emotional literacy in schools, according to a group of Hampshire Head Teachers' Forum

- Teachers are expected to do so many things.
- Too many new initiatives – heads need vision and to manage everything coming into school.
- Heads are driven by academic results and league tables.
- Short-term vision.
- Short-term funding.
- Some colleagues resent having to teach PSHE – it's low priority; there's no training in it; some teachers don't have enough life experience.
- Size of some schools. It's about building relationships – in some large schools, teachers don't even know their colleagues, let alone the children.
- In some schools, the focus is on the failures of staff rather than successes.

■ THE CHARACTERISTICS OF AN EMOTIONALLY LITERATE MEMBER OF STAFF

The kind of qualities that an emotionally literate member of a school staff needs to display have been set out in Chapter 2 which looked at competences in some detail, and we will just bring out a few of the most pertinent here. They need to be high on self-regard, self-knowledge, emotional awareness and the ability to manage their own emotions. They need to be aware of the influence of their own emotions, and set clear professional boundaries between themselves and the students. They need to be emotionally resilient and with a high tolerance of stress: teaching, and especially emotional literacy work, is very demanding. They need to be a 'people person' with strong relationship skills and positive attitudes towards others, a celebrator of others' success and infectiously optimistic. They need to be trustworthy, authentic, honest, clear, and their behaviour congruent with what they claim to believe.

All school staff need emotional literacy, and teachers who work with students on the issue will need especially high levels of it. Emotional literacy work may be new to the students, and may cause them to 'act up' until they get used to it. It will produce strong emotions in students and teachers need to be able to 'hold' those emotions and not respond directly themselves. Certainly not every teacher in a school is likely to be able to work on emotional literacy to the same extent, and those who carry out the core teaching in this area may need to be chosen for their abilities to handle difficult and demanding work.

We need however to support staff to achieve these exacting standards, not blame them if they fall short, not least because in order to be emotionally literate, staff need to have their own needs met, and to be supported by their organization, issues we will examine next.

◼ STAFF NEED TO HAVE THEIR OWN NEEDS MET – INCLUDING STRESS REDUCTION

The starting point for helping create more emotionally literate staff is to take their emotional needs into account, ensure they are given resources and help, and that they feel valued and respected. Teachers may find the idea of taking on responsibility for emotional and social competence difficult because they feel already under stress. Unless they see that the principles of emotional literacy are being applied to their welfare they may well be cynical about emotional literacy work, and feel unable to support it.

There is clear evidence from the research literature of a rise in stress levels among teachers: teachers are the most stressed occupational group of all. In a recent survey, 42 per cent of UK teachers said they were 'highly stressed' compared with an average of 20 per cent across all occupations and had the highest rate of all groups, including comparable groups such as nurses; they also reported that most of this stress was work related (DfES, 2003). The result of this increase in stress is devastating to schools and to education as a whole. It brings with it a decrease in staff morale, difficulties in teacher recruitment, problems with teacher retention, ineffective and 'burnt out' teachers, and days lost through stress-related illness – long-term absence through stress is especially on the increase among teachers (Dean, 1995; Leech, 1995; Kyriacou, 1996).

Working in schools, and especially teaching, is more challenging than ever, for a variety of reasons. Teachers' workloads are increasing and there are many more demands on schools than there used to be (McEwen and Thompson, 1997). Schools are asked to manage themselves and their budgets, and are subject to ever higher expectations by society and governments in terms of standards, test results and accountability. Children and young people are becoming more challenging, difficult and disruptive at the same time that schools are being asked not to exclude the most difficult. In many societies there has been a breakdown in respect for the teaching profession, with teachers feeling underpaid and undervalued, and lacking the support from the children's homes or from the public that they once did. In any case there are some endemic problems in schools: ineffective communication in schools has been cited as the most commonly reported cause of teacher stress, after the inevitable complaint about excessive workload (Rumsby, 2001).

It may be too that, as a self-selected group who tend to be highly interested in other people, teachers are rather prone to stress. Teachers tend to suffer from low self-esteem, which has been shown to correlate with their feeling mentally unhealthy: those with lower self-esteem have a lower commitment to teaching, more negative attitudes to school and higher stress levels (Lin and Lin, 1996). Teachers often blame themselves when things go wrong, such as students misbehaving. Teaching is a job that is never finished and can expand to fit 24 hours a day, seven days a week, so it is easy to overwork. There is a certain culture of masochism and workaholism in teaching: this needs tackling by teachers generally expecting more for themselves and the quality of their working lives. (As an ex-teacher the author reserves the right to claim this!)

■ LINKING THE WELL-BEING OF STAFF WITH EMOTIONAL LITERACY

We are starting to make some progress on understanding and allieviating these unacceptable levels of teacher stress, and international research and practice are now developing on this issue (Vandenberghe and Huberman, 1998). Several attempts to promote emotional literacy and emotional well-being in schools have taken as their starting point the literacy and well-being of school staff. In an investigation by the author of five English Local Education Authorities who were developing work on emotional and social competence, all five Authorities had prioritized work on staff well-being (Weare and Gray, 2002). The National Healthy School Standard which is attempting to promote healthy schools across England has a major strand on teacher well-being, including a booklet on *Staff Health and Well-Being* (DfES, 2003). This contains guidelines and some very convincing case studies of schools in which work on promoting staff well-being has proved very beneficial. The Standard will be discussed in more detail in Chapter 7.

■ AN ORGANIZATIONAL RESPONSE

Promoting staff well-being is not just about working with individuals: it has to start at organizational level, with the kind of whole-school approach to climates and structures this book is promoting. To recap briefly on some of the issues we have looked at and apply them specifically to staff well-being: the school needs to ensure that staff feel heard and valued, are given as high a level of personal responsibility and autonomy as possible, have clear job descriptions and reasonable workloads including non-contact time for marking and preparation, have adequate resourcing and support, and operate in an atmosphere of open and transparent communication, warmth and approval. High levels of support, particularly from the head-teacher have been shown consistently to reduce the likelihood of teacher burnout (Sarros and Sarros, 1992). All staff need to be consulted about and involved in their own professional and personal development, and the development of the school as a whole.

Approaches to tackling stress that attempt to address the problem at a whole-school organizational level have been shown to be highly effective: for example, a stress reduction project in Norfolk, England which included work on worker participation and top management support resulted in improvements in staff perceptions of management, better recruitment and retention, and higher staff motivation and morale (Rumsby, 2001).

■ THE WORK–LIFE BALANCE

The need to promote a proper work–life balance is a major well-being issue that needs tackling at both the organizational and the individual level in schools. To be both effective and happy, staff need to have a rich and rewarding life outside of school, to find time for rest and recuperation, and not be run into the ground with unrealistic expectations about the levels of work they can sustain. Flexible working and the provision of child-care services can help too. Some of this issue is for management to address in ensuring they do not push employees too far, and that they provide supports. Some of the issue needs addressing by staff themselves, who may need to give up their quest to be superman/woman and settle for being 'good enough' in some areas.

■ STAFF WELL-BEING NEEDS CAREFUL PLANNING

The promotion of staff emotional literacy and well-being will not happen by chance – as with all whole-school changes it has to be planned and implemented carefully, within an overall scheme for developing the emotionally literate school. A range of stakeholders such as teachers, support staff and governors can be consulted from the outset, encouraged to see it as a priority and to clarify the benefits they hope it will bring for themselves and the school. A systematic audit and needs assessment to establish the overall picture and get a baseline can be a helpful starting point. Action plans can be made, which set clear and realistic goals, and be accompanied by appropriate staff development and an adequate appropriate budget. Changes can be made at several levels, monitored over time to see if they are effective and adapted as necessary. The issue can be built into agendas, policies, decision-making and school plans, right across the school. It is important to start small, with achievable plans which can actually be realized in a short time span and thus motivate staff and make them believe change is worthwhile and possible.

Some schools in Southampton where emotional literacy is a key priority have found it helpful to establish an 'emotional literacy interest group' in the school, led by a school co-ordinator (Sharp and Faupel, 2002). These groups not only to help develop approaches for students; their prime function is for staff to help them to reflect on their own emotional reactions to events, and set aside time to reflect on their own practice. The group can include staff from right across the school, support staff as well as teachers, and members may then like to act as advocates or champions for the development of emotional literacy across the school.

■ THE ROLE OF TRAINING

Staff benefit greatly from staff development and training on emotional literacy and well-being, not imposed on them but in response to their requests. Many forms of training have proved to be helpful, including training days or short programmes for a whole staff, a school or cluster representative attending a larger event and cascading the outcomes to other staff, or longer, accredited training in an institute of higher education.

Attempts to promote teachers' emotional literacy and well-being at a national and international level have often involved teacher education. A World Health Organization project which attempted to develop mental and emotional health across Europe began with two training courses for various professionals who work in schools, focused mainly on their own needs: these professionals then went and devised their own approaches in schools (Weare and Gray, 1994). Research shows that teacher education has an important role in supporting work on emotional and social competence and well-being. Programmes which include staff development and education are more likely to have an impact on student behaviour (Durlak, 1995; US General Accounting Office, 1995; Durlak and Wells, 1997).

Stress management courses

Stress management courses abound in most Western countries, and can be very helpful for some people. A typical course might cover:

- the signs and symptoms of stress
- the personal and social consequences of stress
- achieving a proper work–life balance
- positive self-talk to avoid unrealistic expectations of self (such as 'I must be perfect in everything I do')
- gaining and giving social support
- communicating assertively – asking clearly for what you need and resisting inappropriate demands
- time management, including goal setting, prioritizing, scheduling and working smarter rather than harder
- giving yourself rewards
- relaxation techniques.

However many involved in the field believe we still have a long way to go and claim there is not nearly enough staff development and education on emotional literacy and well-being. Some attempts are now being made to set up courses on emotional literacy in the UK: the universities of Bristol and Southampton, for example, run in-service courses for a range of professionals, to encourage an appropriately multi-professional approach.

DEVELOPING EMOTIONALLY LITERATE MANAGEMENT AND LEADERSHIP

THE ROLE OF EMOTIONALLY LITERATE MANAGEMENT IN SCHOOLS

Emotional literacy cannot be imposed on people, it is created through the whole school, using a participative, consultative approach which empowers people to get involved in the creation of an emotionally literate climate and organization. However such a participative approach will not happen by chance, and using teamwork by no means removes the need to have a committed school management team who are highly active in fostering emotional literacy and give it the highest priority. The management team needs to fully understand what work on emotional literacy involves, and their own central role in shaping an emotionally literate school culture and ethos, leading from the front, and by example.

Real-life example

When asked to brainstorm their views on 'what kind of school managers we need to promote emotional literacy?' a group of school staff from Essex, England talked about management structures:

- Open leadership.
- Active communication at all levels.
- Teamwork.
- Staff have a good deal of control over their own work.
- Those above listen more than they talk to those below them.
- Flexible – teams came together for different purposes and different lengths of time.
- Clear systems and structures – everyone knows what is expected of them.
- Inclusive.
- Individual skills and strengths recognized, valued and utilized.

They had a good deal to say about headteachers:

- A head who has a sense of purpose and vision.
- A head who doesn't expect anything from staff he or she isn't willing to do him or herself.
- A head with commitment, who 'walks the talk'.
- A head who is positive and rewarding, celebrates achievement.
- The headteacher gets out from behind the desk and gets involved.

What would you say?

There are, in any case, some roles which only management can play. They need to mediate between staff and the outside world and to manage targets in a way that empowers not dispirits their staff. They need to take emotional literacy into account when recruiting staff, not just go for the most technical skilled or academically clever. They need to help staff respond to change appropriately, and prevent and deal with stress, not least by handling the key issues of workload, resources and responsibility which staff can find so stressful, and encouraging staff to achieve a healthy work–life balance. They need to make sure staff have clear and mutually agreeable contracts and job descriptions, and receive regular and sensitive appraisal of their performance – this appraisal does not have to be 'top down' and some schools and local education authorities are starting to use so called 360^0 appraisal (Dulewicz and Higgs, 2000) in which staff receive feedback from those above, below and on the same level as themselves.

▧ THE ROLE OF THE HEADTEACHER

Clearly the most single significant senior manager is the head. There is a strong consensus, both in the literature and in the field, that leadership by the headteacher is essential in the development of an emotionally literate school: a proactive concern with this issue needs to come right from the top, and to permeate every aspect of school life and learning. The relationship between emotional literacy and leadership is two-way: effective leadership requires high levels of emotional literacy, while effective leadership in turn helps create emotional literacy.

All the qualities we have looked at so far as characterizing an emotionally literate person and member of staff of course apply to headteachers, but they will need other qualities in addition. Headteachers need to be prepared to be leaders, and not just administrative managers, and this involves more than efficiency: they need to have a sense of vision and purpose, and the ability to inspire others, to be creative and innovative, and to manage change and uncertainty. They also need to know their own limitations so they can make sure they have others to take care of the tasks and roles they are not good at, and make sure they look after themselves properly in the process.

Being a headteacher is a lonely job, the person with whom the buck stops, the filter through which those above communicate with the school, and the frequent focus of discontent and complaint from below. There is no one in the school who is in the same position or who can help take some ultimate decisions. The workload and weight of responsibility can be enormous, especially for people who went into the job as classroom teachers and may not naturally have the management, leadership or business-like qualities that the role they have taken on now demands. We often expect almost superhuman levels of commitment, competence and the ability to manage stress and conflict from our headteachers. As a result, headteachers are notoriously prone to stress-related breakdowns, and in some parts of the UK it is becoming almost impossible to recruit new ones – the job is increasingly seen as non-'do-able', or at least not worth the stress it creates. Heads need a good deal more emotional and practical support and understanding, within and outside school, than they tend to get at present.

■ THE ROLE OF GOVERNORS/SCHOOL BOARDS

Governors or school boards are often forgotten in accounts of work on emotional literacy, but in some countries they play a pivotal role in the running and management of the school, including its efforts to work on emotional literacy. Southampton City Council has involved governors in whole-school plans to increase emotional literacy (Sharp and Faupel, 2002). They suggest that each school should nominate a governor with a particular focus on emotional literacy who can help, for example, with the development of the school programme, ask questions about emotional literacy of candidates when making appointments, take an active interest in staff welfare and working conditions, liaise with the local education authority on this issue, and induct and mentor new governors. Such a person will need to have a high level of emotional literacy themselves, be prepared to reflect further on how to deepen this, and model emotionally literate responses to the outside world. Southampton found that the whole governing body can usefully be involved from the outset in training, planning, policy-making and monitoring changes. The governing body can be prepared to demonstrate their own emotional literacy by working effectively as a team, engaging in open and democratic communication, listening carefully to one another, tolerating difference, taking risks, making unpopular decisions, and managing change and uncertainty.

WORKING WITH PARENTS IN EMOTIONALLY LITERATE WAYS

■ MAKING PARENTS FEEL INFORMED, LISTENED TO, WELCOMED AND INVOLVED

All effective schools are coming to realize the importance of good home–school relations. In most parts of the world there is increasing involvement of parents in the whole life of the school, with much more regular, steady, open and informal dialogue and information exchange between parents and school than used to be the case (Haynes and Comer, 1996; Webster-Stratton, 1999). Children are bringing home regular and informal communications from school, such as reading record and homework record books in which both home and school exchange comments about progress on a daily basis. School are taking care to ensure that parents can quickly see staff if parents or staff have concerns about a student, rather than wait for the traditional parents' evening with its long queues and exhausted teachers. Some enlightened schools contact parents to tell them when the child has done something well rather than always focusing on the negative, and find that this positive base helps set up a non-defensive communication between the partners that is invaluable if things go wrong. End of term reports are increasingly written in ways that encourage contributions and dialogue between teacher, student and parent. Many schools have set up home–school agreements, with clear information about what each party can expect from the other. Parents' rooms are increasingly common, with information for parents about what the school is doing, resources that can be borrowed, and somewhere for parents to meet.

Good schools will develop a regular exchange of information with the home about emotional needs as well as learning needs. Staff will know about issues at home that may be affecting learning and well-being for good or ill, such as family celebrations, positive or negative changes in the domestic situation such as parental disagreements or separations and bereavements or the birth of a new sibling. Both parties need to be in contact if something about the child's behaviour is suddenly worrying, and attempt to get to the bottom of the problem quickly and without too much fuss.

■ WORKING WITH PARENTS TO PROMOTE EMOTIONAL LITERACY

There is considerable evidence that effective work on emotional and social education is more effective if it involves parents. Schools need to share with parents what they are trying to do in tackling emotional literacy, to make sure that parents understand the goals and the processes. This way we can attempt to ensure that parents do not harbour unfounded fears about work on emotional literacy, fears which may include believing that, for example, students are being encouraged to 'let it all out', to act out anger, or encouraged to bully.

Schools can also work proactively with parents as partners in developing and delivering programmes. Several major reviews of emotional and social education programmes in the USA (Durlak, 1995; US General Accounting Office, 1995; Durlak and Wells, 1997) showed that programmes which actively involve parents, the local community and key local agencies are more likely to have an impact on student learning and behaviour. Some successful projects have asked parents to help students with emotional and social 'homework' for assignments and projects, for example by looking at how social and emotional learning from school can be applied in the home context (Gettinger, Doll and Salmon, 1994; Elias et al., 1997). Specific attempts to reduce bullying and violence in schools (Olweus, 1995; 2001) have been shown to be more effective if they involve the parents of both bullies and victims. Some schools have gone further and have involved parents in helping teach about emotional literacy, in mentoring students with problems, and sitting on their emotional literacy planning, management and community liaison teams (Chapman et al., 1999).

■ RELATING TO 'DIFFICULT' PARENTS

The relationship between home and school is often charged with emotion and does not always go well. Parents can have emotional problems with the school their children attend, and staff can have emotional problems with parents and parents' reactions. Parents may be angry with the school for real or imagined mistakes over the treatment of their children. They may be defensive or overanxious about problems their child has and either be unwilling to face them or make too much of them. They may be unsupportive of what the school is trying to do for their child, including its emotional literacy programme.

However irritating, time-consuming or sometimes downright frightening parents may be, emotionally literate schools will try to work with the assumption that it is likely that parents have what is, from their own point of view, a good reason to be difficult. Of course, this is no reason for a school to put up with aggression, much less violence, from parents, and staff have a right to feel safe when doing their jobs. However, an empathic attitude can often go a long way towards defusing parents' aggression and defensiveness. All good parents are naturally concerned for their children and keen to make sure they are well and fairly treated, and most have no point of comparison, knowing only their own family. Many will have heard only one side of the story, their child's, and have a natural good parent's inclination to believe and support their child. They may themselves be insecure and thus angry or defensive coming into school, due to their own negative experience of school. They may be at the end of their tether with a difficult child and keen to pin the blame elsewhere. They may be defensive because they are only too aware of their own failings as a parent and not know what to do about it. Finally, of course, they may have just cause: the school may indeed have 'got it wrong' in treating a child unfairly, or at least not communicated effectively with parents.

■ PARENTING PROGRAMMES: THE ROLE OF THE SCHOOL

Not all parents are going to be highly emotionally literate, any more than all schools are. Where parenting is less than adequate, the emotionally literate school has an important part to play. Schools have a part to play in attempting to help children cope with the results of harsh, neglectful or overindulgent parenting, and a school's efforts to develop emotional literacy may help in this respect. Schools can also be proactive in helping some parents become more competent at their task: even effective parents can often do with support and new ideas and insights. We now know a good deal about what makes for emotionally literate parenting, and what the characteristics of a good, or at least a 'good enough', parent are (Hartley-Brewer, 1994; Covey, 1998): unsurprisingly they parallel the characteristics of an emotionally literate school. They include treating each child as special and unique, using praise and encouragement rather than punishment, having clear and fair boundaries, rules and consequences, and being consistent about enforcing them, using active and empathic listening, encouraging appropriate levels of independence and autonomy, engaging in fun and play, allowing themselves not to be perfect parents, and looking after themselves properly. Some schools are attempting to help parents by running parenting programmes for parents in tandem with their own emotional literacy programme. Family Links, a UK organization, run their 'Nurturing Programme' which brings together schools, teachers and health professionals in counties across the UK (Family Links, 2001: see also contact lists at the end of this book). Hampshire Local Education Authority in England has run training sessions for parents that are focused on building parents' self-esteem and on the management of the child, which have been very successful, with some parents going on to form self-help groups.

Parenting programmes have been shown to be particularly helpful for parents with children with behavioural and emotional problems. A school in Southampton in England successfully involved parents of adolescent girls with anger management problems by working on parenting skills with their parents (Sharp and Faupel, 2002: 25). In the USA children being taught a social skills programme were much more likely to keep up their new behaviour if their parents were involved in the process through home–school notes (Middleton and Cartledge, 1995). The benefits go both ways, and emotional and social education have been shown to impact on students' behaviour at home (Gentry and Benenson, 1992; Johnson et al., 1995).

To do as a result of reading this chapter

How important do you think the issues covered in this chapter are as indicators of an emotionally literate school climate and environment? What others might you add?

- Warmth, person centredness and involvement.
- Empathic communication.
- Autonomy and self-reliance.
- An emotionally literate physical environment.
- Staff emotional literacy and well-being.
- Emotionally literate management and leadership.
- Work with parents in an emotionally literate way.

In what ways does the school you know or work in attempt to develop these issues? How successful are they at doing this? What helps and what hinders?

CHAPTER SIX

Profiling, Assessing and Evaluating Emotional Literacy

GOALS OF THIS CHAPTER

By the end of this chapter you will

- be clearer about some of the central issues involved in profiling and assessing emotional literacy, and in evaluating interventions
- be aware of some of the most useful and soundly based qualitative and quantitative instruments currently available for profiling, assessment and evaluation.

ISSUES IN PROFILING, ASSESSMENT AND EVALUATION

REASONS FOR THE GROWTH IN INTEREST IN PROFILING AND ASSESSMENT

The rapid rise of interest in emotional literacy has led naturally to the question of how it can be profiled and assessed in individuals, groups and organizations, and how the impact of interventions can be assessed. There are several reasons for this growth in interest:

- We live in a climate where profiling and assessment are increasingly important, in education, as elsewhere. There has been an explosion in the number of interventions designed to promote emotional and social competence and well-being, and to assess their impact.
- The growing emphasis on having a proper 'evidence base' for educational development has led to the need for

'harder' approaches to the collection of evidence in all areas, including emotional literacy.

- There has been a huge rise in the development of testing of academic attainments and some schools are keen to have parallel methods to use for assessing emotional and social competence.

- The realization that most emotional problems are discernable from an early age has led to a need for methods of early identification.

- As schools become more interested in emotional literacy, some become keen to profile their own strengths and shortcomings in their attempt to become more 'emotionally literate schools'.

LACK OF ANY COMMON STANDARDS

The profiling and assessment of emotional competence is now a growth industry, and many different instruments have been, and are being, produced. It is tempting to hope for a few straightforward checklists that can tell us all we need to know about the state of emotional literacy of students, staff and schools, and against which we can measure the impact of interventions. However, given the complexity and value-laden nature of the issues involved, this hope is unlikely to be realized. There is a distinct lack of any standardized measures in this area. There are many different tools to choose from in assessing individuals, while attempts to profile organizations are in their infancy. Efforts to evaluate interventions use many different kinds of indicators that loosely cluster around social and emotional competence and well being, are assessed by all kinds of different tools and scales, and examine a vast range of skills, attitudes, competences, indicators and outcomes.

There are then no 'quick fix' answers, and anyone who is interested in profiling, assessment and evaluation needs to explore some fundamental issues and come to their own conclusions, including about whether to use published tests and, if so, which, and for what purpose. This chapter will attempt to provide some guidance on these issues.

REASONS TO PROFILE, ASSESS AND EVALUATE

Profiling, assessment and evaluation overlap, but broadly speaking profiling involves mapping the competences of groups of people and features of organizations, assessment involves measuring the competences of individuals to make a judgement about them – often in numerical terms – while evaluation involves gauging the impact of an intervention. There are many reasons why a school or other agency might want to profile and assess emotional literacy in students, teachers, classes or the school as a whole, or to see whether the efforts it was making to improve emotional literacy were being effective. All of these different purposes have rather different implications so it is important to be clear from the outset what they are. The reasons include:

- To *profile competences* in individual students, as a basis for planning interventions to help students develop their competences.

- For the *early identification* of students who are having difficulties now or who may do later, in order to give them special help.

- To help *teachers assess their own strengths and weaknesses* to see what they need personally to work on, or to help select the right person for a specific role or task such as being emotional literacy co-ordinator.

- To help *appoint staff* with the right mix of competences to make an effective, well-balanced and emotionally literate team.

- To *profile emotional literacy, and the factors that support it, across the whole school*, to uncover areas of strength and weakness which a whole-school approach might then address, to give information to *aid planning*, for example in devising a teaching and learning programme to teach emotional literacy, or decide on what elements of a whole-school approach need to be tackled and in what priority order.

- To *evaluate an innovation, and monitor change over time*, for example the impact of special initiatives, or education and training designed to promote emotional literacy in students or teachers.

We will examine how schools might realize some of these purposes in the course of this chapter.

PROFILING, ASSESSMENT AND EVALUATION MUST BE DRIVEN BY THE PROGRAMME

Any judgement of worth can only be as good as the teaching and learning programme it sets out to judge. However, there is an increasing tendency in education, and indeed across the whole of society, to confuse worth with the ability of measure, and to only value what we can measure. This is short sighted, as some issues, such as emotional literacy, are very complex, but this does not mean that we should be driven by the items on a checklist to oversimplify and believe this is all there is to it. We need first to focus on what matters, on what we are trying to help our students learn, and then seek ways to assess it that do justice to its complexity, not work from the measuring tools to the programme.

There also needs to be some kind of change at the end of any exercise in judgement, for example a new programme or an improvement to an existing one, or resources to help children identified as having problems. Otherwise the whole exercise will seem pointless and unmotivating to those who have been asked to contribute to it. Profiling, assessment and evaluation must not become just a paper exercise, or another burden for busy schools.

◼ SUMMATIVE OR FORMATIVE

One key difference in forms of assessment and evaluation is the question of whether they are formative or summative. Table 6.1 attempts to summarize the key differences between these two approaches.

TABLE 6.1 KEY DIFFERENCES BETWEEN FORMATIVE AND SUMMATIVE ASSESSMENT AND EVALUATION

Formative assessment:
• Aims at informing and assessing attempts at change and development
• Often involves multidimensional instruments that involve a range of people, including sometimes the person being assessed, and is often ongoing over time
• Takes a good deal of time, skills and commitment
• Can be used as an integral part of teaching and learning process.

Summative assessment:
• Attempts to give a 'one off' judgement on someone
• Can be helpful for gathering statistics through which to compare, for example, the impact of different initiatives on a population
• Often seen by schools as time efficient and thus more acceptable to busy teachers than more complex methods

◼ WHAT DO PRACTITIONERS THINK OF THE VARIOUS TYPES OF ASSESSMENT?

In most countries there appears to be a good deal of concern to use assessments in a way that enhances, not undermines, the educational process. The UK in particular has experienced a massive increase in external testing and assessment in recent years, which appears to have resulted in a good deal of suspicion about the assessment of emotional competence, and concern that, for example, any attempt to assess emotional competence should not result in target-setting and emotional competence league tables for schools. A recent project for the English DfES (Edmunds and Stewart-Brown, 2002) on the assessment of emotional competence canvassed opinions from a wide range of practitioners, such as teachers, advisers, early years managers, those involved in national projects, researchers and educational psychologists. A project carried out by the author of this book (Weare and Gray, 2002) looked at what five local education authorities in England were doing to develop work on emotional and social competence, including its assessment. Both projects uncovered a great deal of interest in emotional competence assessment, which is perhaps not surprising as the practitioners canvassed were heavily involved in it. Practitioners were keen on formative assessment, which they felt was non-judgemental, helped children to develop their own awareness and included children's opinions as well as those of other people. But the practitioners also had many concerns about the feasibility, desirability of using summative assessments, and how they might be introduced and used, or misused in practice. Many were very concerned that crude and judgemental assessment should not be used simplistically to construct targets and league tables, as they felt this would undermine the whole point of working in the area of emotional literacy, stress teachers and lead to confusion, cynicism and apathy in teachers. There was a strong concern that assessment should not be summative and judgemental and a general mistrust of 'checklists' in this area, which were thought to encourage dangerous oversimplification of what is a complex area, to label children, to reduce children's self-esteem and risk children simply learning to give the most acceptable response.

ASSESSING INDIVIDUAL STUDENTS

WHO SHOULD ASSESS? THE NEED FOR A RANGE OF PERSPECTIVES

Many early attempts in the 1960s and 1970s to assess emotional and social competence in individuals were developed by experts from their own observations. They were at the time generally seen as neutral and value free. However, we now know that there is no such thing as a value-free perspective on emotional literacy. The values, beliefs and attitudes, both of the people who devise the approach and those who carry out the assessment, profoundly shape the content of the assessment and how it is interpreted. Any single assessment is bound to be to some extent limited, biased and subjective. There is, therefore, now increasing emphasis on using a range of different perspectives from different people in assessing the emotional competence of individuals, and using a range of methods in order to obtain an 'all round' picture. Clearly any tools we decide to use need to be interesting, quick, and easy to complete if they are to be used by parents and children as well as professionals.

Teachers are the most obvious people to assess children's emotional and social competences. They have the advantage of working with children routinely, and knowing them well, so they can judge how representative their response is of their normal patterns. It is particularly important that those involved in carrying out profiling and assessment are familiar to the children and have their trust, and that children be assessed in familiar environments so they behave naturally. Assessing children's competence takes skill, so it is important that it be carried out by those who are involved in emotional literacy work. Different teachers' judgements about any one child will probably vary a good deal, and children will behave rather differently in different contexts, for example with different teachers, or in the classroom and the playground, so it is important to use a range of teachers to make assessments and look at children in a range of contexts. This is especially important with older children, as variance increases as the children get older.

A key consideration is that most instruments are constructed and administered by adults, and thus fail to reflect the reality and understanding of *children and young people*. There has been a rise in interest in taking children's views into account in education in general, including in assessment. If we wish children to feel empowered and to become reflective and autonomous citizens it is essential that they are genuinely involved in their own assessments, and do not just have assessment imposed on them. Self-assessment is an important part of any assessment, especially if it is to be used to plan changes for an individual child or a group, so it is often important to seek the views of the child themselves on the nature and causes of their behaviour. There is evidence that very young children can contribute to self-assessment in a helpful way (Izard et al., 2001). Harter (1993) developed a self-perception profile for children and found children from the age of 8 could contribute views about their own abilities across six different domains, including self-worth and social competence.

It is important to use methods that are appropriate for the age and stage of the children involved, which in the case of young children or those with limited literacy will mean using discussion, drawings, pictures and symbols, and student-dictated writing. Later in this section we discuss some qualitative illuminative techniques, such as draw and write and bubble dialogue, which invite children to reflect on their own experience, competences and feelings. A few quantitative assessment instruments are attempting to incorporate the child's perspective, and one of them, Talkit, will be discussed later in this chapter. The process of development of some instruments has taken into account what children understand by emotional and social competence in formulating the instrument, working in partnership with children, and have included tools which seek the views of the peer group about an individual, for example, the Enable Project (Banks et al., 2001).

When using instruments that take into account what children think of one another we have to be especially careful about bias, as children can be rating popularity rather than competence, and a child's judgement of another's behaviour will be influenced by their perceptions of what that behaviour means to them. For example, a child with a low tolerance for physical contact may rate a child as aggressive where another would just see the child as boisterous. It is clearly best to use a range of respondents to try to reduce the overall bias.

Parents are often worried about the assessment of emotional and social competence. They may not understand the purpose of the whole enterprise, seeing school as properly concerned only with academic matters: a view of course shared by many teachers. They may fear their child will be stigmatized, or that they will be made to blame for having an 'emotionally incompetent' child. To avoid a rift developing, a wise school would involve the parents in the whole process of the development of an emotional literacy programme, and in particular in any attempts at profiling or assessments, explaining the strategy to them and seeking their views both about the process as a whole and about their own child.

In line with the development of partnerships between home and school, some instruments now include parental views, as we shall see when we examine specific instruments later in this chapter. There have been interesting studies which showed that there tend to be differences between parents' and teachers' views of emotional and social competences (Bibou-Nakou et al., 2001) but these may of course be due to the fact that children behave differently in different contexts, and there is clear evidence that parents tend to have sound judgements about their child's problem behaviours as early as 1 year of age (Carter et al., 1999).

■ BASELINE ASSESSMENTS OF CHILDREN ON ENTRY TO SCHOOL

Many schools are either required, or wish, to conduct baseline assessments on children at school entry, and some of these include the assessment of emotional and social competence, usually using informal measures of the school's devising. Baseline assessment can be kept informal, and involve observation of children in natural settings, for example at play, and be carried out by people who the children trust. Once established in a school, assessment can be ongoing. Formative assessments can include a developing profile, or portfolio for each child, class or perhaps the whole school, and include the celebration of achievement and self-directed goals. Many schools would like to go further and have more standardized measures, so there has been a growth of interest in their development. Some such measures will be discussed later in the chapter.

■ ASSESSMENT FOR EARLY IDENTIFICATION

We have said in Chapter 3 that it is helpful to identify children who are having emotional and social problems early on in their school career so that steps can be taken to help them before the problem escalates too far. However, it is not necessarily helpful to pursue the idea of using one simple 'test' for the purpose, which becomes a form of screening. Screening makes perfect sense in its original context, which is the spotting of a defined medical condition which some people have and some do not. It is much harder to 'screen' in an area such as emotional literacy, where no one has yet defined what is 'normal' and where all of us are 'competent' or 'incompetent' to a degree, and more competent in some areas that others.

It is not possible, and probably not desirable, to have one clear-cut tool or even one method for identifying those with problems in any absolute and final sense. The tendency is becoming to take a 'softer' approach to the issue, and assess children in groups and in relation to one another. Such assessment can be formative, take place over time, include consideration of positive capacity as well as problems, involve several points of view including that of the child, and take place in a natural setting. Early identification need not be reduced to being a one-off judgement of a child and then used to limit expectations of them, or even worse to write them off as unreachable. The resultant help we offer children needs to be flexible, to come and go as needed without the need for elaborate paperwork and process, and to avoid labelling and stigmatizing. If we use this softer approach, help will inevitably be offered to many more children, some of whom will only have mild and transient problems.

EVALUATING INNOVATIONS

■ EVALUATING INNOVATIONS

One major use of assessment is to monitor the impact of innovations designed to develop emotional literacy. There is in general a strong move towards achieving a better 'evidence base' for the practice of education in general, and almost everyone in the field of emotional and social competence is agreed that there is a need for more evaluation of interventions to make sure they are not based on wishful thinking, and to convince the sceptical of the value of work in this area. Work on emotional and social competence and well-being inevitably raises a good deal of emotion itself and is a value-laden area: many people and organizations have invested a great deal of energy and hope in their efforts. It is important to value the energy and the innovative work that has been produced – without this there would be nothing to evaluate – but we do need to sift the evidence carefully, and distinguish hopes from sound demonstrated effect.

■ THE NEED FOR CONTROL, OR BEFORE AND AFTER

It is generally accepted that evaluations need to follow certain basic procedures if they are to stand up to scientific scrutiny and persuade people that the innovation in question was worth doing. They need to at least collect baseline data, as without this we cannot know whether anything has changed. Ideally, too, we need a control group, as without this we cannot know whether it was the intervention that made the difference rather than some other influence. In medicine the standard for evaluation continues to be the randomized control trial, and education has been tussling with the appropriateness of this model for educational innovations.

The experimental approach, using controls, sets a standard for objectivity and the burden of proof that is a useful yardstick, not least in convincing sceptical outsiders and hard-nosed funding bodies. It is also feasible, at least in a limited sense, as experience in the USA shows us. In the USA there is a strong tradition of research and evaluation in relation to specific work on interventions to promote emotional and social learning, which comes from the highly empirical world of experimental psychology where much effort has been put into reviews of social and emotional learning programmes (Durlak, 1995; Durlak and Wells, 1997). Much of this evaluation includes the use of control groups. For example, the large database of projects on emotional and social learning held by the Collaborative for Academic, Social and Emotional Learning (CASEL, 1998) contains reviews of over 700 studies about a quarter of which manage to include elements of control. Several systematic reviews, which only include studies with controls, have been able to be carried out in relevant areas, such as health-promoting schools (Lister-Sharp et al., 2000), and on emotional and social well-being (Wells, 2000; Wells, Barlow and Stewart-Brown, 2003). However, even in the USA, as Mayer and Cobb (2000) point out, educational policy on 'emotional intelligence' appears to be based more on popular journalism than on actual research, and policy in the area has outstripped the science on which it is based.

Evaluation is even less developed in other parts of the world than the USA. It is telling that very few non-US studies ever appear in the many large-scale systematic reviews of work being carried out across the world on the issues around emotional literacy which are being used to provide some of the evidence base for this book: they include large reviews on interventions categorized as relating to: 'emotional and social competence' (CASEL, 2002; Edmunds and Stewart-Brown, 2002); 'mental health' (Durlak and Wells, 1997; Wells, Barlow and Stewart-Brown, 2003); 'prevention programmes' (Durlak, 1995; Carr, 2002); 'behaviour' (Marshall and Watt, 1999); 'positive youth development' (Catalano et al., 2000) and 'health promoting schools' (Lister-Sharp et al., 2002). The predominance of US evidence in all these related areas cannot all be due to national bias of those collecting the information, as some of the reviews have been carried out by researchers who are not US based.

The author's impression is that the situation may be getting a little better in some parts of Europe and that the need for evaluation is finally coming home to those who are working in this area in Europe. The evidence for this is the author's involvement in two large-scale European Union funded projects which are attempting to discover interventions that attempt to promote mental health in young people. The first one collected data in the mid-1990s and almost none of the projects collected used controls and only a few used pre- and post-test evaluation (Henderson, 2001). The most recent project, the results of which are not yet published at the time of writing, collected projects in 2002: of 33 projects collected by 12 countries, 6 used a Randomized Control Trial (RCT), a further 4 used some kind of control and 10 used pre- and post-test evaluation.

In the UK there have been a few rigorous evaluations on educational interventions, most notably and most relevantly in this case that of the English Health Promoting School initiative (HEA and NFER, 1997). To date no one to the author's knowledge has brought together the evaluation that has been done in the UK on emotional and social literacy or on related areas. If a review was done it is likely they would find some qualitative work, but very little quantitative, a smattering of before and after designs, and virtually no use of controls. This assertion is based on the few collections of case studies in the areas (for example, Coram Family, 2002), and the author's experience of reviewing the work of five English local education authorities who are working on emotional and social education. As we will see when we look at their experience in detail in Chapter 7, although all had made an attempt at evaluation none had been very rigourous in their methods.

■ IMPROVING THE QUALITY OF EVALUATIONS

Clearly we need to do more to improve the amount and quality of evaluation of emotional literacy initiatives that are taking place. There should at least be the collection of baseline data before the intervention takes place. Ideally we should use controls, although it needs to be recognized that using controls is expensive, and may be beyond the reach of small initiatives. Control is particularly challenging when assessing initiatives that use a holistic approach, work on emotional and social competence and well-being is invariably very multi-factoral. It is telling that, of the 427 studies, most of them from the USA, looked at in a recent systematic review of health-promoting school approaches in their totality (Wells, Barlow and Stewart-Brown, 2003), only 14 had controls and were deemed rigorous enough to include, but the presence of the 14 does at least suggest it is possible.

Given the low level of evaluative activity at present on emotional literacy, and especially within a whole-school approach, it is important to go carefully, respect where people are starting from, and include current work on formative evaluation and qualitative approaches. The evaluation process needs first and foremost be congruent with the principles of emotional literacy. For example, we need to evaluate emotional education in emotionally sensitive ways that do not result in people feeling they have failed. If we wish to look at schools from a holistic point of view it is best to collect a range of data from a wide range of sources, use a variety of tools within a portfolio approach, and draw on a variety of disciplines and approaches if our evaluations are to do justice to the complexity of the whole-school idea. There needs to be a balance between rigour, the needs and perspectives of all the participants in the process, and the resources available. All parties need to be involved at every stage of the process, consulted about all aspects of it before it begins, involved in the data collection and interpretation and in the implementation of any outcome so they feel they have ownership of the process, have learned something useful from it and have the motivation to put the results into practice.

USING QUALITATIVE APPROACHES

Two vital educational principles in developing work on emotional literacy are 'starting where people are' when planning educational interventions, and then 'using a developmental approach' which builds from there in small steps that are appropriate to the age and stage of the learners. To do this teachers need complex information about what their students feel, know and are able to do in terms of their emotional literacy. Gaining this information may involve quantitative assessments, most usually some kind of question-naire or checklist which requires respondents to tick a scale which is then translated into a composite number or score, and this chapter will later dis-cuss some of the key quantitative approaches and trialled instruments that are currently in use. However, such quantitative instruments can fail to get to the underlying meanings, attitudes and beliefs that children possess that drive their responses. Those that require people to complete questionnaires are off-putting and scary for some children, and even some schools. So, before we look at traditional quantitative approaches, the next section will examine a range of qualitative approaches to the profiling and assessment of emotional literacy. Qualitative approaches use a range of methods, most usu-ally with adults interviews and focus groups of various kinds; with children other 'illuminative' methods such as draw and write and bubble dialogue have proved very appropriate, as we shall see.

THE USE OF INFORMAL ASSESSMENT

In considering the newer focus on the development of tested instruments we need not to forget that good teachers have been informally assessing children's emotional competence for years. At the most basic level teachers can observe and listen to what students are doing and saying normally, for example when they are working together in the class, at play, in corridors and moving to and from classes and school. There are formal checklists that can be used to try to catch some of this which will be discussed later, but there is a lot to be learned 'en passant' by a sensitive and observant teacher about individual or groups of children's emotional and social competences through observing and overhearing, for example: how they squabble or solve interpersonal problems; how they comfort or taunt chil-dren in distress; how they include or exclude their fellows from their games and activities; how they cope or fail to cope with disappointment or teas-ing. All of this can form the basis of interventions at various levels of organ-ization, ranging from informal on the spot coaching to a planned sequence of lessons. At a slightly more formal level, classroom lessons and discus-sion such as 'circle time' which tackle social and emotional issues are an opportunity not just to ensure learning but also to ascertain children's levels of competence and plan the next intervention.

ILLUMINATIVE TECHNIQUES: 'DRAW AND WRITE' AND 'BUBBLE DIALOGUE'

As well as the familiar tools of observation, listening and formal and infor-mal interviews, there is a growing body of knowledge about the use of what are sometimes called 'illuminative techniques'. Illuminative approaches involve presenting children with an invitation to which they are asked to respond in some way. 'Draw and write', and 'draw and talk', invite children to draw plus writing or talking, depending on their age and stage of development. 'Bubble dialogue' asks them to fill in the dialogue over the heads of cartoon figures. As these techniques are much easier to imagine when a concrete example is given, the next box outlines an example.

Example: using illuminative techniques with European school children

The author carried out work in health-promoting schools across Europe developing approaches to emotional and social well-being in schools, including work on emotional literacy (Weare and Gray, 1994). The following are some tools developed with teachers and others across several European countries:

- Students were invited to *draw and write* about someone they met who was 'feeling good about himself or herself', show what they looked like and then draw all around them what was making them feel good. They were then asked to imagine meeting someone 'not feeling good about himself or herself' and do another draw and write.
- *'Bubble dialogues'* were aimed at slightly older students. Students were asked to complete the sentences shown over the heads of two students talking, with one saying 'I'm not feeling good about myself and my life because ...', and the other saying 'I know how you feel: I was just like you once but now I can tell you ...'.
- Further *'incomplete sentences'* were offered to children to complete which were aimed at uncovering elements of their emotional literacy. The sentences included for example 'when I have a difficult decision to make I ...' and 'when things around me are changing I ...'.

Some findings that surprised teachers:

- Children claimed their emotional well-being depended on their relationships rather than on possessions.
- School achievement or failure was a major source of pleasure or distress.
- Worries about bullying were much in evidence.
- Some children's worries were very serious – war, HIV/AIDS and environmental pollution, in 9-year-olds.
- Children had great stores of good sense on how to deal with their own worries and concerns.

The invitation has to be a concrete and attractive one of the kind that involves children giving spontaneous responses about issues they can relate to in real life and which they find fairly easy and natural to explore. It is important to take an indirect approach, so that children feel that any response is possible and acceptable, and so that the right answer is not evident: it is sometimes best to ask children what 'someone of your age' would do or say rather than quizzing them about themselves. Children usually need to complete illuminative techniques individually so as to ensure a proper spread of opinion, and to be assured that their response is anonymous, if they are to disclose as fully as they might.

The children's responses to an illuminative technique can tell us a great deal about what they think, know, feel and do, and at quite a deep level, but without frightening children with a formal checklist or putting ideas into their heads with a set of pre-set questions. The techniques are quick to administer, fun to do and can gather a great deal of data, in a manageable form, from a lot of people in a very short time. They can be repeated later in a process to see whether and how the children's responses have developed. They are, however, time consuming and rather challenging to analyse.

■ USING ILLUMINATIVE APPROACHES AS THE BASIS FOR PLANNING

We have already given an example of an approach that has been used to help plan interventions to promote emotional well-being in schools. Illuminative techniques have been used on a national scale as the basis for developing comprehensive curriculum-based approaches to health education in schools which focus particularly on emotional and social issues as the core. For example, *Health for Life* (Wetton and Williams, 2000) is now found in most UK primary schools, and the materials and the illuminative research that underpins them have been adapted for use in other countries, most notably Hungary (McWhirter, Wetton and Williams, 1998).

■ USING ILLUMINATIVE METHODS TO DEVELOP WHOLE-SCHOOL INDICATORS

Illuminative methods can be used as the basis for monitoring change over time at a whole-school level. *Confidence to Learn* (Wetton and McCoy, 1998) contains a section on how to do this in ways that involve the children in the reflection. These techniques have been used extensively in the UK, and in some parts of Europe, to provide information for the planning of some very large-scale and comprehensive approaches to school health education, including at national level. For example, the National Healthy School Standard in England recently carried out a consultation in primary schools to attempt to develop indicators for a healthy school which used a draw and write (DfES, 2002, available on line). The children were told 'We want to build a new healthy school in your area and we want you to tell us what it should be like'. Children were given boxes to draw and write in, which included being invited to describe what the building and playground would be like, what the children would be like, what teachers and other adults would be like, how they would feel if they went there, anything that would make the school unhappy, unsafe or unhealthy. Their answers are now being used to help in the development of indicators of a healthy school.

Example: using a draw and write used as the basis for planning whole-school programmes in Scotland

The Scottish-based initiative, *Confidence to Learn* (Wetton and McCoy, 1998), is now found in all Scottish primary schools. The resource materials are mainly concerned with helping teachers to use a range of 'draw and write' tools in a careful sequence which they then use to plan teaching initiatives. The draw and write starts with invitations to the children to draw 'healthy people' and what 'helps them be healthy', and the 'signs that a school is health-promoting'. They then move on to explore emotional and social issues, including drawing and writing about:

- 'Me feeling good about being here and feeling I can learn and do my best work' (followed by a 'feeling not so good' invitation).
- 'Children who enjoy learning and take care of each other'.
- 'The kind of person I am'.
- 'Two things I am good at and two things I am not so good at'.
- 'Me helping a new student who is sad and lonely feel better'.

The resource also includes a range of worksheets which use open-ended bubbles to elicit children's ideas about a range of social and emotional issues, including dealing with difficult feelings, bullying, and managing their own behaviour.

PROFILING ORGANIZATIONS

THE NEED TO PROFILE ORGANIZATIONS AS WELL AS INDIVIDUALS

Many accounts of assessment start and end with the individual. However, this book suggests that emotional literacy in individuals can only be achieved by changes to the whole-school environment and ethos, so if we are serious about developing a whole-school approach we need to attempt to profile emotional literacy, and the factors that support it, across the whole school. This can give guidance on areas of strength and weakness and to aid planning, for example a teaching and learning programme to teach emotional literacy.

■ USING BRIEF AUDITS, CHECKLISTS AND PROFILES

Many schools do not want, or are not ready, to use the kind of complex quantitative tools we discuss later in this chapter – what they want is a brief audit, checklist or profile, based on some useful theory, and which they can use to find out what is happening, raise consciousness, plan, and monitor progress.

Short audits, checklists and profiles can often be found in the many books that have been published on developing emotional literacy/intelligence in organizations: they usually have been developed locally to meet the needs of a particular context. In a recent book, Sharp (2001) outlines two straight-forward and useful audits to measure an 'Emotionally Literate Local Education Authority' and 'Emotionally Literate Organization' which were used by Southampton Local Education Authority in their far-reaching project to develop emotional literacy within the LEA, an effort that will be discussed in more detail in Chapter 7.

A typical example of a straightforward audit that has been developed is the 'Emotional Health Audit' of Leicestershire Local Education Authority, who use it within their 'Emotional Health and Wellbeing Strategy' which is part of its National Healthy Schools Strategy, along with their guidelines – *A Toolkit for Schools* (Leicester Local Education Authority, 2001). The intention is that schools will use the audit to identify strengths and areas for development, to update policies and practices and to use the toolkit as a basis to promote health and well-being throughout the school. All schools have received a copy via the headteachers' development group, and Leicestershire is now working with heads to develop training courses to support the work.

There have been many attempts to profile aspects of emotional literacy at an organizational level. Across the world the Healthy School/Health-Promoting School approach has carried out considerable work on the development of indicators of the extent to which whole-schools' environments promote health, including emotional and social well-being. This approach will be discussed in Chapter 7, when we look at this approach in more detail. In addition to these audits and indicators, there are a few

Record of Assessment for Emotional Literacy Checklist

This instrument is being used in *Mason Moor Primary School Southampton* in the UK and was developed by the *Southampton Emotional Literacy Interest Group*. It is used to benchmark at the start of every term, and to assess progress in individual students and classes.

The checklist invites the teacher to grade each child A–D on the following criteria.

A = Consistently and independently
B = With adult guidance, sometimes independently
C = With difficulty or with a high level of adult support
D = Not at all yet, or very rarely

Handling relationships: the child can …
• express feelings and needs appropriately
• respect the property of others
• respect the personal space of others
• work with others without conflict.

Managing and knowing own emotions: the child can …
• understand behavioural norms at school
• control anger
• manage stress
• recognize the effect he/she is having on others
• ignore negative peer pressure
• ask for/accept help appropriately
• be helpful to other children (adults).

Recognizing emotion in others/motivating own self and others: the child can …
• behave in a consistent manner with adults
• take responsibility for own actions
• control impulsive behaviour
• understand the feelings of others
• show empathy
• compromise in disagreements
• express needs clearly and calmly
• accept fair blame
• accept praise without the expectation of concrete gratification
• show that he/she knows the difference between feelings and action
• show that he/she values and respects themselves and others.

tested and validated instruments that have been and are currently being produced. The Child Development Project Questionnaire (Roberts et al., 1995) is probably the most established, and will be discussed later in this chapter, as will the 'Emotional Litearcy Audit' developed by Antidote, and the set of 'Emotional Literacy Indicators' currently being produced by the University of Bristol.

QUANTITATIVE TESTS AND INVENTORIES

Quantitative approaches involve the use of standardized tools such as tests, inventories and questionnaires. We will next examine some of the issues that surround using quantitative tests and inventories, followed by a look at some of the best examples currently available.

HOW WELL ARE THE TESTS TESTED?

As with cars, a crucial criterion for a useful quantitative test is that it is 'reliable'. In the case of those tests of emotional and social competence that are designed to be used by just one type of person (for example, teachers) the standard of reliability is that the tests need to give similar results when used by different raters. Tests which are to be used to monitor changes in children over time, either to assess the child or to assess the impact of an intervention need to have particularly good 'inter-rater reliability' because they will be carried out by different people during different periods of time. Tests designed to be used by different types of people that make up a portfolio (such as teachers, parents, children) need not give all give the same result as one another, as the final outcome will be determined by 'triangulation' in other words comparing the results, but they need to have 'test-retest reliability' when given by the same person a little later. Tests also need to be 'valid', in other words to be shown by some independent measure to be assessing what they are supposed to assess. They need to be 'norm referenced', in other words have standards that are set by testing large numbers of a specific population or group, and the people they are subsequently used on need to have the same characteristics (for example, age, cultural background, level of education, gender, and/or occupation) as the ones people were tested on. They need to be 'sensitive' enough to pick up what can be quite minor changes in a child or a group.

Meeting these criteria is a major challenge in the case of tests that attempt to assess emotional and social competence in children. Reliability is difficult, as we know that children behave very differently with different people and in different contexts, so it is overoptimistic to hope for one test for that can be quickly administered by one teacher. Even when we soften this requirement and rely on 'triangulation' using different points of view, validity is difficult to ensure when so much of what we are seeking to assess is a matter of degree rather than absolutes, when the whole area is value-laden and culturally specific, and when there is rightly so much dispute about what is 'normal' and 'desirable' behaviour. 'Norm referencing' is difficult when, again, so much of what is seen as 'normal' in emotional literacy is culturally specific, not only to a particular country, but to particular social and cultural groups. When choosing an instrument we need to think about whether the group on whom the test was norm referenced is the same as ours. This applies not only to children, but to adults too, and we need to be careful of applying tests to teachers that have been validated for very different populations. In the case of the many tests of 'emotional intelligence' the 'guinea pigs' have mostly been corporate and very well paid businessmen, a very different population from the predominantly female, more altruistic and underpaid workforce that is teachers. Sensitivity can also be difficult when changes may be quite small, but some outside agency is demanding instant and spectacular results.

There are then no easy answers in this field, no one 'off the shelf' checklist is going to meet all our needs all of the time. None of us can get around the need to look very carefully at the tests available and tread warily. We need, for example, to look at what the test is actually measuring, and make sure that it makes sense to us and to anyone else who is using it, and is clearly assessing what we want to assess, in other words that it has so called 'face validity'. It makes the search for a generalizable test that is valid across many different populations of children very challenging.

◼ THE NEED TO BE AWARE OF BIAS

We need to bear in mind that there is no such thing as a neutral instrument. All have been produced in a particular context, for a particular purpose and developed on a particular population. Many have strong vested interests behind them, sometimes of a commercial nature. We may not receive much help in spotting bias from the literature that accompanies the instrument, nor from papers written about it, which do not often comment on such things.

When the instrument was developed may be an indication of its usefulness: there is a long history to the development of instruments in this area, which parallels the development of thinking about the whole issue. Many early instruments that were developed in the 1960s and 1970s were designed to identify children with specific 'conditions' and problem behaviour, and did so in a piecemeal fashion, and as a result their content was entirely negative and problem focused. Schools beware: many such instruments are still in use. Over time more instruments were developed which included positive measures of emotional and social competence such as abilities and strengths, and were aimed at wider 'normal' populations. There has been an accompanying change in language over the years, with earlier instruments using the language of 'social behaviours' and 'behavioural problems', while more recent instruments use the language of 'abilities', 'attributes' and 'competences'. Later, instruments were developed that took into account the emotional factors that underlie behaviour, and the contextual and holistic nature of behaviour, rather then fragmenting it into isolated behaviours. Recently there has been an effort to develop instruments that recognize the complex and positive nature of emotional literacy/intelligence and which attempt to measure the kind of competences outlined earlier in this chapter. Newer instruments are more likely to help make formative assessments, to profile competences across a normal range of ability, and aid the development of programmes, rather than the earlier emphasis on summative assessment.

Instruments can be culturally specific. We need to be aware that many instruments are standardized on white middle-class populations and to consider their appropriateness for other populations carefully. For example, assessing a child on the amount of eye contact they make can disadvantage girls from some Eastern cultures where eye contact with adults, especially respected ones such as teachers, is discouraged. Afro-Caribbean culture may encourage boys to be more boisterous than is normal for white boys. This book has argued that autonomy is an essential component of emotional literacy, but many of the instruments that have been developed, including recent ones, and especially those that come from North America, conflate emotional and social competence with conformity and compliance. The measures of competence are often concerned with behaviours that benefit adults rather than children and young people. It is important therefore for the school to make sure that the instrument they intend to use actually measures what matters to them and to the people being assessed, has been developed on the same population as the one for which they want to use it, and that they are aware of its biases. Finally, the media used by the test may be biased against certain types of learner. As we saw in Chapter 2, there are different types of learning styles, and a test that uses predominantly words, may be biased against visual or kinaesthetic learners.

SOME QUANTITATIVE INSTRUMENTS THAT ASSESS EMOTIONAL AND SOCIAL COMPETENCE

■ THE CHOICE OF QUANTITATIVE INSTRUMENTS FOR MEASURING EMOTIONAL AND SOCIAL COMPETENCE

There are many quantitative instruments that are available and schools may be confused by the apparently wide choice. However, many instruments in the area have been designed for use only on adults, and are not suitable for use with children. Edmunds and Stewart-Brown (2002) who carried out a thorough investigation of existing instruments for the English DfES started with 56 that are aimed at children and which initially looked promising. They rejected most of them as not really being measures of emotional competence/literacy for the following reasons:

- Many only assess negative, problem behaviours thought undesirable by adults, not positive behaviour and not emotional competence.

- Some measure emotional development, and emotional states (for example, smiles, seems happy) rather than emotional literacy/competence.

- Some only measure a few aspects of emotional competence, for example, bully/victim problems, self-esteem, worry, and do not present a well-rounded picture.

■ SOME TESTED AND AVAILABLE INSTRUMENTS FOR SUMMATIVE ASSESSMENT

If we look for published and easily available instruments that assess a range of aspects of emotional compe including positive capacities, use multiple perspectives and have been tested for validity and reliability there are very few to choose from. Those that there are have been described overleaf.

The EQi (Bar-On and Parker, 2000)

- US instrument.
- *Appropriate content*: matches well with the competences put forward in Chapter 2 as being central to emotional literacy. It has five scales: intrapersonal (the ability to express feelings and needs), interpersonal (ability to identify and respond to the feelings of others), adaptability (problem-solving and flexibility), stress management (dealing with anger and anxiety, and impulse control), and general mood (optimism, happiness).
- *Well tested*: it has been shown to have good reliability and validity when tested against other instruments.
- *Wide range*: can be used for both 'normal' and 'abnormal' populations; for a range of populations and age groups, from adults to very young children (for whom statements can be read out).
- *Flexible*: it is available for self-completion or completion by others, and is therefore useful for peer appraisal. It comes in paper and computerized forms. The full version contains 133 items, but there are short versions too.
- *Expensive*: property of a commercial organization, EQi Limited; may be rather expensive for schools to use.

Behavioural and Emotional Rating Scale (BERS) (Epstein, Ryser and Pearson, 2002)

- *Appropriate content*: focus is entirely on strengths and there are no negative items. It includes five subscales: 'interpersonal strengths' which measure a child's ability to control emotions or behaviours and treat others with respect and empathy; 'intrapersonal strengths' which assesses the child's confidence and optimism; 'affective strengths' measuring a child's ability to acknowledge painful feelings, give and receive affection and trust others; 'family involvement' assessing the child's participation and relationship with family; and 'school functioning' which covers competence in school.
- *Uses multiple perspectives*: is based on the statements provided by 250 UK parents and health professionals which, over time, were summarized into 52. It was standardized on a representative population sample of 2,176 'normal' children aged 5–18 years and 861 children with emotional and behavioural disorders. It is now aimed at 5–18-year-olds.
- *Tested for validity and reliability*.
- *Published and freely available*.

Strengths and Difficulties Questionnaire (SDQ) (Goodman, 1997)

- *Mixed content*: measures social rather than emotional competence. Some regard it as a useful test for mental health in general, and it includes some positive behaviours. Strongly psychiatric focus, and focuses mainly primarily on conduct problems, emotional symptoms, and hyperactivity.
- *Quick*, brief and easy questionnaire (25 items).
- *Covers children*: covers the 4–16 year age range and there is a self-report version from about 9 years and older.
- *Well tested*: based on well-regarded work by the child psychiatrist Michael Rutter on the 'Health and Behaviour Checklist' and is based on rigorous UK trials and normalized on a large population.
- *Much used*: popular with researchers and practitioners and has been used as the basis for other instruments such as the screening instrument used with 8-year-olds for admission to the Pyramid Trust clubs in the UK.
- *Identifies problems, not 'normal' range*: is said to identify between 10 and 20 per cent of the school population as in need of specialist help and most of these children are likely to have low levels of social competence, but it will miss many other children with even slightly higher levels of competence.

■ ASSESSMENTS IN DEVELOPMENT

Many of the most promising instruments are currently in development. The following boxes give a brief account of the best of them.

Process-Oriented Monitoring System (POMS) (Laevers, 1994)

- *European*: developed at the Centre for Experiential Education, Univeristy of Leuven in Belgium.
- *Process, not outcome, oriented*: assessment during the learning process of the development of emotional and social competencies, rather than measuring skills acquired as an outcome.
- *Appropriate content*: was developed to assess children's well-being and involvement in class. The instrument covers a range of developmental and educational areas, including social and emotional competence. Includes children's basic need for affection, warmth, tenderness, need for safety, clarity, continuity, need for recognition, need to experience

---

oneself as competent, need for moral correctness and for a meaning to life. Positive signs of well-being are openness and receptivity, flexibility, self-confidence and self-esteem, able to defend oneself and assertiveness, vitality, relaxation, enjoyment without restraints, being in touch with one's self.

- *Multi-use*: the first stage screens the whole class for children with social and emotional problems. The second stage is a closer observation of individual children and analysis of their behaviour, with the intention of identifying the children with low well-being scores. Here the child's well-being is assessed in four domains of social activity, with peers, teachers, family and in class or at play depending on age. The manual contains examples of well-being at each level, together with conclusions, interpretations and suggestions for interventions to tackle whatever problems are found.
- *Currently being tested.*

Social Competence Test (ScoT)

- Available from Professor Laevers, Centre for Experiential Education, University of Leuven in Belgium.
- *European*: Centre for Experiential Education, Univeristy of Leuven in Belgium.
- *Process, not outcome, oriented*: assessment during the learning process of the development of emotional and social competencies, rather than measuring skills acquired as an outcome.
- *Appropriate content*: the focus of the assessment is feelings and emotions, and the child's ability to observe and understand their own behaviour, predict what someone would do next, and act in a socially competent way.
- *Limited age range*: the instrument for assessment is aimed at 4–8-year-olds and asks for their responses at various points when watching a puppet show and a 'Mr Bean' video individually.
- Is in the process of *being rigorously tested.*
- *Time-consuming*: its drawback for busy teachers is that it takes 25 minutes to complete for each child individually and teachers need careful training to administer it reliably.
- The test is *supported by a resource pack* to improve emotional and social competence called the 'Box Full of Feelings' which contains materials covering the four basic emotions of anger, fear, sadness and happiness which the test is designed to assess.

The next two instruments discussed are currently being developed and attempt to use indicators of emotional literacy at the student, class and school level.

Emotional Literacy Audit (ELA)

- Developed by Antidote, the Campaign for Emotional Literacy (see list of contacts at the end of the book) in London, England.
- *Research based*: based on Antidote's 'matrix of organisational emotional literacy' (Antidote, 2003), which was built through their research in primary and secondary schools in England. At the time of writing a pilot ELA has been developed from work with three schools in Newham in London, based on one-to-one interviews and focus groups with selected members of staff and students of 6–14 years.
- *Appropriate content*: it looks at how individuals experience the emotional and social atmosphere of the whole organization, the factors that inhibit or facilitate individuals in processing their emotional and social experience and how emotional literacy can be fostered at an organizational level. The framework of the matrix lays out the three domains where emotional literacy is needed; *communication, relationships and organizational systems and structures*. It outlines the qualities that need to inform practice in these domains such as *transparency, engagement and warmth* in the way people communicate, *trust, empathy and respect* in the way people relate to each other, and *alignment, reflection and collaboration* in the way an organization supports its members. These qualities correspond to 'six important core organizational' values, *safety, openness, compassion, connection, reflection and growth orientation*.
- *Multi-method*: the ELA aims to provide a general audit on what is going on in a school to which the school itself can add its own specific indicators. There is a *questionnaire for children* with statements on how they feel about their school, and a *draw and write questionnaire for younger children* is currently being developed.
- *Developing*: research is currently being carried out with parents to generate an instrument for them to complete and the audit is being trialled in further schools. The tools are currently *being tested for inter-rater reliability*.
- The instrument will be *used with a toolkit* that attempts to change the emotional climate of the school.

Emotional Literacy Indicators: The School of Emotional Literacy
www.schoolofemotional-literacy.com (Morris and Scott, 2002)
This UK-based group from the University of Bristol has produced and is currently trialling three sets of indicators:

- The 'Whole-School Emotional Literacy Indicator'. Areas covered include motivation, class climate, self-management, managing relationships, openness, tolerance of difference.
- 'Class Emotional Literacy Indicator'. Areas covered include motivation, conflict handling, class climate, self-management, relationship management, openness.
- The 'Emotional Literacy Indicator for Adults to Use with Students'. Areas covered include self-awareness, self-management, other awareness, other management, relationship management.

Each of these is assessed on a continuum which respondents are invited to check.

The next instrument currently being tested uses student views of emotional literacy.

Talkit (Tew, 2003)

- *UK based*: being developed out of a PhD at Bristol University in the UK and in conjuction with the Calouste Gulbenkian Foundation.
- *Uses the views of children*: it was developed from statements of what 11-year-old children themselves thought would demonstrate the most important issues or factors that enable students to 'be effective at school'.
- *Appropriate content*: mixture of positive and negative statements. The five aspects of emotional competence that reflect what the children thought important are, controlling your emotions and using anger well, understanding other people/empathy, keeping motivated (both internally and staying on track with the expectations of the school), confidence and integrity ('being true to yourself') and getting on with other people including communicating well.
- *Flexible*: the programme allows individuals to self-assess and can also be filled in by peers, teachers and parents in order to provide the student with an 'in the round' view of themselves.
- It has now been *computerized* and the software is compatible with that used in many UK schools.
- It is *about to be tested for validity and reliability*.

AN INSTRUMENT WHICH ASSESSES THE WHOLE SCHOOL

We have said that it is important to see the development of emotional literacy as taking place at a whole-school level, as including emotional well-being in addition to competence, and as being as much about whole-school climates and practices as it is about individual students and teachers. The assessment of emotional literacy at a whole-school level is, however, a very underdeveloped area, and few of the instruments that have been developed have been properly tested. Most instruments are the kind of qualitative checklists and audits we examined earlier. There is one fully tested, summative instrument.

> **Child Development Project Questionnaire (CDP)** (Roberts et al., 1995)
>
> - *Appropriate content*: covers the kind of issues that this book suggests are central for an emotionally literate school. Assesses aspects of the social and emotional environment of the school or classroom that affect emotional well-being.
> - *Multi-perspective*: measures three key attributes of healthy interpersonal relationships, respect, trust and empathy. The items include statements which imply emotional competence, for example, 'when someone in my class does well, everyone in the class feels good' and 'people care about each other in this school'. The student scale assesses perceptions of collaborative and supportive relationships among students, positive relations between students and teachers, closeness and intimacy, student participation and influence and ethnic caring. The teacher's version assesses perceptions of collaborative and supportive relationships among staff, closeness, teacher participation and influence and shared goals and values.
> - *Grounded in research and development on a whole-school/whole-community approach*: part of the CDP Programme at the Developmental Studies Centre in California led by Professor Battistich (Battistich et al., 1989; Battistich et al., 1996), cited in Chapter 5 as a demonstrably effective project, which aims to create caring schools and communities.
> - The instrument was developed with 550 teachers and approximately 4,000 8–12- year-olds.
> - *Well tested*.

To do as a result of reading this chapter

- Decide whether you need to profile and/or assess emotional competences, whether it is at individual or organizational level, and what is the purpose of the exercise.
- Think about how broadly you would tackle it; for example, who will do it, who they will assess and when, whom they will consult, and what general methods they will use, where to use a qualitative or a quantitative approach.
- Decide whether any existing qualitative or quantitative instrument might suit your purpose, or whether there are any you could build on and adapt.
- If you are thinking of introducing an innovation into your school, or you are supporting a school which is trying to do this, think about what baseline data you will collect, and whether it is possible to identify a control group who can act as a yardstick to tell you whether it is the innovation that has had an impact. It might be sensible to contact a university that is working in this area to see if you can form a partnership with them to help you evaluate your intervention.

CHAPTER SEVEN

Wider Support for the Emotionally Literate School: The Role of Local Education Authorities and of Healthy School Approaches

GOALS OF THIS CHAPTER

By the end of this chapter you will have explored some of the ways in which schools can gain support from those outside schools, and in particular at the part local education authorities (LEAs) and Healthy School initiatives can play.

THE NEED FOR SCHOOLS TO MAKE LINKS WITH WIDER INITIATIVES

No effective school is an island, and approaches to emotional literacy which actively link with those outside the school, in the local community and key local and national agencies and initiatives are much more likely to be effective. There is now a wealth of interest in emotional literacy right across society, both under this title and many others that are closely related, and a huge range of statutory and voluntary agencies are working in this field in various ways. In some countries governments take an interest too. So there is potentially a great deal of support for schools.

Schools traditionally have often seen their relationship with local agencies as one in which they themselves are gatekeepers, making an initial identification of a behavioural or emotional problem, then passing the problem students on to the appropriate agencies. Other than that, they deal with their own problems. Of course, schools will need to continue to seek help with their problems but the relationship between schools and outside agencies can go beyond the crisis management of individual students. Agencies can work with schools to give schools broader, preventive, in-school, support for whole-school programmes. These programmes may be on emotional literacy, or may be on closely related areas such as behaviour management, healthy school approaches, special needs, inclusion, disaffection, crime and disorder, truancy and the management of drug-related incidents.

Looking in detail at the role of all the agencies who are potentially involved in the vast range of work that constitutes emotional literacy and related areas is beyond the scope of this book, but this chapter will explore the principles involved by looking in particular at the role of two that are providing strong support in some places, namely local education authorities and Healthy School/Health Promoting School approaches, networks and schemes.

THE ROLE OF LOCAL AUTHORITIES

■ THE INVESTIGATION OF FIVE LEAs

Most countries have some kind of local education agency (LEA) which acts at an interim level between the government's education ministry and schools, organizing education in a region. Those who work there can have a key role in shaping the development of work on emotional literacy in schools. Recently the author undertook an investigation for the Department for Education and Skills of England and Wales which looked at five 'cutting-edge' LEAs in England that were prioritizing work on emotional and social education. Those who were leading the initiatives were interviewed, and the documents they had produced analysed. Their experience of what they found helped and hindered was remarkably similar, and their experience may be useful for the many local/supportive agencies in other places who would like to do more to support the work of schools on emotional literacy. The lessons learned by these LEAs very much echo the messages in the rest of this book, and so also serve to illustrate the principles put forward in these pages with some real-life cases.

In the account which follows, the extracts from the interviews will not be credited to any individual, or indeed to any specific LEA, as the numbers interviewed from any one LEA were small and it is important not to identify any individual.

The leaders of the five LEAs working on emotional and social competence were asked 'What benefits is this work bringing?'

- *Improvement in teacher performance and confidence*: 'In schools where it's embedded it's made a huge difference. Teachers, who were thinking of leaving the profession have regained their ability to teach. It has given them the confidence to carry on.'
- *Less bad behaviour in students*: 'There is a noticeable difference in the queue of children outside the head-teacher's door waiting to be reprimanded.'
- *Increased teamwork in schools*: 'One thing that is good is that it leads to teachers working together.'
- *Increase in multi-agency work.*
- *Linking LEAs working on this issue*: 'We now have links with (another LEA involved). One member of our team has been involved in their audit.'
- *Increased student involvement*: 'There have been unexpected spin-offs. We asked students to comment on the framework for students age 8–11 and the youngsters made very sensible suggestions.'
- *Improvements to whole school*: 'It has a knock-on effect between weekly meetings and can lead to things being affected at whole-school level. It encourages teachers and students to look at how the environment impacts on the child – what changes need to be made.'
- *Saves money*: 'It seems expensive in the short term, but in fact should save money in the long term by freeing up special school places.'
- *Wholism*: 'It helps schools see the need to look after a youngster in a holistic way, not just academic.'
- *Coherence*: 'Emotional literacy is a unifying concept around which a lot of activity is occurring.'
- *Links educational agendas*: 'Emotional literacy forms a powerful bridge between a standards agenda (Feel good, learn good) and an inclusion agenda (Feel good, I attend).'

■ THE NATIONAL CONTEXT IN THE UK

In the UK LEAs have long supported schools in working with students with emotional and behaviour problems, through their teams of Educational Psychologists and advisers on Special Needs. In the last decade all LEAs have been required to have 'Behaviour Support teams'. The focus is now increasingly on 'whole-school' approaches: this is largely in recognition of the widespread nature of disruptive behaviour, and the realization that the whole-school context plays a major role in influencing how all students behave. Meanwhile most LEAs in the UK have adopted the National Healthy School Standard (NHSS), which has usually included the promotion of the mental and emotional well-being of all students as a significant focus for their work. The NHSS has been highly instrumental in encouraging the development of whole-school approaches to emotional well-being, including in particular the issue of bullying. (The actual and potential links between emotional literacy and the NHSS will be discussed in more detail later in this chapter.)

■ THE FIVE LEAs

Five LEAs were looked at in the course of the project, and illustrate a range of approaches to this work. One, Southampton, was the first LEA to use the term 'emotional literacy' to organize its work in this area, and to see emotional literacy as one of its key priorities, along with numeracy and literacy. Southampton created a 'Southampton Emotional Literacy Interest Group' or 'SELIG' and took the national lead on emotional literacy at LEA level. It set up the National Emotional Literacy Interest Group (NELIG) with a website (http://nelig.com.htm) and encouraged other local education authorities to become 'ELIGs'. At the time of writing seven local education authorities have set up formally constituted 'ELIGs'. Across the world, many local and national agencies are finding the term 'emotional literacy' to be a useful one in organizing multi-professional approaches to support this work in schools. So we will look at the learning from the Southampton experience in some detail in this chapter.

The other four LEAs investigated were Cumbria, Leicestershire, North Tyneside and Birmingham. These LEAs were looking at emotional literacy within other organizing frameworks which also take a wide, whole-school, preventive approach to emotional and social issues. As we have seen, if we look across the world, there are many possible names and unifying frameworks for this work: the two used by these four LEAs were to do with the 'management of behaviour' and 'healthy schools', both of which are typical of work in LEAs in the UK at present. So the experience of these four LEAs trying to integrate emotional literacy into other frameworks may have some general interest.

SUPPORT AND BARRIERS TO WORK ON EMOTIONAL LITERACY

Those who were leading the initiatives in the LEAs were asked what the supports and barriers to the work were. Table 7.1 outlines their responses.

We will explore their reflections on what helps and hinders in what follows.

USING AN OVERALL FRAMEWORK

All five LEAs found that their attempts to develop work on emotional and social competence had been helped by developing an overall framework to focus their work. These frameworks varied in name but they were all holistic and general ones under which a range of professions could unite. Southampton was the only LEA to use the term 'emotional literacy' for its framework, the others used a range of other terms such as 'Framework for Intervention' (Birmingham), 'Behaviour Support Plan' (Cumbria) and the 'Child Behaviour Intervention Initiative' (Leicestershire).

There are many ways forward in attempting to develop work on emotional literacy in schools, and it is important not to 'ghettoize' emotional literacy by insisting it is always the name of the main framework used. At the same time we need to make sure that specific work on emotional literacy, in other words, work which supports the learning of emotional competences and promotes the emotional well-being of staff and students, has a prominent place within other sympathetic approaches, and does not get lost in the process. Southampton had given emotional literacy the highest possible profile and had embedded it in the LEA policy as a leading priority, third after literacy and numeracy. In contrast, a leader from Birmingham LEA said that they have not yet managed to get their work on what they called 'emotional and social competence' linked with broader LEA policy. So it would appear that using the actual words 'emotional literacy' for the framework may be helpful in giving the work priority.

CREATING COHERENCE AND TEAMWORK

A vast number of agencies are potentially or actually working on emotional literacy and emotional well-being, and related issues. Work in these five LEAs had involved an enormous number of different agencies, professions and projects, all attempting to work together to meet commonly defined goals

TABLE 7.1 SUPPORTS AND HINDERANCES TO LEAs' WORK ON EMOTIONAL LITERACY

What LEAs said supported their work on emotional literacy	What LEAs said hindered their work on emotional literacy
Developing an overarching framework under which a range of professions could unite	Lack of coherence at LEA level: 'too many initiatives, not enough strategy'
Linking with other key initiatives, plans, structures, locally and nationally	
Teamwork and a multi-professional, multi-agency approach	Different agendas of the various professions involved
Having something concrete for the different agencies to do together, e.g. write guidelines, policies, curriculums	
Having a strong Healthy School Standard within the LEA within which to embed their work	
Using a whole-school approach, aimed at all children and the whole-school organization	Schools' lack of understanding of the whole-school approach
Emphasizing the link between emotional literacy and the improvement of learning and standards	Government seen as only interested in league tables and standards and not emotional literacy
Emphasizing the link between emotional literacy and the improvement of behaviour	Government seen as wanting schools to be inclusive but only recognizing schools for academic standards
Linking between emotional literacy and approaches to behaviour management, especially low key, non-stigmatizing approaches	Schools just want difficult children managed, punished or removed, not interested in underlying emotional reasons for problem behaviour
Having a high profile for Personal, Social and Health Education	Personal, Social and Health Education seen as low status overall
Having inspirational leadership to start it off and sustain work on emotional literacy	Real change takes time and commitment, schools and government want 'quick fix'
	Problems of sustainability if key people leave
Imaginative and flexible use of existing funding to support emotional literacy	Not enough funding in the whole area
	Too many strings attached to funding to be able to use it flexibly
	Feeling in schools that emotional literacy is manipulative
	Fear in schools that work on emotional literacy will be imposed on them by government
Focusing on the emotional well-being of teachers	Teachers too stressed to prioritize emotional literacy or take on anything new
Work on emotional literacy helps build teachers' confidence	Teachers find working on their own emotional literacy 'scary'
Being a small, new LEA: easier to prioritize emotional literacy and makes communication easy	Being a large LEA which already has a great deal going on: produces inertia and lack of coherence
Involvement of outside bodies in evaluation, e.g. universities	Lack of rigorous evaluation: no baselines and no controls

and targets. All five LEAs found that their chosen framework had been essential in helping them try to develop clear joint goals, coherence, teamwork and a multi-professional approach. All the frameworks emphasized multi-professional work, making links between those in education and a wide range of relevant agencies and professions in an organised and coherent way.

> We have got together with police, health, school nurses, behaviour service, educational psychology and so on, to work in partnership. We are planning a whole system event – auditing current things which are happening. Participants will include CAMHs, Child and Adolescent Mental Health Services, senior managers, PSHE coordinators, some-one in the LEA who is responsible for personnel, to make the link with governors.

The strongest links tended in practice to be between schools and Educational Psychology, Special Needs teams, Behaviour Support teams, Child and Adolescent Mental Health Services and Healthy School schemes.

In order for there to be effective support for, and liaison with, whole-school programmes, support needs to be organized in a coherent, planned and developmental way. There is a need for high levels of co-ordination and teamwork across and at all levels, and active steps need to be taken to ensure that that all parts of the whole are working efficiently and effectively together, in full knowledge of their own and other's roles, complementing but not duplicating one another's work. The LEAs attempted to achieve this by setting up multi-professional steering groups which met regularly and had produced copious policy and guidance documents.

> The working party has been meeting since last November and the agencies have been working together in the production of the pack on emotional well-being in schools. This is the first time they have all come together.

It is clear that all five LEAs had found the creation of a coherent, multi-professional, teamwork approach both essential to their mission and a major challenge. When asked about 'what helped', all the leaders from the LEAs had tales to tell of successful teamwork, and it was generally felt that one benefit of work on emotional literacy and well-being was that it promoted greater congruence and coherence. However, when asked what the 'barriers' were, they often mentioned persistent problems with multi-professional working.

> Keeping a multi-professional team together has been difficult. There is no team manager or co-ordinator, although maybe there are also positives in that.

Although they were working hard to produce coherence, nevertheless all said they experienced an overall lack of co-ordination and strategy at some level or other – between LEAs and schools, between emotional literacy work and Personal, Social and Health Education, between various agencies, between agencies and projects, and between themselves and the government.

> Our LEA is massive, with pockets of wonderful ideas, but not co-ordi-
> nated. We need an overview of where we are heading: there are too
> many initiatives – not enough strategy.

Difficulties in producing a coherent approach were seen as being due to the
different agencies each having their own objectives:

> Each agency has their own goals and objectives which they want to
> see the initiative as helping to achieve. Each agency wants proof of
> success – but their own particular version of success.

■ LINKING WORK ON EMOTIONAL LITERACY WITH LEARNING AND STANDARDS

All those in the LEAs felt that emotional and social education can help
promote high standards, and that this should be more widely appreciated.
All were keen to make clear that their work on educational and social competence and well-being was directly linked with learning, and had direct
benefits for learning.

> There is a general fear that emotional literacy is 'touchy, feely'. The
> term emotional literacy has negative connotations for some. We need
> to get across that it is tuned to achievement. It is not just about
> making people happy.

> Achievement and inclusion are often seen as mutually exclusive.
> Emotional literacy is a bridging concept – you need to feel good to
> be able to achieve and to attend.

■ CONCERNS THAT THE STANDARDS MOVEMENT NEEDS BALANCING

Although they were obviously in favour of high standards of learning, the LEA
leaders felt strongly that standards and testing have been overemphasized in
the UK recently, and which risks excluding and undermining emotional and
social learning. They saw the drive for standards and accountability as generally having had a detrimental effect on the teaching profession, by giving
teachers a great deal of stress, sapping their morale and devaluing their
autonomy and professional confidence. Some felt there was an overemphasis on the cognitive and the intellectual side of learning at the expense of the
other areas, including personal, emotional and social aspects of education,
and that the time and priority now given to testing meant that teachers felt
they could no longer afford to prioritize emotional and social learning.

> An over emphasis on standards and league tables means there is no
> time for emotional and social matters. Standards agenda – league
> tables – pressure on the curriculum – means sometimes that things
> like circle time get pushed out. The best things in education can't be
> measured.

> There is an over emphasis on assessment and measurement. Schools are under pressure to achieve – and to be competitive – league tables don't help. It is a disincentive to spending time on social and emotional growth – academic results are all that count.

> There is a conflict between the aims of this type of work and the emphasis on assessment and achievement. Many schools believe they have no time on the time-table to devote to this type of work.

Some suggested that an overemphasis on achievement was devaluing the social role of school in producing rounded people, active in their communities.

> We need to get the message across that the most important task for schools is: 'How do I, living in a community, protect my own self-esteem at the same time as protecting the self-esteem of others?' The message currently is 'standards, standards, standards.'

> There needs to be a long-term view – that education is about our environment, about justice to future generations, about justice for the present community, about living together.

Several were keen to emphasize that work on emotional literacy should not itself be used as part of the standards agenda, and that checklists on emotional and social competence should not be used for teacher appraisal or to contribute data for school league table grading.

■ LINKS WITH BEHAVIOUR AND INCLUSION

All in the LEAs were keen to make links between their work on emotional literacy and the improvement and management of behaviour. The starting point for their work on emotional literacy tended to be their behaviour support plans, which were set up originally to target those with behavioural and emotional problems. The link between emotional literacy and behaviour had continued, with all five LEAs feeling that their work on emotional literacy was having a beneficial effect on behaviour in schools. They were keen that this link should be more widely known:

> What people need is 'sock it in your face figures', proof that emotions affect behaviour. We need a body of literature that convinces people that by investing in this will lead to improved behaviour.

They were all inspired by the need to reduce exclusion, and all saw their work as contributing directly to this goal. One of the authorities, Southampton in particular, was keen to emphasize the significant drop in exclusions that followed the introduction of emotional literacy into schools.

Many felt that it would help if government rewarded schools for inclusion as well as for academic results:

> We need some measure to recognize inclusive schools. Our LEA has no special schools for children with moderate learning difficulties. They are all in mainstream schools. But as a result the average school score comes down in the league tables. Inclusion needs to be recognized in the league tables.

■ TENSIONS BETWEEN LEAS' AND SCHOOLS' VIEWS OF THE MANAGEMENT OF BEHAVIOUR

All the LEAs had a very specific view of behaviour, which concurs with that put forward in Chapter 4 of this book: they agreed that it was essential to focus on understanding and working with the underlying emotional, social and contextual causes of behaviour and use positive approaches, not just manage or, even worse punish, the behaviour itself. All had blurred the boundaries within their own work on special needs, to minimize labelling and procedures, and to speed up getting practical help for problem students into schools quickly.

However, they did not feel that schools always shared their perspective on behaviour. Many felt that schools often called in the behaviour support team because they wanted their problems dealt with by someone else. 'We don't take the children away and deal with the problem, which is what a lot of schools are wanting', said one leader, while another said, 'they want the fire engine as well as the fire prevention officers.' They felt that schools tend to concentrate on individual children, not the environment in which behaviour occurs or its underlying emotional causes:

> It was an uphill struggle to start with to get across the idea that you can change behaviour without the focus being on the child.

> It is moving it from being the child's problem to being the school's problem.

> Schools want behaviour management rather than emotional literacy. One of the tasks is helping staff to realize that behaviour is communication about emotional states.

■ TAKING A WHOLE-SCHOOL APPROACH

All in the LEAs emphasized the importance of taking a whole-school/environmental approach to understanding, preventing and responding to behaviour, and the importance of positively understanding and shaping the whole-school context, not just concentrating on individual students with problems. All felt that there was no conflict between taking a holistic approach and a concern to tackle behavioural and emotional problems; indeed they believed the holistic approach is the most effective in helping those with problems. They emphasized that their whole-school work was intended to continue to meet the needs of students with behavioural and emotional problems, to prevent the onset of such problems where possible, and to attempt to minimize or manage them where they occur. Again, however, they felt that schools did not always appreciate this point of view, and had a lack of understanding that it is possible to use both an individual and a whole-school approach together.

> People think that our approach is all about the environment and that if that doesn't work then you go to more traditional methods of working with individual children. Not the case. Our framework covers both the environment and work with specific children.

■ CURRICULUM

All five LEAs encouraged the teaching of the skills of emotional and social competence in schools. They varied in the extent to which they had developed and/or promoted specific and explicit programmes that teach emotional and social competences. Cumbria had done most to develop an explicit curriculum. They had produced a 'Behaviour Curriculum' which had been developed with a group of teachers and which taught the skills and abilities underpinning positive behaviour. Southampton had not itself developed one programme but they asked every school in the LEA to put emotional literacy 'at the heart of the curriculum'. Their guidelines to schools outline a set of key competences they thought should be taught, which include self-awareness, self-regulation, motivation, social competence and social skills, which they asked schools to teach them through their 'emotional literacy curriculum'. This LEA provided lists of commercially available materials which schools might use. In Leicester the Behaviour Support Team taught whole-class work on social and communication skills, through circle time, drama groups, performance and Lifeskills work. North Tyneside used circle work extensively, not just by setting aside a certain time a week for circle time, but as a way of working in the classroom all the time. Birmingham mainly focused on special needs students in their teaching and learning. They had a scheme, 'circle of friends', which is a support group for special needs students. All the LEAs were also keen to make links between emotional literacy and existing curriculum areas: three that were mentioned explicitly were Personal, Social and Health Education, literacy and oracy.

CLARITY

Many of those interviewed were keen to stress that work on emotional and social competence and well-being is not a 'soft, woolly' option but a hard-nosed and rational strategy that needs considerable clarity and strategic thinking to implement. As the Southampton plan puts it: 'emotional literacy is not hugs, cakes and mopping up tears on the classroom floor' (Sharp and Faupel, 2002: 8). All of the five LEAs felt they owed their success to the level of strategic thinking and planning they had brought to bear on this issue, all based their strategies on clear target setting and all had integrated this work into their behaviour support strategies.

PARTICIPATION

A recurrent theme in the interviews was the importance of actively involving people in all parts and stages of the process, not imposing solutions on them. The leader of the Cumbria initiative was keen to point out how much consultation and involvement of students there had been in the development of the Cumbrian Healthy School standard. Southampton City Council prioritized the need to involve as many people as possible to increase a sense of ownership, and to make the policy reflect what people actually want to do. They suggested that 'the whole-school staff need to wrestle with definitions, rationale, aims, principles and scope and commit their shared understanding to paper' (Sharp and Faupel, 2002: 10).

AUTONOMY

Many interviewed were keen to stress that emotional literacy should not be imposed on people. 'We don't want an emotional literacy hour … we don't want another checklist' were typical responses. Some reported that schools were 'punch drunk' with imposed initiatives and might respond adversely if they felt that emotional literacy was yet another.

> Heads are very disillusioned. They don't like outsiders saying what's best for their school. One head is very disillusioned and is likely to tell them 'on your bike'.

Some reported that there were concerns in schools that emotional literacy itself is manipulative and coercive:

> Schools staff wonder if they are being manipulated. What is the hidden agenda of people trying to promote this work?

■ DEVELOPING THE EMOTIONAL LITERACY OF STAFF AND MANAGERS

All the LEAs felt that teacher emotional well-being was essential to attempts to develop emotional and social competence in schools.

> We need to foster the emotional well-being of teaching staff. They need time to do their job well and to be reflective practitioners.

All five LEAs had themselves emphasized teacher support, development and training to develop teachers' own emotional literacy. This had sometimes been an uphill struggle as teachers and heads could be resistant:

> The main principle is starting with the grown ups not with the young people. If you start with the young people and then put them back in the same settings with the same adults, they will soon revert back – you achieve nothing. Heads find the subject scary – the idea that they themselves may be emotionally illiterate ... One difficulty is finding out how to present this to grown ups in a way which does not scare them off.

■ LEADERS NEED TO 'WALK THE TALK'

Linked with the concern for teacher well being, there was a strong feeling that change needs to start at the top, and those who want to encourage emotional literacy should practise what they preach. Southampton had started its emotional literacy project with an attempt to raise the emotional literacy of its education managers. All managers took part, although it was optional. Almost all managers were reported to have become very involved and enthusiastic. They had first benchmarked the managers' emotional intelligence using an instrument designed for managers (Dulewicz and Higgs, 2000). They then held 360° appraisals, involving rating of managers by a subordinate, peer and superior on the same questions. Managers then formed a learning partnership with a colleague to draft a learning plan to promote their own emotional literacy. They ran developmental and experiential workshops for managers on emotional literacy. Southampton has continued to focus on staff emotional literacy and training to promote the overall strategy. The current aim is that all managers are involved in the emotional literacy programme, and all sections, services and divisions have a published emotional literacy programme.

The leaders from the LEAs were keen that government take a role in this process, and do more to ensure that teachers' workloads were reasonable, their achievements were celebrated, that they felt empowered and their confidence was bolstered.

Characteristics of an 'emotionally literate' local authority

- It listens to those it serves.
- It provides many opportunities for face-to-face contact, communication would be good.
- There is respect and understanding between members of the authority for each other's roles.
- There is sharing of ideas and vision – colleagues would be allowed to take risks and to fail.
- Colleagues are supportive of each other as professionals.
- All take responsibility for the success of the organization.
- Colleagues actively seek contributions from across the organization and between the local authority and other organizations.
- In making appointments and in all selection procedures there is a regard for the emotional literacy of the candidates – this may involve a range of selection techniques and procedures.
- There is a range of different skills and personal qualities in the team.

Sharp and Faupel (2002: 29–30), writing about the experience of Southampton LEA.

We need positive messages about the good work teachers are doing. We know that students respond better to praise than criticism – teachers are the same. We should shift the emphasis from pointing out what the 5% are doing badly to pointing out what the 95% are doing well.

■ USING FUNDING TO ENCOURAGE WORK IN THIS AREA

The LEAs were clear that developing emotional literacy costs money, and had many inventive ideas for gathering together funding for this area from a wide range of government initiatives. Several sources of existing funding were mentioned, but they said they would like more flexibility on how existing funding, more specific funding for emotional literacy and more long-term money they could rely on.

■ EVALUATION

All the LEAs had made some attempt at evaluation of their initiatives, usually involving some outside agency such as a local university, a partnership which all had found useful. However the picture that emerged was of an embryonic and confused field. The evaluation that was being carried out tended not to have been systematic, and those involved usually thought it needed better co-ordination.

> I feel rather embarrassed about this – there is a shortfall of evidence – we've been bad on this. We have collected a variety of data, of students' perceptions, but it hasn't been analysed … I would welcome some form of evaluation. We should encourage schools more to do their own.
>
> As there are various projects happening at the same time, it is difficult to know which project has made a difference. I could not put my hand on my heart and say that it is definitely A, B, or C which has caused X, Y, or Z.

Most of the data collected were qualitative, and the evaluations formative, not summative. The most easily remediable weakness, shown by most of the evaluations, was a failure to benchmark at the outset, in other words to collect baseline data.

> The University carried out an evaluation, but there had been no collection of baseline data so it was difficult to know what had made a difference.
>
> They did have someone from (name of local college) carry out an evaluation, but it wasn't quantitative.

Some LEAs had used some simple benchmarking/baseline indicators, mostly those schools and LEAs were using anyway, such as exclusion and attendance figures and examination grades – these are, of course, useful and telling, but not in themselves measures of emotional literacy. Some LEAs had collected the comments of inspectors to demonstrate the effectiveness of their approaches. Some schools and LEAs had linked with attempts at targeting by their local National Healthy Schools scheme.

This picture that emerged would support the suggestions made in Chapter 6 for ways in which evaluation could be improved. There is an urgent need for more good quality evaluation, for rigour, for co-ordination and a more systematic approach. Local education authorities need to be encouraged to collect baseline data before embarking on new initiatives. However, given the low level of evaluative activity at present it is important to go carefully, respect where people are starting from, including current work on formative evaluation and qualitative approaches. Local education authorities need to be encouraged to work with local research centres/Universities, and to make use of existing data, for example attendance figures, SATs to monitor the impact of their interventions.

Developing a strategy at local authority level

Southampton Local Education Authority have outlined what they call the 'steps to success' in developing an emotional literacy strategy, based on what they have learned in trying to achieve this. The steps include:

- Establish a partnership involving at least two senior officers to champion the strategy.
- Begin with the individual – managers explore their own levels of emotional literacy.
- Hold an awareness-raising programme of seminars, presentations and publications.
- Publish widely that emotional literacy is a priority, ranked with literacy and numeracy.
- Establish an emotional literacy interest group.
- Plan the evaluation of the implementation of emotional literacy at the outset, ideally by independent evaluators.
- Undertake demonstration or pilot projects in schools, carried out on an action research basis with pre- and post-project measures.
- Incorporate emotional literacy into all major plans, including the education development plan, behaviour support plan, early years plan, etc.

LINKING EMOTIONAL LITERACY AND WHOLE-SCHOOL APPROACHES: THE EXAMPLE OF THE HEALTHY/HEALTH-PROMOTING SCHOOL

■ LINKS IN THE FIVE LEAs BETWEEN EMOTIONAL LITERACY AND HEALTHY SCHOOLS

In England the National Healthy School Standard (NHSS) is having a major impact on work on emotional well-being, and has enormous potential for being a highly effective framework for work on emotional literacy. The five LEAs being discussed here either mainly organized work on emotional and social competence and well-being within its local NHSS scheme or had made strong links between their work on emotional literacy and that of their local NHSS. As Health Promoting School networks can be now be found over much of the globe it is worth taking a little time to look specifically at advantages of linking emotional literacy with a Health Promoting School approach, as this may be one of the most fruitful ways forward for embedding emotional literacy in whole-school approaches, and giving it appropriate support.

■ THE SETTINGS APPROACH

The English NHSS exists within a broad and long tradition, and is just one example of a phenomenon, usually known as 'Health Promoting Schools', that has taken off across the world. In the 20 or so years since it was started, the Health Promoting School approach has been the subject of a massive amount of theorizing, discussion and evaluation through a wealth of conferences, meetings, publications and projects.

The Health Promoting School approach is in any case only one example of a whole-school approach that has the potential to focus on emotional literacy. As we said in Chapter 2, whole-school approaches and movements go under many titles, including 'universal', 'environmental', 'comprehensive' and 'multi-dimensional' approaches, and there are several movements which also use a whole-school approach, including the 'safe schools' of the USA and the Netherlands and 'the environmental schools movement' in Sweden and Denmark. So unpacking the relationship between emotional literacy and Health Promoting Schools may have wide relevance to encouraging a holistic approach to emotional literacy in a range of countries.

The World Health Organization (WHO) was the theoretical powerhouse in the development the Health Promoting School approach. The approach evolved from an overall 'settings' approach which has been heavily promoted by the WHO since the mid-1980s. The 'settings' approach recognizes the myriad interconnected and interacting physical, social and psychological factors that make up the total overall context in which any development takes place. It suggests that those organizations, agencies and individuals who wish to promote key developments in education or health should pay attention to providing an overall policy, social, psychological, and legislative climate and context that is supportive of that development, rather than focusing on the behaviour of individuals. In the mid-1980s, following on from its success in implementing the 'settings' approach through 'Healthy Cities', the WHO evolved the 'Health Promoting School' idea. In this approach, the school is the setting. The whole-school organization, including its management, ethos, communication systems, physical environment and community context are the focus for development, not just the curriculum for the individual student. This approach rapidly turned into an international network of 'Health Promoting Schools' which has now spread across all countries in Europe, East as well as West, including the UK. Led by the WHO supported by the EU and the Council of Europe. Healthy/Health Promoting School networks are also to be found in other parts of the world, most notably Africa, the Western Pacific and Latin America.

■ SOUND TRACK RECORD

The Health Promoting School movement has a long and distinguished pedigree. The lengthy involvement of countless respected researchers and practitioners has resulted in a tried and tested approach, with high acceptability, a growing evidence base, rigorous and large-scale evaluations (HEA and NFER, 1997; Lister-Sharp et al, 2000; Piette et al., 2001) a well thought through coherent and holistic framework that includes emotional and social well-being, and strong links with mental health. For example, in England the NHSS is a major national project with widespread acceptability and coverage. All 150 LEAs have signed up and achieved the standard at some level. Fourteen thousand schools have some involvement through projects or attendance at a training course, while just over 8,000 are involved on an intensive level, having this as a key priority area for development in a health development plan.

■ STRONG TRADITION OF WORK ON EMOTIONAL WELL-BEING

In Europe at least the Health Promoting School approach has almost invariably taken a close interest in developing work on mental, emotional and social well-being. Of the original '12 criteria for a health promoting school' with which the approach began in the mid-1980s, three criteria were directly concerned with emotional and social well-being:

- active promotion of the self-steem of all students by demonstrating that everyone can make a contribution to the life of the school

- the development of good relations between staff and students and between students and the daily life of the school

- the clarification for staff and students of the social aims of the school.

Five more criteria were concerned with other aspects of school life which this book has argued have a direct bearing on emotional and social well-being:

- the development of good links between the school, home and the community

- the active promotion of the health and well-being of school staff

- the consideration of the role of staff exemplars in health-related issues

■ the realization of the potential of specialist services in the community for advice and support in health education

■ the development of the education potential of the school health services beyond routine screening towards the active support for the curriculum.

Since then most Health Promoting School approaches have built on this emphasis, adding detail and specificity.

Health Promoting School approaches link in directly with work on Health Education, PSHE and Citizenship, which have a long tradition of work on the development of emotional and social competences and well-being. There have been international examples of specific emotional and social health projects developed by the Health Promoting School approach, and we will cite just two here. In Australia a major national project, 'MindMatters' (see contact list at the end of the book), has developed a whole-school approach to teaching about mental health in schools. Serious consideration is now being given to adapting 'MindMatters' for use across Europe. In Europe the author of this book has been involved in a long-term WHO project working with teachers in the networks in almost all the 36 countries in the European Network of Health Promoting Schools to develop teachers' competences in promoting mental, emotional and social

---

Including emotional health and well-being in the criteria for the Western Pacific Health Promoting Schools
The WHO regional guidelines for the Western Pacific Region lists as one of its six themes for developing Health Promoting Schools 'the school's social environment'. Some 'components' of this theme include:

• 'the school ethos is supportive of the mental health and social needs of students and staff'
• 'the school creates an environment of care, trust and friendliness which encourages student attendance and involvement'.

Some of the 'criteria' or 'checkpoints' by which the components can be assessed:

• 'the school actively discourages physical and verbal violence, both among students and by staff towards students'
• 'students are encouraged to be active participants in the learning process' (WHO, 1996: 10).

---

well-being, which has included the production of a training manual which has accompanied the six-day training workshops (Weare and Gray, 1994; Gray, 1996). The research techniques it encouraged teachers to use to find out where students are starting from have been described in Chapter 6.

The Health Promoting School approach has always emphasized the well-being, including the emotional and social well-being, of teachers as well as students. For example, the English NHSS has recently produced support material for schools and local partners on staff health and well-being in liaison with the Teachers' Support Network. The NHSS is also leading, in partnership with the Department of Health and the Department for Education and Science a national programme of teacher education and certification of Personal, Social and Health Education.

■ INCLUSIVITY

Although the European Network of Health Promoting Schools originally set up 10 schools in each country to be 'exemplar' schools, this has in recent years given way, as planned, to a more inclusive approach. The emphasis with the European Network is now on a range of key principles (WHO, 1997), which schools are invited to interpret as they wish, and on case studies of 'what works' (Parsons et al., 1997) rather than on any kind of prescription.

The English NHSS has strongly emphasized the importance of creating a sense of ownership of the scheme and is giving it widespread acceptability among teachers. One of the strengths of the NHSS, and one which is particularly valued by schools and their local communities, is that targets are negotiated with schools informed by needs assessment activity with staff, students and parents to define specific priorities and needs, as well as through undertaking supported self-review whereby the school is encouraged to identify what it does well and would want to build on alongside areas for improvement and development. Schools therefore decide on their own starting points/entry point into the Standard, based on priorities, community needs and stage of development.

■ EMPHASIS ON PARTNERSHIPS

Health Promoting Schools have always attempted to work with both health and education agencies in their development: a process which has probably been the single most difficult aspect to sustain.

The English NHSS has worked hard to make the rhetoric of partnerships

and multi-professional working a reality. It carried out an initial consultation through regional networks, national seminars and workshops which
have given a sense of ownership to participants. There is a strong emphasis
within the NHSS on partnerships, between local education and health partnerships, between LEAs and Health Authorities (and more recently Primary
Care Trusts), between management and schools. The scheme is hoping to
move more towards multi-disciplinary teams within local government
offices, a development which many cities are doing already. They are creating local strategic partnerships, involving a wide range of bodies, including
Health through Primary Care Trusts, education, local authorities,
Connexions, organizations which aim to prevent teenage pregnancy, Sure
Start, drug agencies, Neighbourhood Renewal, and children and young
people's strategic partnerships.

■ NEED FOR MORE SPECIFIC WORK ON EMOTIONAL AND SOCIAL COMPETENCES WITHIN HEALTHY SCHOOL APPROACHES

We have said that work on emotional literacy can benefit from being
embedded within work on Health Promoting Schools. However, this cuts
both ways, and work on Health Promoting Schools could do more to prioritize work on emotional literacy.

There is a tendency for Health Promoting Schools' approaches to include a
concern with emotional and social well-being in their rhetoric but, in practice, to 'default' to a simplistic physical model of health which concentrates
for example on healthy eating, the physical environment, the health services and the prevention of disease. A typical example is the guidelines for
the Western Pacific Region (WHO, 1996), where the components to do
with the school as a social environment are included at the start of the
document but have become an optional part of the award scheme outlined
at the end, while components to do with sanitation and healthy eating
remain compulsory!

Although some international programmes aimed at promoting mental
health at international level have included a concern to transmit specific
and detailed competences, usually called in this context 'Lifeskills', such an
approach is rare within health promoting school initiatives. The ways in
which teachers and students are expected to promote their own well-being
remain unspecified, and something of a 'black box', within most Healthy
School/Health Promoting School approaches, with the result that it often
does not happen (Buczkiewicz and Carnegie, 2001). More work on emotional literacy, including specific and detailed work on the development of

emotional and social competences, within the Health Promoting School approach would do a great deal to help schools to achieve their apparent goal of promoting health and well-being.

To consider as a result of reading this chapter

- What, if anything, is your local education authority doing to promote emotional literacy? If something positive, can you join in? If nothing, could you encourage them to? What services do they have to offer (for example, educational psychology, special needs teams, behaviour support teams, inclusion teams, curriculum advisory, PSHE advisory) that you could make use of in your efforts to develop emotional literacy in your school?
- Is there a Healthy School initiative in your area? If so what is it doing to prioritize emotional literacy/emotional well-being/mental health? Is there work on the development of emotional competence as part of that work? If not, can you encourage those involved to do more in this area?
- Think about the links your school has with other key agencies. Is there any way of introducing a more co-ordinated approach that brings them all together to consider what they can do to help work on emotional literacy (bear in mind they may prefer to use other labels for it)?
- Find out what other schools in your area are doing about emotional literacy (bear in mind they may call it something else). Would it be helpful to join with them to start a local forum or interest group to learn from one another's experience?
- Look through the list of contacts at the end of the book. Are there any there that would be useful for your school?

Overview: Key Steps in Becoming a More Emotionally Literate School

Clarify what the various members of the school think the term 'emotional literacy' means and how it relates to other terms with which the school is familiar – see Chapter 1.

Clarify what the school hopes work on emotion literacy might add to the school to make it different and better – see Chapters 1, 4 and 6.

Consider what competences various groups (students, teachers, parents, governors) feel are important for students and for staff to learn – see Chapter 2. Keep your list close at hand to compare with any checklists and tools for assessment that are proposed, and only adapt if convinced.

Look at the school as a whole, and think about what aspects or features of it are the most important ones to start to change, or to work on further if the school has already started work on emotional literacy – see Chapters 3 and 5.

Clarify what problem behaviours students have, and whether there is any room for improving the way the school is tackling them, using the principles of emotional literacy, positive responses and an inclusive, whole-school approach – see Chapter 3.

Explore links between the school's programme of learning and teaching and emotional literacy. Consider ways in which the school might develop or adopt a taught programme, work through school projects, and/or link with work on accelerated learning – see Chapter 4.

Carry out an audit of the whole school, and including the competences of students and staff, to establish a baseline, using self-devised tools, or those used elsewhere that fits in with the school's self chosen competences, principles and values – see Chapter 6.

Make links with those in the local area to see what other supports are available to help with this work – see Chapter 7.

Contacts for Developing Emotional Literacy and Emotional Well-being in Schools

PROJECTS AND TAUGHT PROGRAMMES

(Some of these have been evaluated, as described in the table of programmes (Table 4.2) in Chapter 4)

CHILD DEVELOPMENT PROJECT

US based, the Child Development Project is a comprehensive educational reform model intended to transform schools into 'caring communities of learners'. Its focus is on enhancing protective factors, including school bonding, and recognizing the role of the social context in healthy child development. The theory behind it is that satisfying students' basic needs will lead to greater attachment or bonding to the school community and its norms and values. The programme concentrates on creating a co-operative and supportive school. Components include school training in the use of cooperative learning and a language arts model, cross-grade buddying activities, a developmental approach to discipline that fosters self-control through active participation in classroom decision-making. School-wide community building activities are used to promote attachment to school, and parent involvement such as interactive homework assignments reinforce the family–school partnership.
www.prevention.psu.edu/CDP.htm

FAMILY LINKS

UK based. Runs 'The Nurturing Programme' in many counties across the UK. Teaches courses for teachers, health professionals and families, on emotional literacy, nurturing, positive discipline, building self-esteem and relationship skills, using a whole-school approach, with the aim of creating a calm and disciplined school community.
familylinksuk@aol.com

■ JENNY MOSLEY CONSULTANCIES

UK based, producing materials and running training using the 'whole school quality circle time model', an interactive group work method.
www.circle-time.co.uk

■ MINDMATTERS

MindMatters is a health promotion resource for all 4,000 Australian schools with secondary enrolments: government, Catholic and independent. The core component of the programme is a resource kit which provides advice to schools about how to adopt a whole-school approach to mental health. The topics range from a planning framework for implementing the process, working with diversity for well-being, understanding mental illness, a guide for preventing and addressing self-harm and suicide, dealing with bullying, loss and grief, enhancing resilience, and managing challenges and change. The curriculum materials are offered free of charge to all secondary schools in Australia. It has developed a national database that links MindMatters activities to curriculum outcomes for each State and Territory. The 'weblinks' section of the MindMatters site provides a range of links to sites. It is intended to adapt this project for use in Europe.
http://www.curriculum.edu.au/mindmatters

■ PATHS CURRICULUM

The PATHS (Providing Alternative THinking Strategies) curriculum is a programme for educators and counsellors designed to facilitate the development of self-control, emotional awareness, and interpersonal problem-solving skills. The curriculum consists of an instructional manual, six volumes of lessons, pictures and photographs, and additional materials. A research book is also available. PATHS is designed for use with elementary-school aged children. The purposes of the PATHS Curriculum are to enhance the social competence and social understanding of children, as well as to facilitate educational processes in the classroom.
http://www.prevention.psu.edu/PATHS/

■ PEOPLEMAKING

Australian bookshop producing personal and professional development books and training resources.
www.peoplemaking.com.au

■ RESOLVING CONFLICT CREATIVELY PROGRAMME

A US, research-based, secondary school programme in social and emotional learning. It is the US's longest running school programme, focusing on conflict resolution and intergroup relations. It has been disseminated to over 350 schools in the USA. It is a comprehensive strategy for preventing violence and creating caring and peaceable communities of learning. It works to change school cultures so that these skills are both modelled and taught as part of the basics in education.
www.esrnational.org/about-rccp.html

■ SMALLWOOD PUBLISHING GROUP

UK based. Produces catalogues of books, games and simulations, pictures and photos, videos, puppets, etc. materials from several publishers on emotional literacy and related issues.
www.smallwood.co.uk

SUPPORTIVE ORGANIZATIONS
■

(Some of these produce the tests, audits and inventories described in Chapter 6.)

■ UK

ABC PEER SUPPORT SCHEME

Creates the opportunity for a broad range of students to learn about dealing with conflict and bullying in a safe and positive environment. Works upon the principle that young people can be empowered through trust, training and support to help their peers find solutions to the issue of bullying in the school community.
www.aclandburghley.camden.sch.uk

ANTIDOTE

National pressure group that works to create an emotionally literate society. Provides a focus for the work of a growing number of organizations that see emotional literacy as an effective way to achieve their objectives in the settings where they operate. Carrying out research with schools to develop work on emotional literacy, an audit of emotional literacy, and guidelines. Organizes conferences and publications on emotional literacy, including a newsletter.
www.antidote.org.uk

BRAHMA KUMARIS WORLD SPIRITUAL UNIVERSITY

International organization on the roster of the United Nations Economic and Social Council, dedicated to the promotion of peace, co-operation and social and spiritual values. Organizes conferences, courses and projects, including those with a focus on schools.
www.bkwsu.com (international) and www.bkessex.org.uk (UK site)

BUCKHOLDT ASSOCIATES

Company offering consultancy, advice and training on emotional literacy. Has produced the 'Whole School Emotional Literacy Indicator', 'Emotional Literacy Indicator for Adults to Use with Pupils' and 'Class Emotional Literacy Indicator'.
www.emotionalintelligence.co.uk and www.schoolofemotional-literacy.com

BULLY ONLINE

The website of the UK National Workplace Bullying Advice Line provides insight and information on all aspects of bullying with the long-term aim of eradicating the behaviour altogether.
www.successunlimited.co.uk

THE CASPARI FOUNDATION

(Formerly the Forum for the Advancement for Educational Therapy & Therapeutic Teaching.) Aims to develop the theory of educational therapy and disseminate knowledge of it to teachers, and to promote the insight of teachers into emotional factors in learning.
www.psychotherapy.org.uk

CENTRE FOR APPLIED EMOTIONAL INTELLIGENCE

Provides innovative training solutions for human performance problems in organizations, based on the use of emotional intelligence theory, skills and attitudes.
www.emotionalintelligence.co.uk

CHANCE UK

A charity seeking to provide an early and transforming intervention in the lives of vulnerable children, so that, together with their families, they may begin to build a brighter future. Provides specific, targeted solution-focused mentoring for children aged 5–11 years, based on individual needs.
www.chanceuk.com

THE CITIZENSHIP FOUNDATION

An independent educational charity supported by the Law Society to encourage informed and active citizenship, especially among young people. It has been foremost in promoting a programme of citizenship education in schools.
www.citfou.org.uk

CORAM FAMILY

Works with vulnerable children and young people to promote resilience, enabling them to take responsibility for their own lives and achieve their full potential.
www.coram.org.uk

EMOTIONAL INTELLIGENCE SERVICES

A company which provides information, resources and tools to improve personal effectiveness and organizational performance.
http://ei.haygroup.com

FRAMEWORK FOR INTERVENTION

An approach introduced by Birmingham Education Department in 1997 which

attempts to shape schools' students' behaviour, aimed at all ages and all settings.
www.frameworkforintervention.com

HEALTH DEVELOPMENT AGENCY

It is the main national body with overall responsibility for public health in England. This includes overall responsibility for school health education in England. It co-ordinates the National Healthy Standard (see below) and has information on this and many other related topics through its pages 'Wired for Health'. See also Chapter 7. www.hda-online.org.uk

HEALTH EDUCATION BOARD FOR SCOTLAND

Woodburn House, Canaan Lane, Edinburgh, EH10 4SG. It is the main national body with overall responsibility for school health education in Scotland. Co-ordinates the Scottish Network of Health-Promoting Schools. www.hebs.scot.nhs.uk

HEALTH PROMOTION AGENCY FOR NORTHERN IRELAND

18 Ormeau Avenue, Belfast, BT2 8HS. It is the main national body with overall responsibility for school health education in Northern Ireland. Co-ordinates the Northern Ireland Network of Health Promoting Schools. www.healthpromotionagency.org.uk

HEALTH PROMOTION WALES

The main national body with overall responsibility for school health education in Wales. Co-ordinattes the Health Promoting School Network in Wales. Ffynnon-las, Ty Glas Avenue, Llanishen, Cardiff, CF4 5DZ. www.hpw.wales.gov.uk

LEARNING THROUGH ACTION TRUST

Fair Cross, Stratfield Saye, Reading, RG7 2BT. Offers interactive in-service education and consultancy, in the community, and in schools on social and emotional education. www.learning-through-action.org.uk

MEDIATION UK

Alexander House, Telephone Avenue, Bristol, BS1 4BS. A coalition of and network of projects, organizations and individuals interested in mediation and conflict resolution, including those based in schools. www.mediationuk.org.uk

MENTAL HEALTH FOUNDATION

20/21 Cornwall Terrace, London, NW1 4QL. National charity which aims at improving services for those with mental health problems and learning disabilities. Develops community projects, and educates the public, policy-makers and profes-

sionals, including those who work in schools.
www.mentalhealth.org.uk

NATIONAL CHILDREN'S BUREAU

A registered charity which promotes the interests and well-being of all children and young people across every aspect of their lives. Advocates the participation of children and young people in all matters affecting them. Challenges disadvantage in childhood.
www.ncb.org.uk

NATIONAL COUNCIL FOR VOLUNTARY CHILD CARE ORGANIZATIONS (NCVCCO)

The NCVCCO is an umbrella organization whose members are all registered charities that work with children, young people and their families.
www.ncvcco.org

NATIONAL EMOTIONAL LITERACY INTEREST GROUP (NELIG)

Website pooling information from UK organizations promoting emotional literacy in education. At the time of writing the site contains a news section, an information archive, a discussion forum, a resource database, a weblinks section, a 'friends of Nelig' section for those working to promote emotional literacy, and a parents' information area.
www.nelig.com

NATIONAL HEALTHY SCHOOL STANDARD

The National Healthy School Standard (formerly known as the National Healthy Schools Scheme) is a government scheme which identified the school as a setting to improve the health of children, including their mental and emotional well-being. All 150 Local Educational Authorities and 14,000 schools are involved.
www.wiredforhealth.gov.uk/healthy/healsch.html

THE NATIONAL PYRAMID TRUST

Helps primary-school aged children to fulfil their potential in school and in life by building their self-esteem and resilience. The Trust, through local partnerships of statutory and voluntary agencies, runs programmes for 7- to 10-year-olds who are causing concern as a result of significant emotional, social and behavioural difficulties. The work involves checking the emotional and behavioural needs of all children in a year group and offering help to those who need it, including therapeutic activity groups.
www.nptrust.org.uk

NATIONAL YOUTH AGENCY

Aims to advance youth work to promote young people's personal and social development, and their voice, influence and place in society.
www.newhorizons.org

NORTHERN IRELAND ASSOCIATION FOR MENTAL HEALTH (NIAMH),

80 University Street, Belfast, BT7 1HE.
www.caritasdata.co.uk

NURTURE GROUPS UK

Aim to support school improvement by promoting emotional development and improvements in behaviour.
www.nurturegroups.org

PAPYRUS

A voluntary organization committed to the prevention of young suicide and the promotion of mental health and well-being.
www.papyrus-uk.org

PARENTLINE PLUS

A UK registered charity which offers support to anyone parenting a child – the child's parents, step-parents, grand parents and foster parents. Parentline Plus runs a freephone helpline, courses for parents, develops innovative projects and provides a range of information.
www.parentlineplus.org.uk

THE PEER SUPPORT FORUM

Created by a partnership between the Mental Health Foundation and Childline. The aims of the forum are to promote peer support as a process of enhancing and developing the social and emotional well-being of children and young people in schools.
www.mentalhealth.org.uk/peer/forum.htm

Q-METRICS

A company offering advice on how to measure emotional literacy.
www.qmetricsseq.com

RE:MEMBERING EDUCATION

Promotes a concern with relationships in education.
www.remember.mcmail.com

SCOTTISH ASSOCIATION FOR MENTAL HEALTH (SAMH)

www.samh.org.uk

SOUTHAMPTON PSYCHOLOGY SERVICE/LOCAL EDUCATION AUTHORITY

A pioneer in the development of work relating to emotional literacy in schools. Manages the NELIG website (q.v.).
www.southampton.gov.uk

VALUES EDUCATION COUNCIL

Established to promote and develop values education and values in education, and to help individuals develop as responsible and caring persons and live as participating members of a pluralist society.
www.vecuk.org.uk

YOUNG MINDS

A national charity committed to improving the mental health of all children. The Young Minds Parents' Information Service (0800 018 2138) provides information and advice for anyone worried about the mental health of a child or young person.
www.youngminds.org.uk

YOUNG VOICE

Makes the views of young people heard and tries to get something done about it. Latest publication was *Bullying in Britain: Testimonies from Teenagers*.
www.young-voice.org

■ EUROPE

MENTAL HEALTH EUROPE

Mental Health Europe is the Regional Council for Europe for the World Federation for Mental Health. It is a non-governmental organization committed to the promotion of positive mental health and the prevention of mental distress, including for children and young people. It organizes projects and events, and publishes reports, including a newsletter on events related to mental health in Europe, and has links with many other European organizations.
www.mhe-sme.org

WORLD HEALTH ORGANIZATION REGIONAL OFFICE FOR EUROPE

Organizes the European Network of Health Promoting Schools which include a strong component of work on mental, emotional and social well-being.
www.who.dk

■ USA

AMERICAN SCHOOL HEALTH ASSOCIATION (ASHA)

Unites the many professionals working in schools who are committed to safeguarding the health of school-aged children. The Association advocates high-quality school health instruction, health services and a healthful school environment. Publishes peer-reviewed *Journal of School Health* which publishes research on health issues of school-aged children.
http://www.ashaweb.org

CENTRE FOR EFFECTIVE COLLABORATION AND PRACTICE (CECP)

Fosters the development and adjustment of children with or at risk of developing serious emotional disturbance. Collaborates both at Federal and local level in exchange and use of knowledge about effective practice. Website has details of resources on issues of emotional and behavioural problems ranging from fact sheets, articles to on-line journals and databases.
http://cecp.air.org

CENTRE FOR HEALTH AND HEALTH CARE IN SCHOOLS (CHHCS)

A non-partisan policy and programme resource centre established to explore ways to strengthen the well-being of children through effective health programmes and health care in schools. Centre staff and consultants work with institutional leaders, state officials and clinical providers. Site contains brief outlines of some of the more common mental, emotional and behavioural disorders and has links to related sites such as child and adolescent health data, policy and school-based health centres.
www://gwis.circ.gwu.edu/~mtg

CENTRE FOR RESEARCH ON THE EDUCATION OF STUDENTS PLACED AT RISK (CRESPAR)

This is a collaborative effort between Howard and Johns Hopkins Universities. This research and development centre has launched an important comprehensive school initiative designed to enhance the achievement, academic environment, and quality of life for students, teachers and parents.
http://crespar.law.howard.edu

CENTRE FOR SCHOOL MENTAL HEALTH ASSISTANCE (CSMHA)

The Centre for School Mental Health Assistance provides leadership and technical assistance to advance effective interdisciplinary school-based mental health programmes. They give support to schools and communities in the development of programmes that are accessible, family centred, culturally sensitive and responsive to local needs. Site also has comprehensive guide to resource links assembled by the UCLA School Mental Health Project/Centre for Mental Health in Schools.
http://csmha.umaryland.edu

CENTRE FOR SOCIAL AND EMOTIONAL EDUCATION (CSEE)

The Centre for Social and Emotional Education is a non-profit, international organization founded in 1996 by leading educators, parents and health care professionals. Provides parents, educators, and mental health professionals with resources, tools and educational offerings that promote social and emotional skills and knowledge in children and adolescents. There are links to a number of organizations that can support parents' and professionals' understanding of children, social emotional education including: professional associations and organizations; special education; school counsellors and mental health professionals. There are

also links to a range of resources including: substance abuse/prevention; violence prevention; creating safe, caring and responsive classrooms/schools and publications/journals/articles
http://www.csee.

COLLABORATIVE FOR THE ACADEMIC, SOCIAL AND EMOTIONAL LEARNING (CASEL)

Major US network of educators, academics and professionals who are engaged in promoting academic, social and emotional learning in schools. Website has details of vast number of projects worldwide, off-prints of articles and details of ongoing work.
www.casel.org

EDUCATION DEVELOPMENT CENTRE

Works with practitioners and professionals in all sectors of the health care system, as well as with schools and communities and projects around the globe, to design, implement and evaluate strategies to reduce and prevent alcohol, tobacco and other drug use; HIV infection; injuries and violence, working with communities to devise evidence-based programmes that are sensitive and responsive to local needs, concerns and resources.
http://www.edc.org

GEORGETOWN UNIVERSITY CENTRE FOR CHILD AND HUMAN DEVELOPMENT

Interdisciplinary approach to service, training programmes, research, community outreach and public policy. The Centre serves both vulnerable children and their families as well as influences local, national, and international programmes and policy such as poverty, homelessness and violence. The Centre has many web links to an ongoing collection of resources on issues of importance to children, youth and families.
http://www.georgetown.edu/research/gucdc

MHS EMOTIONAL INTELLIGENCE

Produces the Bar-On Emotional Quotient Inventory, a series of questionnaires measuring emotional intelligence. Adult, youth and child versions are available.
www.mhs.org.

NATIONAL ASSEMBLY ON SCHOOL-BASED HEALTH CARE (NASBC)

The 1998–99 national census of school-based health centres, conducted by the National Assembly on School-Based Health Care, provides the most comprehensive analysis to date of school-based health centres in the USA. The survey's findings, compiled from more than 800 responding programmes, include information on school-based health care characteristics, sponsors, operations, scope of services and policies.
http://www.nasbhc.org

NATIONAL MENTAL HEALTH AND EDUCATION CENTRE FOR CHILDREN AND FAMILIES

A public service of the National Association of School Psychologists, is an information and action network to foster best practices in education and mental health for children and families – building upon strengths, understanding diversity and supporting families. Primary goal is to provide leadership to address the critical issues that affect education and improve the outcomes for children and their families for such problems as school failure, classroom disruptions, violence and drug abuse, and works to provide support for children and families and improve the professional training and practices of school psychologists and pupil service. Resources include fact sheets, position statements on ADHD, Tourettes and so on. Guides for parents on special education, youth violence, suicide, depression and emotional first aid.
http://naspweb.org/centres

OFFICE OF SAFE AND DRUG-FREE SCHOOLS

Administers, co-ordinates and recommends policy for improving quality and excellence of programmes and activities including Health, Mental Health, Environmental Health and Physical Education. Site has links to other Drug Abuse Prevention Internet Resources, such as School Violence Prevention, and Healthy Schools Internet Resources.
http://www.ed.gov/offices/OESE/SDFS

OFFICE OF SCHOOL HEALTH, UNIVERSITY OF COLORADO HEALTH SCIENCES CENTRE

This site contains information and resources to assist school health services personnel, school board members, school administrators, classroom personnel, staff, parents and students, school health faculty, local, state and national school health consultants and policy analysts for health and education agencies and organizations.
http://www.uchsc.edu/schoolhealth

POLICY LEADERSHIP CADRE FOR MENTAL HEALTH IN SCHOOLS

Has catalogue of special materials including guides to practice, training tutorials and aids, for example Behaviour Problems in Schools, attention problems, and Bullying Prevention and a net exchange for schools and MH Practitioners interchange to allow them to share ideas and experiences.
http://smhp.psych.ucla.edu/coalitin.htm

PUBLIC EDUCATION NETWORK

The School and Community Services Initiative aims to develop and strengthen the links between public schools and community-based services. The goal is to provide children and youth with a comprehensive set of support services that will help them achieve both in and out of school. Looks at how to address the non-academic needs

of poor, disadvantaged children without distracting schools from reaching their aca-demic goals. The Initiative takes a child-centred, co-ordinated perspective that recog-nizes the role of schools, families and community agencies in the lives of children.
http://www.publiceducation.org

UCLA CENTRE FOR MENTAL HEALTH IN SCHOOLS

Operating under the auspices of the School Mental Health Project is a national training and technical assistance centre focusing on approaches to mental health and psycho-social concerns from the broad perspective of addressing barriers to learning and promoting healthy development. Specific attention is given to enhancing collaboration between school and community programmes. The Centre was established in 1995 as part of a major initiative to foster mental health in schools.
http://smhp.psych.ucla.edu

■ AUSTRALIA

AUSTRALIAN ASSOCIATION OF INFANT, CHILD, ADOLESCENT AND FAMILY MENTAL HEALTH

The association's aim is to actively promote the mental health and well-being of infants, children, adolescents and their families and/or carers in Australia. Has links to information on the latest conferences happening in infant, child, adoles-cent and family mental health and related fields. Categories are *Consumers* – this provides links to consumer involvement in infant, child, adolescent and family mental health; *Documents – Surveys – Reports* – this area provides links to relevant documents, reports, studies in the area of infant, child adolescent and family mental health; *Key Organizations* – contains links to key international health organ-izations; *Mental Health* links to topics specifically relating to mental health, for example promotion, information, networks and services. *Professional Associations* – contains links to relevant professional association websites; *Youth* – contains links to sites of interest to young people
http://www.aicafmha.net/

CUBBY HOUSE

Six to 12-year-olds can find information about positive mental health and ways of looking after their mental health. They can learn more about feelings, problem-solving, bullying, stress and friendships, as well as share ideas on the bulletin board, have art work published in the gallery and explore on-line games and links.
http://www.headroom.net.au/cubby/index.html

FAMILY ROOM

For parents and caregivers with information about promoting the positive mental health of children and young people. Includes things like 'what is emotional intel-ligence and why is it important?' and 'who or what are "emotionally intelligent"

parents and how can they help?' It provides up-to-date information about parenting now and the changes that have occurred over the years. It is intended to help parents plan ahead in their parenting, rather than be reactive. It gives information about what is normal for parenting and for young people's behaviour.
http://www.headroom.net.au/family/index.html

HEADROOM

A site dedicated to the positive mental health of children and adolescents and the adults in their life. The information in the 'Lounge' has been written by young people.
http://www.headroom.net.au

■ NEW ZEALAND

ATTITUDE

Is an educational division of 'Parenting with Confidence Inc.'. Attitude programmes are designed to build, complement and synergize with health teachers' own programmes. The goal is to creatively teach lifeskills that will assist the teenagers to make life-enhancing choices. Attitude has a variety of programmes that can be packaged as classroom sessions and provides presentations to secondary schools.
http://www.attitude.org.nz/

MENTAL HEALTH RISK FACTORS FOR ADOLESCENTS

A collection of electronic resources is intended for parents, educators, researchers, health practitioners and teens.
http://education.indiana.edu/cas/adol/mental.

MINISTRY OF YOUTH AFFAIRS TE TARI TAIOHI

A website with information on the policies, programmes, legislation and services that concern young people in New Zealand. Provides policy advice to the government on youth affairs. Aims to promote the direct participation of young people aged between 12 and 25 years in the social, educational, economic and cultural development of New Zealand, both locally and nationally.
http://www.youthaffairs.govt.nz/

NEW ZEALAND ASSOCIATION FOR ADOLESCENT HEALTH AND DEVELOPMENT (NZAAHD)

A national network organization for people working with young people (those aged 12 to 25) in health, education, social work and other sectors to promote adolescent health and development. Over 800 people scattered throughout New Zealand who are trained to support young people.
http://www.nzaahd.org.nz/

PARENTING WITH CONFIDENCE INC.

A charitable organization established in 1994 for the purpose of providing education, inspiration and resources to enable parents to grow confident and competent children, as well as inspiring and equipping adolescents to become great future parents. Is a not-for-profit community organization dedicated to improving the lives of families throughout New Zealand through the provision of Hot Tips for Parents and Hot Tips for Marriage and Relationships seminars and other strategic resources to inspire and equip parents with the tools and the belief that they can raise a great family.
http://www.parenting.org.nz/

SKYLIGHT

A New Zealand support agency for children and young people who are facing change, loss and grief, provides support both in urban and rural areas. Individuals, groups and organizations access includes information, resource and training services. Staff travel all over New Zealand and throughout the year a free phone support service is available. Will be developing a national network of approved skylight counsellors, who are skilled and experienced in supporting children, and teens, through change, loss and grief. Has established effective links with a wide range of New Zealand agencies.
www.skylight.org.nz

URGE/WHAKAMANAWA

A website by and for young people from Aotearoa/New Zealand with a focus on health and well-being.
www.urge.org.nz or www.whakamanawa.co.nz

References

Aber, J.L., Jones, S.M., Brown, J.L., Chaudry, N. and Samples, F. (1998) 'Resolving conflict creatively: evaluating the developmental effects of a school-based violence prevention program in neighborhood and classroom context', *Development and Psychopathology*, 10 (2): 187–213.

Antidote (1998) *Realising the Potential: Emotional Education for All*. London: Antidote.

Antidote (2001) *Emotional Literacy Initiative: Project Update 2002*. London: Antidote.

Antidote (2003) 'The matrix of organisational emotional literacy'. *Handbook for Emotional Literacy*. London: Antidote.

Antonovsky, A. (1987) *Unraveling the Mystery of Health*. San Francisco, CA: Jossey-Bass.

Arenio, W. and Fleiss, K. (1996) 'Typical and behaviourally disruptive children's understanding of the emotional consequences of socio-moral events', *British Journal of Developmental Psychology*, 14 (2): 173–86.

Balding, J. (1998) *Young People in 1997*. Exeter: University of Exeter, Health Education Unit.

Bandura, A. (1989) 'Human agency in social cognitive theory', *American Psychologist*, 44 (9): 1175–84.

Banks, T., Bird, J., Gerlach, L., Henderson, M. and Lovelock, R. (2001) *ENABLE Emotional Needs, Achieving, Behaving and Learning in Education*. Modbury, Devon: The Modbury Group.

Bar-On, R. and Parker, J.D.A. (2000) *Bar-On Emotional Quotient Inventory: Youth Version. Technical Manual*. New York: Multi-Health Systems Inc.

Batten, A. (2001) *Mainstreaming Mental Health in Schools: Report of a Seminar Held at the Institute for Public Policy Research*. London: Institute for Public Policy Research.

Battistich, V., Solomon, D., Watson, M., Solomon, J. and Schaps, E. (1989) 'Effects of an elementary school program to enhance pro-social behaviour on children's cognitive–social problem-solving skills and strategies', *Journal of Applied Developmental Psychology*. 10: 147–69.

Battistich, V., Watson, M., Solomon, D., Schaps, E. and Solomon, J. (1991) The Child Development Project; a comprehensive program for the development of prosocial character, in W. Kurtines and J. Gewirtz (eds), *Handbook of Moral Behavior and Development*. Hillsdale N.J.: Lawrence Erlbaum Associates Inc.

Battistich, V., Schaps, E., Watson, M. and Soloman, D. (1996) 'Prevention effects of the Child Development Project: early findings from an ongoing multi-site demonstration trial', *Journal of Adolescent Research*, 11 (1): 12–35.

Battistich, V., Solomon, D., Watson, M. and Schaps, E. (1997) 'Caring school communities', *Educational Psychologist*, 32, (3): 137–51.

Bibou Kakou, I., Kiosseoglou, G. and Stogiannidou, A. (2001) 'Strengths and difficulties of school aged children in the family and school context', *Psychology: The Journal of the Hellenic Psychological Society*, (8): 506–25.

Black, I. (1991) *Information in the Brain: A Molecular Perspective*. Cambridge, MA: MIT Press.

Blackman, C. (1982) 'Cognitive styles and learning disabilities', *Journal of Learning Disabilities*, 2 (15): 106–15.

Bowlby, J (1969, 1973, 1980) *Attachment and Loss, vols. 1–3*. New York: Basic Books

Briggs, S., MacKay, T. and Miller, S. (1995) 'The Edinbarnet Playground Project: changing aggressive behaviour through structured intervention', *Educational Psychology in Practice*, 11: 37–44.

Bruun Jensen, B. (1997) 'A case of two paradigms within health education', *Health Education Research*, 12 (4): 419–28.

Buchanan, A. (2000) 'Present issues and concerns', in A. Buchanan, and B. Hudson (eds), *Promoting Children's Emotional Well-Being*. Oxford: Oxford University Press.

Buczkiewicz, M. and Carnegie, R. (2001) 'The Ugandan Life Skills initiative', *Health Education*, 101 (1): 8–13.

Byrk, A. and Driscoll, M. (1988) *The High School as Community: Contextual Influences and Consequences for Students and Teachers*. W: National Center on Effective Secondary Schools.

Caplan, M., Weissberg, R.P., Grober, J.S., Sivo, P.J., Grady, K. and Jacoby, C. (1992) 'Social competence promotion with inner-city and suburban young adolescents: effects on social adjustment and alcohol use', *Journal of Consulting and Clinical Psychology*, 60: 56–63.

Carr, A. (ed.) (2002) *Prevention: What Works With Children and Adolescents?* London: Taylor and Francis.

Carter, A.S., Little, C., Briggs-Gowan, M.J. and Kogan, N. (1999) 'The infant–toddler social and emotional assessment (ITSEA): comparing parent ratings to laboratory observations of task mastery, emotion regulation, coping behaviors, and attachment status', *Infant Mental Health Journal*, 20 (4): 375–92.

CASEL (2002) *The Collaborative Centre for the Advancement of Social and Emotional Learning*, Website address: Chicago: University of Illinois in Chicago. http://www.cfapress.org/casel/casel.html

Catalano, R.F., Arthur, M.W., Hawkins, D.J., Berglund, L. and Olson, J.J. (1998) 'Comprehensive community and school based interventions to prevent anti-social behaviour', in R. Loeber and D.P. Farrington (eds), *Serious and Violent Juvenile Offenders: Risk Factors and Successful Interventions*. Thousand Oaks, CA: Sage, pp. 24–283.

Catalano, R.F., Berglund, L., Ryan, A.M., Lonczak, H.S. and Hawkins, J. (2002) 'Positive youth development in the United States: research finding on evaluations of positive youth development programmes,' *Prevention and Treatment*, (5), article 15. http://journals.apa.org/prevention/volumne5/pre005001a.html

Chapman, S., Lister-Sharp, D., Sowden, A. and Stewart-Brown, S. (1999) *Systematic Review of Reviews of Health Promotion in Schools*, York: Centre for Reviews and Dissemination, University of York.

Cheney, D. and Barringer, C. (1995) 'Teacher competence, student diversity and staff training for the inclusion of middle school students with emotional and behavioural disorders', *Journal of Emotional and Behavioural Disorders*, 3 (3): 174–82.

Cherniss, C. and Goleman, D. (eds) (2001) *The Emotionally Intelligent Workplace*. San Francisco, CA: Jossey-Bass.

Cohen, J. (1993) *Handbook of School-Based Interventions: Resolving Student Problems and Promoting Healthy Educational Environments*. San Francisco, CA: Jossey-Bass.

Coram Family (2002) *Intervening Early: A Snapshot of Approaches Primary Schools Can Use to Help Children Get the Best from School*. Nottingham: DfES.

Covey, S. (1998) *The Seven Habits of Highly Effective Familes*. London: Simon and Schuster.

Damasio, A. (1994) *Descartes' Error: Emotion, Reason and the Human Brain*. New York: Grosset/Putnam.

Damasio. A. (2000) *The Feeling of What Happens*. London: Vintage.

De Beauport, E. (1996) *The Three Faces of Mind: Developing Your Mental, Emotional and Behavioural Intelligences*. Wheaton, IL: Quest Books.

Dean, C. (1995) 'Angry adieu to years of experience', *Times Educational Supplement*, 4120, 16 January: 4–5.

Dennision, P. and Dennison, G. (1986) *Brain Gym: Simple Activities for Whole Brain Learning*. Ventura, CA: Edu-Kinesthetics.

Devlin, T. (1998) *Public Relations and Marketing for Schools*. London: Pitman.

DfEE (Department for Education and Employment) (1999) *National Healthy School Standard*. London: http://wiredforhealth.gov.uk/healthy/Brochurenew.pdf

DfES (Department for Education and Skills) (2002) *National Healthy School Standard: Primary School Indicator Consultation*. London: DfES. http://wiredforhealth.gov.uk/healthy/sci.pdf

DfES (Department for Education and Skills) (2003) *Staff Health and Well Being*. London: Health Development Agency.

Dilts, R. and Epstein, T. (1995) *Dynamic Learning*. Capitoa, CA: Meta Publications.

Dulewicz, V. and Higgs, M. (2000) *Emotional Intelligence Questionnaire*, Henley: Henley Management College.

Durlak, J. (1995) *School Based Prevention Programmes for Children and Adolescents*. London: Sage.

Durlak, J. and Wells, A. (1997) 'Primary prevention mental health programs for children and adolescents: a meta-analytic review', *American Journal of Community Psychology*, 25 (2): 115–52.

Edmunds, L. and Stewart-Brown, S. (2002) *Assessing Emotional Competence in Primary School and Early Years Settings: A Review of Approaches, Issues and Instruments*. London: DfES.

Elias, M. (1995) 'Primary prevention as health and social competence promotion', *Journal of Primary Prevention*, 16: 5–24.

Elias, M. and Kress, J. (1994) 'Social decision making and life skills development: a critical thinking approach to health promotion in the middle school', *Journal of School Health*, 64 (2): 62–6.

Elias, M., Zins, J., Weissberg, R., Frey, K., Greenberg, M., Haynes, N., Kessler, R., Schwab-Stone, M. and Shriver, T. (1997) *Promoting Social and Emotional Learning*. Alexandria, VA: ASCD.

Elton, Lord (1989) *Discipline in Schools: Report of the Committee of Enquiry Chaired by Lord Elton*. London: HMSO.

Epstein, M.H., Ryser, G. and Pearson, N. (2002) Standardization of the behavioral and emotional rating scale: factor structure, reliability, and criterion validity', *Journal of Behavioral Health Services and Research*, 29: 208–16.

Epstein, T. and Elias, M. (1996) 'To reach for the stars. How social/affective education can foster truly inclusive environments', *PHI Delta Kappan*, 78 (2): 157–62.

Fahlberg, V. (1996) *A Child's Journey Through Placement*. London: British Association for Fostering and Adoption.

Family Links (2001) *The Nurturing Programme* (handbooks and videos). Oxford: Family Links.

Fantuzzo, J., Polite, K.C., David, M. and Quinn, G. (1988) 'An evaluation of the effectiveness of teacher- vs. student-management classroom interventions', *Psychology in the Schools*, 25: 154–63.

Farmer, T. and Hollowell, J. (1994) 'Social networks in mainstream classrooms: social affiliations and behavioural characteristics of students with EBD', *Journal of Emotional and Behavioural Disorders*, 2 (3): 143–55.

Felner, R., Brand, S. Adan., A., Mulhall, P., Flowers, N. and Sartain, B. (1993) 'Restructuring the ecology of the school as an approach to prevention during school transitions: longitudinal follow ups and extensions of the School Transitional Environment Project (STEP)', *Prevention and Human Services*, 10 (2): 103–36.

Felner, R., Ginter, M. and Primavera, J. (1982) 'Primary prevention during school transitions: social support and environmental structure', *American Journal of Community Psychology*, 10 (3): 277–90.

Fertman, C. and Chubb, N. (1992) 'The effects of a psycho-educational program on adolescents' activity involvement, self-esteem, and locus of control', *Adolescence*, 27 (107): 517–26.

Fiske, S. and Taylor, S.E. (1984) *Social Cognition*. Reading, MA: Addison-Wesley.

Gable, R., Arllen, N. and Hendrickson, J. (1994) 'Use of students with emotional/behavioral disorders as behavior change agents', *Education and Treatment of Children*, 17: 267–76.

Gardner, H., Kornhaber, M. and Wake, W. (1995) *Intelligence: Multiple Perspectives*. London: Harcourt Brace College Publishers.

Gelb, M. (1998) *How To Think Like Leonardo Da Vinci*. London: Thorsons.

Gentry, D. and Benenson, W. (1992) 'School-age peer mediators transfer knowledge and skills to home setting', *Mediation Quarterly*, 10: 101–9.

Gettinger, M., Doll, B. and Salmon, D. (1994) 'Effects of social problem solving, goal setting, and parent training on children's peer relations', *Journal of Applied Developmental Psychology*, 15 (2): 153–7.

Goleman, D. (1996) *Emotional Intelligence*. London: Bloomsbury.

Goodman, G., Powell, E. and Burke, J. (1989) 'The Buddy System: a reintegration technique', *Academic Therapy*, 25: 195–9.

Goodman, R. (1997) 'The Strengths and Difficulties Questionnaire: a research note', *Journal of Child Psychology and Psychiatry*, 38: 581–6.

Gordon, J. and Grant, G. (1997) *How We Feel*. London: Jessica Kingsley.

Gordon, J. and Turner, K. (2001) 'School staff as exemplars: where's the potential?', *Health Education*, 101 (6): 283–91.

Gottfredson, D., Gottfredson, G.,and Hybl, L. (1993) 'Managing adolescent behavior: a multiyear, multischool study', *American Educational Research Journal*, 30: 179–215.

Gray, G. (1996) 'Training to promote mental health in the European Network of Health Promoting Schools', in R.N. Trent and C.R. Reed (eds), *The Promotion of Mental Health Volume 1996*. Aldershot, Avebury.

Greenberg, M., Kusche, C., Cook, E.,and Quamma, J. (1995) 'Promoting emotional competence in school-aged children – the effects of the PATHS curriculum', *Development and Psychopathology*, 7 (1): 117–36.

Greenhalgh, P.(1994) *Emotional Growth and Learning*. London: Routledge.

Haertel, G., Walberg, H. and Haertel, E. (1981) 'Socio-psychological environments and learning: a quantitative analysis', *British Educational Research Journal*, 7: 27–36.

Hains, A. (1992) 'Comparison of cognitive-behavioral stress management techniques with adolescent boys', *Journal of Counseling and Development*, 70 (5): 600–605.

Harter, S. (1993) 'Causes and consequences of low self-esteem in children and adolescents', in: R.F. Baumeister (ed.), *The Puzzle of Low Self-Regard*. New York: Plenum, pp. 87–116.

Hartley-Brewer, E. (1994) *Positive Parenting: Raising Children with Self Esteem*. London: Vermillion.

Hartley-Brewer, E. (2001) *Learning to Trust and Learning to Learn*. London: IPPR.

Hawkins, J.D. and Catalano, R. (1992) *Communities That Care: Action for Drug Abuse Prevention*. San Francisco, CA: Jossey-Bass.

Hawkins, J.D., Catalano, R.F., Kosterman, R., Abbott, R. and Hill, K.G. (1999) *Preventing Adolescent Health-Risk Behaviours by Strengthening Protection During Childhood*. Cited in R.F. Catalano (2002) 'Positive youth development in the United States: research findings on evaluation of positive youth development programmes', *Prevention and Treatment*, (5), article 15.

Hayden, C. (1997) *Children Excluded from Primary School*. Buckingham: Open University.

Haynes, N. and Comer, J. (1996) Integrating schools, families and communities through successful school reform. *School Psychology Review*, 25: 4.

HEA and NFER (Health Education Authority and National Foundation for Educational Research) (1997) *The Health Promoting School: Final Report of the ENHPS Evaluation in England*. London: HEA.

Henderson, J. (ed.) (2001) *A Directory of Mental Health Projects in Europe*. Brussels: Mental Health Europe, pp. 4–7.

Hendren, R., Birell Weisen, R. and Orley, J. (1994) *Mental Health Programmes in Schools*. Geneva: WHO, Division of Mental Health and Substance Abuse.

Hopkins, D. (2002) *Improving the Quality of Education for All: A Handbook of Staff Development Activities*. 2nd edition. London: David Fulton.

Hughes, D. (2000) *Facilitating Developmental Attachment: The Road to Emotional Recovery and Behavioral Change in Foster and Adopted Children*. London: Jason Aronson.

Izard, C., Fine, S., Schultz, D., Mostow, A., Ackerman, B. and Youngstrom, E. (2001) 'Emotion knowledge as a predictor of social behavior and academic competence in children at risk', *Psychological Science*, 12: 18–23.

Jensen, E. (1995) *The Learning Brain*. San Diego, CA: The Brain Store.

Johnson, D., Johnson, R., Dudley, B., Ward, M. and Magnuson, D (1995) 'The impact of peer mediation training on the management of school and home conflicts', *American Educational Research Journal*, 32: 829–44.

Kamps, D. and Tankersley, M. (1996) 'Prevention of behavioral and conduct disorders: trends and research issues', *Behavioral Disorders*, 22 (1): 41–8.

Kyriacou, C. (1996) 'Teacher stress: a review of some international comparisons', *Education Section Review*, 20 (1): 17–20.

Laevers, F.R. (1994) *Leuven Involvement Scale for Young Children LIS-YC*. Leuven: Centre for Experiential Education, University of Leuven.

Lantieri, L. and Patti, J. (1996) *Waging Peace in Our Schools*. Boston, MA: Beacon Press.

Lazerson, D. (1980) '"I must be good if I can teach": peer tutoring with aggressive and withdrawn children', *Journal of Learning Disabilities*, 13: 152–7.

LeDoux, J. (1998) *The Emotional Brain*. London: Phoenix.

Leech, A. (1995) 'Missing, presumed ill', *Education*, 185 (24): 11.

Leicester Local Education Authority (2001) *Emotional Health and Wellbeing: A Toolkit for Schools*. Leicester: Leicester City Council.

Lin R. and Lin H. (1996) 'A study of Junior High School teachers' mental health in Taiwan', in D. Trent and C. Reed (eds), *Promotion of Mental Health. Volume 5*. Aldershot: Avebury.

Lister-Sharp, D., Chapman S., Stewart-Brown, S.L. and Sowden A. (1999) 'Health Promoting Schools and health promotion in schools: two systematic reviews', *Health Technology Assessment*, 3 (22).

Little, R. (1982) 'Norms of collegiality and experimentation; workplace conditions of school success', American Educational Research (78): 178–85.

Locke, E.A. and Latham, G.P. (1990) 'Work motivation and satisfaction: light at the end of the tunnel'. *Psychological Science*, (1): 240–6.

Loeber, R. (1990) 'Development and risk factors of juvenile antisocial behaviour and delinquency', *Clinical Psychology Review*, 10: 1–41.

Macklem, G. (1987) 'No one wants to play with me', *Academic Therapy*, 22: 477–84.

MacLean, P. (1990) *The Triune Brain in Education*. New York: Plenum.

Marmot, M., Bosma, H., Hemingway, H., Brunner, E. and Stanfield, S. (1997) 'Contribution of job control and other risk factors to social variations in coronary heart disease incidence', *Lancet*, 350: 235–9.

Marshall, J. (2000) 'Investing in early life to prevent crime: the opportunities and the challenges', paper presented at the conference 'Reducing Criminality: Partnerships and Best Practice', convened by the Australian Institute of Criminology in association with the WA Ministry of Justice, Department of Local Government, Western Australia Police Service and Safer Western Australia, Perth, 31 July–1 August.

Marshall, J. and Watt, P. (1999) *Child Behaviour Problems: A Literature Review of its Size and Nature and Prevention Interventions*. Perth, Western Australia: Interagency Committee on Children's Futures.

Maslow, A. (1970). *Motivation and Personality: 2nd Edition*. New York: Harper and Row.

Mayer, J.D. and Cobb, C.D. (2000) 'Educational policy on emotional intelligence: does it make sense?', *Educational Psychology Review*, 12 (2): 163–83.

Mayer, J. and Salovey, P. (1997) 'What is emotional intelligence?', in P. Salovey and S. Shulter (eds), *Emotional Intelligence and Emotional Development*. New York: Basic Books.

McEwen, A. and Thompson, W. (1997) 'After the national curriculum: teacher stress and morale', *Research in Education*, 57: 57–66.

McGinnis, E. (1990) *Skillstreaming in Early Childhood: Teaching Prosocial Skills to the Preschool and Kindergarten Child*. Champaign, IL: Research Press.

McMillan, J. (1992) *A Qualitative Study of Resilient At-Risk Students: Review of Literature*. Richmond, VA: Metropolitan Educational Research Consortium.

McWhirter, J.M., Wetton, N.M. and Williams, D.T. (1998) *Egeszseges Elet* (4 vols), Budapest: Real Med.

Meese, J., Wigfield, A. and Eccles, J. (1990) 'Predictors of math anxiety and its influence on young adolescents' course enrolment intentions and performance in mathematics', *Journal of Educational Psychology*, 82: 60–70.

Middleton, M. and Cartledge, G. (1995) 'The effects of social skills instruction and parental involvement on the aggressive behaviors of African American males', *Behavior Modification*, 19: 192–210.

Moos, R. (1991) 'Connections between school, work and family settings', in B. Fraser and H, Walberg (eds), *Educational Environments*. Oxford: Pergamon.

Morgan, S. (1983) 'Development of empathy in emotionally disturbed children', *Journal of Humanistic Education and Development*, 22: 70–9.

Morris, E. and Scott, C. (2002) *Whole School Emotional Literacy Indicator; Emotional Literacy Indicator for Adults to Use with Pupils; and Class Emotional Literacy Indicator*. Frampton on Severn, Gloucestershire: School of Emotional Literacy Publishing.

Munn, P., Cullen, M., Johnstone, M. and Lloyd, G. (1999) *Exclusions and In School Alternatives*. Edinburgh: Scottish Office Education and Industry Department.

New Policy Institute (1998) *Second Chances: Exclusion from School and Equality of Opportunity*. London: New Policy Institute.

Olweus, D. (1995) 'Bullying or peer abuse at school: facts and interventions', *Current Directions in Psychological Science*, 4: 196–200.

Olweus, D. (2001) *Olweus' Core Program Against Bullying and Anti-Social Behaviour: A Teacher Handbook*. Bergen: Hemil Research Centre for Health Promotion.

Ornstein, R. and Thompson, R. (1986) *The Amazing Brain*. Boston, MA: Houghton-Mifflin.

Palardy, J. (1992) 'Behavior modification: it does work, but … ', *Journal of Instructional Psychology*, 19: 127–31.

Palardy, J. (1995) 'Dealing with misbehavior: two approaches', *Journal of Instructional Psychology*, 22: 135–40.

Parsons, C. (1999) *Education, Exclusion and Citizenship*. London: Routledge.

Parsons, C., Stears, D., Thomas, C., Thomas, L. and Holland, J. (1997) *The Implementation of the ENHPS in Different National Contexts*. Canterbury: Centre for Health Education and Research.

Pauley, J., Bradley, D. and Pauley, J. (2002) *Here's How to Reach Me: Matching Instruction to Personality Types in Your Classroom*. London: Paul H. Brookes.

Piette, D., Roberts, C., Prevost, M., Tudor-Smith, C. and Bardolet, J. (2001) *Tracking Down ENHPS Successes for Sustainable Development and Dissemination: The EVA2 Project*. Copenhagen: WHO Regional Office for Europe.

Rickert, V., Jay, S. and Gottlieb, A. (1991) 'Effects of a peer counselled AIDS education programme on knowledge, attitudes and satisfaction of adolescents', *Journal of Adolescent Health*. 12: 38–43.

Riding, R. and Rayner, S. (1998) *Cognitive Styles and Learning Strategies: Understanding Style Differences in Learning and Behaviour*. London: David Fulton.

Roberts, W., Ham, A. and Battistich, V. (1995) Assessing students' and teachers' sense of the school as a caring community. Presented at American Educational Research Association: San Francisco, April.

Rogers, B. (1994) *Behaviour Recovery: A Whole-School Program for Mainstream Schools*. Camberwell, Victoria: Australian Council for Educational Research.

Rotter, J.B. (1966) 'Generalised expectancies for internal versus external control of reinforcement', *Psychological Monographs*, 80 (1), whole of no. 609.

Rumsby, R. (2001) *Evaluation of the Norfolk Education Staff Well-Being Project: Booklet One – What We Are Learning*. Norwich: Norfolk County Council.

Rutter, M., Hagel, A. and Giller, H. (1998) *Anti-social Behaviour and Young People.* Cambridge: Cambridge University Press.

Rutter, M., Maughan, B., Mortimore, P. and Ouston, J. (1979) *Fifteen Thousand Hours: Secondary Schools and Their Effects on Children.* London: Open Books

Salimi, S. and Callias, M. (1996) 'Self esteeem in adolescents with conduct problems and depression', *European Psychiatry,* 11 (4): 328–9.

Sarros, J., and Sarros, A. (1992) 'Social support and teacher burnout', *Journal of Educational Administration,* 30 (1): 55–69.

Schaps, E., Lewis, C. and Watson, M. (1996) 'Building community in school', *Principal,* November: 29–31.

Seligman, P. (1998) *Learned Optimism: How to Change Your Mind and Your Life.* London: Pocket Books.

Sharp, P. (2001) *Nurturing Emotional Literacy.* London: David Fulton.

Sharp, P. and Faupel, A. (eds) (2002) *Promoting Emotional Literacy: Guidelines for Schools, Local Authorities, and the Health Services.* Southampton: Emotional Literacy Group, Southampton City Council Local Education Authority.

Shipman, V. and Shipman, F. (1983) 'Cognitive styles: some conceptual methodological and applied issues', in E.W. Gordon (ed.), *Human Diversity and Pedagogy.* Westport, CT: Mediax.

Shonkoff, J. and Philips, D. (eds) (2000) *From Neurons to Neighbourhoods: The Science of Early Childhood Development.* Washington, DC: National Academy Press.

Smith, A. (1996) *Accelerated Learning in the Classroom.* Bodmin: MPG Books.

Smith, A. (1998) *Accelerated Learning in Practice.* Bodmin: MPG Books.

Solomon, D., Watson, M., Battistich, V., Schaps, E. and Delucchi, K. (1992) 'Creating a caring community: a school based programme to promote children's prosocial competence', in E. Oser, J. Patty and A. Dick (eds), *Effective and Responsible Teaching.* San Francisco, CA: Jossey-Bass.

Sperry, R. (1968) 'Hemisphere disconnection and unity in conscious awareness', *American Psychologist,* 23: 723–33.

Steiner, C. and Perry, P. (1997) *Achieving Emotional Literacy,* London: Bloomsbury.

Sternberg, R.J. (2001) 'Measuring the intelligence of an idea: how intelligent is the idea of emotional intelligence?', in J. Ciarrochi, J. Forgas and J. Mayer (eds), *Emotional Intelligence in Everyday Life.* London: Psychology Press/Taylor and Francis, pp. 187–94.

Stewart-Brown, S. (1998a) *Evaluating Health Promotion in Schools: Reflections From the UK.* Oxford: Health Services Research Unit, Department of Public Health, University of Oxford.

Stewart-Brown, S. (1998b) 'Public health implications of childhood behaviour problems and parenting programmes', in A. Buchanan and B. Hudson (eds), *Parenting, Schooling and Children's Behaviour.* Aldershot: Ashgate.

Stewart-Brown, S. (2000) 'Parenting, well being, health and disease', in A. Buchanan and B. Hudson (eds), *Promoting Children's Emotional Well-being.* Oxford: Oxford University Press, pp. 28–47.

Surber, J. (1999) *Student Assistance Programmes.* Website address: http://www.sicom.com./~surber/

Sylwester, R. (1995) *A Celebration of Neurons: An Educator's Guide to the Human Brain.* Alexandria, VA: ASCD.

Tew, M. (2003) Personal communication. The Talkit is available from Marilyn Tew at 'Ailsa

Craig', Greens Lane, Wroughton, Swindon, SN4 0RJ.

Torrance, P. and Ball, O. (1978) 'Intensive approach alters learning styles in gifted', *Journal of Creative Behaviour*, 12 (2): 48–52.

Tuettemann, E. and Punch, K. (1992) 'Teachers' psychological distress: the ameliorating effects of control over the work environment', *Educational Review*, 44 (2): 181–94.

US General Accounting Office (1995) *School Safety: Promising Initiatives for Addressing School Violence. Report to the Ranking Minority Member, Subcommittee on Children and Families, Committee on Labor and Human Resources. US Senate.* Washington, DC: General Accounting Office.

Vandenberghe, R. and Huberman, A. (eds) (1998) *Understanding and Preventing Teacher Burnout: A Source Book of International Research and Practice.* Cambridge: Cambridge University Press.

Walker,H. (1995) *Antisocial Behavior in School: Strategies and Best Practices.* Pacific Grove, CA: Brooks/Cole.

Weare, K. (2000) *Promoting Mental, Emotional and Social Health: A Whole School Approach.* London: Routledge.

Weare, K. (2001) 'Building bridges between mental health and education', *The International Journal of Mental Health Promotion*, 3 (4): 35–44.

Weare, K. and Gray, G. (1994) *Promoting Mental, Emotional and Social Health in the European Network of Health Promoting Schools.* Copenhagen: World Health Organization Office for Europe.

Weare, K. and Gray, G. (2002) *What Works in Promoting Children's Emotional and Social Competence?* Report for the Department of Education and Skills, London.

Webster-Stratton, C. (1999) *How to Promote Children's Social and Emotional Competence.* London: Paul Chapman Publishing.

Weisinger, H. (1998) *Emotional Intelligence at Work.* New York: Jossey-Bass.

Wells, J. (2000) 'Promoting emotional wellbeing in schools', in A. Buchanan and B. Hudson (eds), *Promoting Children's Emotional Well-being.* Oxford: Oxford University Press.

Wells, J., Barlow, J. and Stewart-Brown, S. (2003) 'A systematic review of universal approaches to mental health promotion in schools', *Health Education*, (4), in press.

Wenger, A. (1996) *The Einstein Factor.* CA: Prima Publishing.

Wetton, N. and McCoy, M. (1998) *Confidence to Learn: A Guide to Extending Health Education in the Primary School.* Edinburgh: Health Education Board for Scotland.

Wetton, N. and Williams, T. (2000) *Health for Life: Healthy Schools, Healthy Citizens.* Waltham on Thames: Nelson.

WHO (World Health Organization) (1996) *Regional Guidelines: Development of Health-Promoting Schools – a Framework for Action.* Manila: WHO Regional Office for the Western Pacific.

WHO (World Health Organization) (1997) *The Health Promoting School: An Investment in Education, Health and Democracy: Case Study Book. First Conference of the European Network of Health Promoting Schools, Thessaloniki, Greece.* Copenhagen: WHO Regional Office for Europe.

Wubbels, T., Brekelmans, M. and Hooymayers, H. (1991) 'Interpersonal teacher behaviour in the classroom', in B. Fraser and H. Walberg (eds), *Educational Environments.* Oxford: Pergamon.

Zohar, D. and Marshall, I. (2000) *Spiritual Intelligence, the Ultimate Intelligence.* London: Bloomsbury.

Index

DATE DUE